THE JOURNAL OF THOMAS JUXON, 1644–1647

THE JOURNAL OF
THOMAS JUXON, 1644–1647

edited by

KEITH LINDLEY and DAVID SCOTT

CAMDEN FIFTH SERIES
Volume 13

 **CAMBRIDGE**
UNIVERSITY PRESS

FOR THE ROYAL HISTORICAL SOCIETY
University College London, Gower Street, London WC1E 6BT
1999

Published by the Press Syndicate of the University of Cambridge
The Edinburgh Building, Cambridge CB2 2RU, United Kingdom
40 West 20th Street, New York, NY 10011–4211, USA
10 Stamford Road, Oakleigh, Melbourne 3166, Australia

First published 1999

A catalogue record for this book is available from the British Library

Library of Congress cataloguing in publication data

Juxon, Thomas, 1614–1672.
    The Journal of Thomas Juxon, 1644–47 / edited by Keith Lindley and David Scott.
    p.   cm. -- (Camden fifth series : vol. 13)
    Includes bibliographical references and index.
    ISBN 0–521–65259–6 (hb)
    1. Great Britain--History--Civil War, 1642–1649--Personal narratives. 2. Juxon,
Thomas, 1614–1672--Diaries. I. Lindley, Keith. II. Scot, David. III. Title. IV. Series.
DA20.C15 vol. 13
[DA410]
942.06'2'092--dc21   99–28023
                                                      CIP

ISBN 0 521 65259 6 hardback

SUBSCRIPTIONS. The serial publications of the Royal Historical Society, *Royal Historical Society Transactions* (ISSN 0080–4401), Camden Fifth Series (ISSN 0960–1163) volumes and volumes of the Guides and Handbooks (ISSN 0080–4398) may be purchased together on annual subscription. The 1999 subscription price (which includes postage but not VAT) is £60 (US$99 in the USA, Canada and Mexico) and includes Camden Fifth Series, volumes 13 and 14 (published in July and December) and Transactions Sixth Series, volume 9 (published in December). Japanese prices are available from Kinokuniya Company Ltd, P.O. Box 55, Chitose, Tokyo 156, Japan. EU subscribers (outside the UK) who are not registered for VAT should add VAT at their country's rate. VAT registered subscribers should provide their VAT registration number. Prices include delivery by air.

Subscription orders, which must be accompanied by payment, may be sent to a bookseller, subscription agent or direct to the publisher: Cambridge University Press, The Edinburgh Building, Shaftesbury Road, Cambridge CB2 2RU, UK; or in the USA, Canada and Mexico: Cambridge University Press, 40 West 20th Street, New York, NY 10011–4211, USA.

SINGLE VOLUMES AND BACK VOLUMES. A list of Royal Historical Society volumes available from Cambridge University Press may be obtained from the Humanities Marketing Department at the address above.

Printed and bound in the United Kingdom by Butler & Tanner Ltd, Frome and London

CONTENTS

PREFACE

This volume has been a most rewarding work of collaboration for its two editors, each of whom, quite independently, came to recognise the need for a published edition of Juxon's journal to rescue a relatively neglected text from obscurity, and to make its contents known to a wider readership than a few academic specialists. The editors subsequently agreed to pursue this important task on a joint basis. Anyone who has ventured into Dr Williams's Library to consult the journal will be only too aware of the difficulties facing the reader when trying to make consistent sense of its text. In particular, Juxon's use of capitals, commas and colons frequently obscures his meaning, and his eccentric paragraph structure compounds the problem. Furthermore, although Juxon generally writes in plain and accessible prose, there are occasions when his syntax and compressed narrative, and, to a lesser extent, his chronology and factual references, can lead to confusion. The editors began the work, therefore, with a determination to make the journal as accessible as possible by modernising the text, in terms of its spelling, capitalisation, punctuation and paragraph structure, and by providing a high level of editorial intervention, by means of footnotes and a full introduction, to clarify, explain and set in context. There was clearly a further need to rescue Thomas Juxon himself from his relative obscurity; to flesh out his life and to identify his beliefs, achievements and personal significance in the context of seventeenth-century England. This is provided in the introduction and also accounts for the decision to include appendices containing his will, and its subsequent confirmation, as well as the will of his father, John Juxon. It is to be hoped, therefore, with both the journal and its author rescued from relative neglect and obscurity, fresh light might be shed on a complex and controversial period of history.

Debts of gratitude are due to a number of individuals, libraries and archives. John Adamson, Jane Cox, Don Gilbert, Robert Hunter, Patrick Little, Frances Mannion, Jason Peacey, Alan Peacock, Stephen Roberts, David Sturdy and Elliot Vernon drew upon their knowledge or expertise to provide welcome advice or assistance. John Creasey, the former librarian of Dr Williams's Library, made the manuscript of the journal repeatedly available to the editors and drew upon his long familiarity with it, and the question of its provenance, when faced with queries; and his successor, David Wykes, has been most helpful during the latter stages of the enterprise. Raymond Refaussé, librarian and archivist of the Church of Ireland Representative Church Body Library, Dublin, and Jane Maxwell, assistant librarian in the department of manuscripts, Trinity College Library, Dublin, dealt with questions about a possible Dublin parish of residence for Juxon and his family promptly and efficiently. Gerry Lyne of the genealogical office in the National Library of Ireland kindly agreed to search the funeral entries for information on Juxon's death and burial. Help and courtesy have also been gratefully received from the staffs of the British Library, the Coleraine campus library of the University of Ulster, the Corporation of London records office, the Guildhall Library, the House of Lords record office, the Institute of Historical Research, Lambeth Palace Library, John Rylands Library, the Public Record Office and the library of Queen's University, Belfast. Our thanks are also due to the University of Ulster and the director and trustees of the History of Parliament for granting us the time and encouragement needed to complete the work. And finally, we would like to express our gratitude to the trustees of Dr. Williams's Library (with whom the copyright of the manuscript remains), for granting us permission to publish the journal, a sentiment that we are sure would have been shared by Juxon himself.

Keith Lindley and David Scott
January 1999

ABBREVIATIONS

Add. Mss.	Additional Manuscripts
Baillie	D. Laing (ed.), *The letters and journals of Robert Baillie* (3 vols., Edinburgh, 1841–2)
Boyd	Boyd's index of the inhabitants of London
BL	British Library
Bruce	J. Bruce and D. Masson (eds.), 'The quarrel between Manchester and Cromwell', *Camden Society*, 1875
CSPD	*Calendar of State Papers Domestic*
C	Chancery
Clarendon	E. Hyde, earl of Clarendon, *The history of the rebellion and civil wars in England*, ed. W. D. Macray (6 vols., Oxford, 1888)
CJ	*Journals of the House of Commons*
CLRO	Corporation of London Records Office
DNB	*Dictionary of National Biography*
E	Exchequer
Firth and Rait	C. H. Firth and R. S. Rait (eds.), *Acts and ordinances of the Interregnum, 1642–60* (2 vols., 1911)
Fortescue	G. K. Fortescue, *Catalogue of the pamphlets, books, newspapers and manuscripts ... collected by George Thomason, 1640–61* (2 vols., 1908)
Gardiner	S. R. Gardiner, *History of the great civil war* (4 vols., 1893)
Gentles	I. Gentles, *The New Model Army in England, Ireland and Scotland, 1645–53* (Oxford, 1992)
Greaves and Zaller	R. L. Greaves and R. Zaller (eds.), *Biographical dictionary of British radicals in the seventeenth century* (3 vols., 1984)
Guild.	Guildhall Library, London
Harl. Mss.	Harleian Manuscripts
Harl. Soc.	Harleian Society
HMC	Historical Manuscripts Commission
HLRO	House of Lords Record Office
Jor.	Journals of common council
Kishlansky, *New Model Army*	M. A. Kishlansky, *The rise of the New Model Army* (Cambridge, 1979)
Lindley	K. Lindley, *Popular politics and religion in Civil War London* (Aldershot, 1997)
LJ	*Journals of the House of Lords*

PROB	Probate
PRO	Public Record Office
Rushworth	J. Rushworth, *Historical collections* (8 vols., 1721)
VCH	*Victoria County History*
Visitation, 1633–35	J. J. Howard and J. L. Chester (eds.), *The visitation of London 1633, 1634 and 1635* (2 vols., 1880–83)

London is the place of publication of all published works cited unless otherwise stated.

INTRODUCTION

Thomas Juxon (1614–72)

Thomas Juxon was born on 24 June 1614 and baptised in his father's London parish of St Stephen Walbrook on 30 June.[1] He was the second son of John Juxon, a citizen of London free of the merchant taylors, who earned a lucrative living as a sugar baker/refiner. John was of genteel lineage, the son of Raph Juxon of Christ Church, Newgate, by Sara Hawkins, daughter of John Hawkins of Rugby, Warwickshire, and a cousin of William Juxon, the future bishop of London and archbishop of Canterbury.[2] Thomas's mother was Elizabeth Kirrell, the daughter of John Kirrell of St Michael Queenhithe and East Sheen in the Surrey parish of Mortlake.[3] Both parents died during Thomas's childhood, his mother in November 1619 and his father in August 1626, and were buried in St Lawrence Pountney.[4]

Juxon attended Merchant Taylors' School in 1619–21 at the remarkably young years of five to seven, from shortly after his mother's death until his father's remarriage in 1621.[5] Arthur Juxon, John Juxon's youngest brother,[6] acted as guardian for the young family, after the latter's death, arranging for Thomas to be bound apprentice to William Allott, a liveryman of the merchant taylors' company, for nine years on 29 November 1630 on a bond of £100.[7] However, Thomas eventually gained his freedom of the merchant taylors by patrimony rather than

[1] C. J. Robinson, *Register of Merchant Taylors' School* (2 vols., Lewes, 1882), i. 100; W. Bruce Bannerman and W. Bruce Bannerman (eds.), *The registers of St Stephen's Walbrook, and of St Benet Sherehog, London* (Harl. Soc. xlix, 1919), p. 14.

[2] Wills of John and Thomas Juxon in appendices, pp. 171–92; *Visitation, 1633–35*, ii. 23; Boyd 3723. John Juxon was baptised on 10 April 1579 in Christ Church: W. A. Littledale (ed.), *The registers of Christ Church, Newgate, 1538 to 1754* (Harl. Soc. xxi, 1895), p. 28. In his 1662 will, Archbishop Juxon made a bequest to 'my cousin Thomas Juxon of Mortlake': H. F. Waters, *Genealogical gleanings in England* (2 vols, Boston, Mass., 1901), ii. 1379.

[3] Boyd 3725.

[4] Guild., Ms. 7670, fos. 106, 111.

[5] Thomas was the youngest boy in his class when admitted to the school on 9 December 1619 (all of his classmates had been born between 1607 and 1612) and was last included in the probation list on 11 March 1621: Guild., Merchant Taylors' Company School, probation books, vol. 1 (1607–1651), fos. 88, 90, 92, 97.

[6] Arthur Juxon was free of the salters' company and was also engaged in the family's trade of sugar baking in Walbrook: *Visitation, 1633–35*, ii. 23; W. J. Harvey (ed.), *List of the principal inhabitants of the City of London, 1640* (1886), p. 18.

[7] Guild., apprentice binding book of the merchant taylors' company, 1629–35 (MF 316/10), fo. 120.

service on 25 October 1637.[8] His initial schooling and continuing education during his apprenticeship, as the journal testifies, produced a soundly educated, literate and informed individual with some knowledge of Latin and French, the classics and history, and an intellectual curiosity ready to feed on the great array of published news, information and controversy during the unprecedented press freedom of the early 1640s.

Thomas was born into, and enjoyed the benefits of, a family of rising prosperity and influential social connections, and his own career was to build upon that success. His father acquired the Surrey manor of East Sheen and Westhall in 1619, and subsequently divided his time between residing in his new home, set among orchards and gardens in the parish of Mortlake, and managing his sugarhouse in Walbrook.[9] The move to East Sheen, and his second marriage on 18 December 1621 to Judith Lawrence, née Rainton, the daughter of Alderman Nicholas Rainton,[10] confirmed that John Juxon had arrived socially. His 1626 will was that of a prosperous tradesman, with considerable property accumulated in Mortlake and London, stock in the East India Company, and jewels, plate and other furnishings of an affluent household. Among his bequests were an addition to the merchant taylors' plate, sums for several 'godly ministers' and towards the maintenance of lectures in seven London parishes, provision for four poor widows in Mortlake (who were to wear gowns embroidered with his initials) and other charitable bequests. Funeral arrangements included mourning cloth for Alderman Rainton and his wife and other prominent relatives, a dinner for fellow liverymen of the merchant taylors, and an attendance of the company's almsmen and boys from Christ's Hospital. Most of the property in Mortlake was bequeathed to the eldest son, John Juxon junior, who later married Susan Langham, the daughter of George Langham, a London merchant.[11] Good City connections for the Juxons were also cemented by the 1627 marriage of Thomas's elder sister, Elizabeth, to Maurice Gethin, an affluent woollen draper.[12] Thomas was given the brick house recently built by his father in East Sheen and approximately a hundred acres of surrounding property.

[8] Presentment books of the merchant taylors' company (MF 324/28), vol. 2, unfol.: 25 October 1637.

[9] VCH, Surrey, iv. 71; below, appendices, pp. 178, 180–82.

[10] Boyd 3726. Nicholas Rainton served as sheriff in 1621–22, lord mayor in 1632–33 and was knighted on 5 May 1633: Beaven, ii. 55.

[11] George Langham was alderman's deputy for the ward of Vintry in 1634 and a City militia captain: Boyd 35379; Visitation, 1633–35, ii. 45 where John Juxon is mistakenly called John Jackson of Mortlake.

[12] International Genealogical Index, London, St Augustine Watling Street, marriages 27 November 1627; Woodhead, p. 76; Lindley, p. 206 & n. 35.

After the completion of his apprenticeship, Thomas entered into partnership with his half-uncle, Matthew Sheppard – another wealthy sugar baker residing in the London parish of St Thomas the Apostle but also possessing property at Mortlake.[13] Within a few years Thomas was beginning his rise to respectable positions in the civic arena. By 1642 he was serving as colonel's ensign in the green regiment of the City trained bands commanded by Alderman John Warner; he had become a captain in that regiment by 1643 and major and lieutenant-colonel in 1647.[14] He was also admitted to the livery of the merchant taylors on 8 July 1646.[15] Yet there is no evidence that he ever became a common councillor, despite his intimate knowledge of that assembly's internal politics, although his uncle and former guardian, Arthur Juxon, was one of the councillors for Walbrook[16] and may have been at least one channel of information.

Thomas's marriage on 2 March 1647 at St Giles-in-the-Fields to his first wife Elizabeth Carent, the daughter of Maurice Carent of Toomer Park, Somerset, esquire, put the final seal on his social respectability. The Carents were an old established county family and Elizabeth's mother was the eldest daughter of Sir James Ley, first Lord Ley and earl of Marlborough, who had served as lord treasurer in 1624–28.[17] The marriage produced two children, Elizabeth and William, baptised on 6 December 1647 and 14 October 1649 respectively at St Thomas the Apostle. According to the terms of a settlement made by Maurice Carent, these children and their heirs were to inherit the lands of Toomer and other property should his son and heir, James Carent, die without children.[18] Thomas was sufficiently proud of his late wife's ancestry (she died in September 1669) to leave bequests in his 1672 will for the erection of a

---

[13] BL, Harl. Ms. 986, fos. 19, 21. Matthew Sheppard was the half brother of John Juxon, senior, by his mother's third marriage: *Visitation, 1633–35*, ii. 23, 234. He had a very high rating of £50 in the 1638 London tithe assessment and in 1641 he and Thomas were jointly assessed in London at £8 42s [sic] 8d for the first two subsidies: Dale, p. 182; PRO, E 115/444/57. Sheppard was assessed at £1 1s 4d for the latter in Mortlake.

[14] *The names, dignities and places of all the colonels, lieutenant-colonels, sergeant majors, captains, quarter-masters, lieutenants and ensigns of the City of London* [April 1642], BL, 669 f. 6/10; BL, Harl. Ms. 986. fo. 19; L. C. Nagel, 'The militia of London, 1641–49' (unpublished Ph.D. thesis, University of London, 1982) pp. 317–19. On 29 May 1638, Thomas had become a member of the Honourable Artillery Company: G. A. Raikes (ed.), *The ancient vellum book of the Honourable Artillery Company* (1890), p. 54.

[15] Guild., court minute books of the merchant taylors' company, vol. 9, fos. 233–33v.

[16] He was a councillor in 1643–45 and 1648: PRO, SP 19/79/86; CLRO, Jor. 40, fos. 100, 128; Firth and Rait, i. 1146.

[17] Below p. 150 & n. 565 and appendices, pp. 189–90 & n. 659; *VCH, Somerset*, iv. 44; *Somerset archaeological and natural history society*, xv (1868–9), i. 41–6; G. E. C., *The complete peerage* (1932), viii. 488–9.

[18] *The parish register of St Thomas the Apostle* (Harl. Soc. vi, 1881), p. 57; below appendices, p. 190.

funeral monument to her parents in their parish church, and a marble
plaque on the wall of St Mary Islington near the spot where his wife
was buried, recounting her lineage and displaying his own coat of arms
alongside that of the Carents'.[19] The marriage had also brought Thomas
into close social contact with the Somerset MP John Harington, who was
related to the Carents through marriage and came to refer to Thomas as
'cousin Juxon' after the latter's marriage to Elizabeth Carent.[20] Within a
year or so of his first wife's death, and shortly before his own, Juxon was
to remarry. His second wife was Elizabeth Meredith, the daughter of the
late Sir Robert Meredith of Greenhills, county Kildare, who had been a
leading member of the new wave of pre-1641 English Protestants settlers
in Ireland. Sir Robert had been a member of the Irish privy council and
had served as chancellor of the exchequer from the 1630s until his death
in October 1668. He had also been a member of several important committees concerned with Irish lands or revenues in the 1650s.[21] The marriage brought Juxon into close acquaintance with another leading settler
family, the Cootes. His new wife's sister, Alice, had married Charles
Coote, the second earl of Mountrath, in 1653.[22]

The 1642 scheme to finance the reconquest of Ireland through the Irish
adventurers drew initial investments from Thomas, his elder brother
John, and his uncle Arthur Juxon, who had previously been engaged in
trade with Dublin.[23] Thomas subsequently became a substantial investor
in Irish land, acquiring 3,491 acres (for subscriptions to the Irish adventurers totalling £2,145) in Meath and Queen's counties, Leinster.[24] During
the 1650s he purchased Irish land from other original investors to con-
solidate his holdings,[25] and by the time of his death could refer in addition

[19] Boyd 35385; below, appendices, pp. 189–90. Unfortunately, there is no surviving
plaque to examine in St Mary Islington as the church was destroyed by bombing during
the second world war.

[20] M. F. Stieg (ed.), *The diary of John Harington, MP, 1645–53* (Somerset Record Soc. 74,
1977), pp. 28–9, 32, 34, 46, 61, 68.

[21] *DNB*, xxi. 387; G. E. C., *Complete baronetage* (Exeter, 1903), iii. 306; H. F. Kearney,
Strafford in Ireland 1633–41: a study in absolutism (Manchester, 1959), pp. 73, 83, 254–5; R.
Dunlop (ed.), *Ireland under the Commonwealth: being a selection of documents relating to the government
of Ireland from 1651 to 1659* (2 vols., Manchester, 1913), ii. 603, 655, 698–9; *CSP Ireland,
1666–69*, p. 651.

[22] Burke, *Peerage and baronetage* (1967), p. 597. Juxon's will also refers to a loan made by
him of £1,000 on statute staple to Colonel Thomas Coote, the brother of Sir Charles
Coote, the first earl of Mountrath. Thomas Coote died without issue on 25 November
1671 (below, p. 189). Like Juxon, the Merediths and Cootes held lands in Meath and
Queen's counties.

[23] K. S. Bottigheimer, *English money and Irish land: the 'adventurers' in the Cromwellian
settlement of Ireland* (Oxford, 1971), p. 185; National Archives Ireland, salved chancery
pleadings, 2/688.

[24] Bottigheimer, pp. 185, 205.

[25] PRO, C 54/3829/39–40, 43–5; ibid., 3918/4, 6; ibid., 3921/17; ibid., 4038/7; *CSP
Ireland: adventurers 1642–1659*, pp. 22, 188, 215, 284, 343, 344, 347, 353.

to his 'castles, houses and lands' in county Limerick. This accumulation of Irish property took him over to Ireland where he could enjoy the status of being one of the kingdom's new generation of English landowners, and his second marriage was to signal his social arrival. He was living in Dublin around the time of the Restoration when he was a key figure among Irish adventurers anxious to retain possession of the lands they had acquired under the scheme in what became the act of settlement of 1662.[26] Apart from his Irish interests, Thomas had also temporarily benefited from the sale of dean and chapter lands. Acting jointly with another, on 21 March 1650 he had purchased the manor and prebend of East Marden, Sussex, for the sum of £1,312 10s.[27] There is also the possibility that his sugar interests had developed in the late 1650s to include direct involvement in trade with Barbados.[28] Clearly Thomas Juxon was a man who had prospered in life. Yet he was to be reminded of his childhood experience of the precariousness of human existence by the mental illness of his only son, who was unable to reap the material rewards of that prosperity.[29] Thomas's death was followed by an apparent legal wrangle over the terms of his will which pitted Elizabeth Juxon, his daughter and executrix, against his nephews, Thomas and George Juxon, the two surviving sons of his elder brother, John. Final judgement went in Elizabeth's favour.[30]

So far as Thomas's religious background and convictions were concerned, he was born into a godly family and remained at the heart of the godly network in London in the 1640s. His mother was a woman of exceptional piety if the author of her funeral sermon is to be believed.[31]

[26] Below, p. 11.

[27] PRO, C 54/3547/31. His joint purchaser was Michael Handcorne of High Holborn, gentleman.

[28] In his 1659 will, John Juxon (Thomas's nephew) left a bequest of £20 to 'my kinsman William Juxon in the Barbados' with the request that his uncle, Lieutenant Colonel Thomas Juxon, should take care of it. This may be the same William Juxon, cousin of Thomas Juxon, who was described as 'late of Virginia' in the latter's will: PRO, PROB 11/295/206 will of John Juxon of London, merchant; below, p. 190.

[29] His 1672 will records that his son William had been left in Dublin to be cured of his 'melancholy distemper'. It also reveals that he was hopeful that his second marriage would produce a son: below, appendices, p. 188.

[30] Below, appendices, pp. 193–6. John Juxon's eldest son, John, had died in 1659 and been buried near his father in St Lawrence Pountney: PROB 11/295/206 the will of John Juxon. Legal action over Thomas Juxon's will may have been taken by agreement among the parties to ensure its implementation and defend it against claims under any previous will or wills. The relevant entry in the probate act books, dated 17 February 1673, gives the opinion that, as the will relates to property in Ireland, it should be sent to Ireland for the authorities there. There is also a reference to material witnesses in Chester and that the bishop of Chester should take evidence from them there: PRO, PROB 29/56, fo, 402.

[31] She had undergone a conversion experience in her early twenties and had subsequently become extremely devout (for example, when resident in London, she heard

In his 1626 will, Thomas's father left bequests for mourning gowns for eleven 'godly ministers' to accompany his corpse at the funeral. The ministers included two celebrated preachers, the extremely influential Richard Sibbes and Nathaniel Culverwell, the curate of St Lawrence Pountney, Elias Crabtree, the vicar of Mortlake, one of the preachers at St Antholin's, and his brother, Rowland Juxon.[32] John Juxon also left bequests for the maintenance of lectures in seven London parishes and made provision for one of his nephews to be placed an apprentice with 'some honest religious tradesman'. John Juxon junior (Thomas's elder brother) was to die 'in the faith of the gospel' of wounds sustained in the first battle of Newbury in October 1643. In his will, John urged his brothers and sisters that 'they would Christianly, and carefully see to the godly, and religious educating' of his children after his death and he asked that the Presbyterian Lazarus Seaman would preach at his funeral.[33] Thomas's uncle and guardian, Arthur Juxon, was to become a follower of the Independent divine Thomas Brooks, who was to preach his funeral sermon in 1652.[34]

Thomas Juxon's own will, made in June 1672, contains few clues as to his religious leanings apart from a fairly conventional godly preamble and an emphasis on the doctrine of the Trinity. The only clergy to receive bequests were two Dublin parsons. No provision was made for aiding nonconformist clergy or laity, and no minister was named to preach the funeral sermon.[35] He has all the appearance of a godly yet conforming

nine or ten sermons each week) and she opposed the stigmatising of the godly as 'puritans and precisians, and irregular persons, or the like.' She was also said to have had a strong influence on the religious development of her husband: Stephen Denison, *The monument or tombstone: or a sermon preached at Lawrence Pountney's church in London, November 21, 1619, at the funeral of Mrs Elizabeth Juxon, the late wife of Mr John Juxon* (1620), pp. 85–7, 89, 103, 115.

[32] Below, p. 175 & nn. 652–4. John Juxon had especially close relations with another minister, Stephen Denison, described as 'mine especial friend', a beneficiary of the will and one of its overseers. Denison had apparently lived in the Juxon household for twelve years or more and preached the funeral sermons for both John and his wife. Those sermons had an unmistakenly godly tone, and he was from the very start a determined opponent of Arminianism: below, pp. 174–5, 185; Denison, *The monument or tombstone*; idem, *Another tombstone; or a sermon preached at Lawrence Pountney's church, London, upon the last day of August . . . 1626 at the celebration of the funeral of Mr John Juxon, late citizen of the honourable City of London*; N. Tyacke, *Anti-Calvinists: the rise of English Arminianism c. 1590–1640* (Oxford, 1987), pp. 258–9, 262–3.

[33] J. S. Burn, *Registrum ecclesiae parochialis* (1862), p. 107; Lambeth Palace Library, VH 96/1508, the will of John Juxon of Mortlake, Surrey.

[34] PRO, PROB 11/221/69 will of Arthur Juxon. Brooks had been a preacher at St Thomas the Apostle and had previously preached the funeral sermon for Colonel Thomas Rainborowe, who may also have been a member of his church: Greaves and Zaller, i. 101–2; M. Tolmie, *The triumph of the saints: the separate churches of London 1616–1649* (Cambridge, 1977), pp. 118, 171, 178. Arthur Juxon also left a bequest of £15 to be distributed to 'some godly poor people' chosen by his wife, one of his sons and Thomas Brooks.

[35] Below, pp. 187, 190.

member of his parish church, and his more radical past is effectively hidden from view.

That past is first visible in June 1641, when he was numbered among the parish zealots of St Thomas the Apostle, one of the first London congregations to forcibly remove their Laudian altar rails.[36] The journal itself provides further, and much more extensive, evidence concerning Thomas's religious beliefs. One prominent religious theme running through the journal is the repeated statement of a belief in a providential God who intervenes in the affairs of man and moulds events according to His divine will. Thomas's Erastianism is equally clear: he writes approvingly of parliament's determination to resist clerical pretensions and keep ultimate control over religious matters in its own hands, and depicts London's Presbyterian clergy as schemers and initiators of political action to serve their own ends. Presbyterianism on the Scottish model is unacceptable to him, and he sees parliament and its privileges under threat if ever the Presbyterians managed to establish a general assembly on Scottish lines. Yet he was content to have his Presbyterian brother-in-law, Richard Byfield, officiate at his wedding in March 1647, and there is a possibility that he was one of the ruling elders chosen in the third classis in October 1649.[37] His attitude to Independency is a mixed one. He recognises the injustice of Independents facing banishment, following the imposition of a coercive Presbyterian church, when they had been so active in defence of liberty, and the only clergyman to be singled out for any praise in the journal is the Independent preacher, Jeremiah Burroughs, whose death is 'much lamented'.[38] On the other hand, Thomas is totally opposed to a legal recognition of religious toleration as opening the floodgates to religious anarchy.[39] Like a number of other prominent godly Londoners, his preferred religious settlement was most probably one in which the parish structure of the church was maintained, ultimate authority in ecclesiastical affairs rested with parliament, and gathered churches were

---

[36] Lindley, pp. 39–40, 68–9.

[37] Below, pp. 49, 50, 58, 61, 70, 72, 74–5, 80, 85, 86, 87, 88–90, 94–5, 97, 99, 106, 107–8, 112, 115, 121, 128, 134, 138, 145, 150. A 'Juxon' without a forename is recorded as one of the ruling elders chosen on 30 October 1649 for the third classis in the records of the London provincial assembly: Lambeth Palace Library, Sion College Mss., I 40.2/E 17, records of the provincial assembly 3 May 1647 – 15 August 1660, fo. 101v. However, Thomas Juxon's parish of St Thomas the Apostle (where his son William was baptised on 14 October 1649) was located in the second classis: Firth and Rait, i. 750. It is more likely, therefore, that the Juxon referred to is Thomas's uncle, Arthur Juxon of St Stephen Walbrook in the third classis, despite the fact that he was apparently a religious Independent: above p. 6 & n. 34.

[38] Below, pp. 86, 140. He may also have come under the influence of Thomas Brooks when he preached in St Thomas the Apostle, possibly through his uncle Arthur, but this is purely conjectural.

[39] Below, pp. 95–6.

accorded a pragmatic toleration. Again, like other Londoners, he too probably regretted the divisions in the ranks of the godly, and numbered among his close relations and friends both Presbyterians and Independents.[40]

There is much clearer evidence about his political beliefs in the 1640s. Both Thomas and his elder brother, John, were dedicated parliamentarians. Thomas and his business partner, Matthew Sheppard, were two of the assessors for parliamentarian levies in the ward of Vintry in December 1642, and Thomas himself was still contributing towards the support of the City's forces in April 1646.[41] All three men also experienced direct military action as officers in the first battle of Newbury. Thomas Juxon and Matthew Sheppard were captains in the green regiment under the command of Colonel John Warner, while John Juxon served as captain in Colonel Edmund Harvey's London regiment of horse. John was mortally wounded at Newbury, and died within a few days of being carried to London, and Thomas himself may also have been less seriously wounded in the same battle.[42] A royalist commentator on the London militia officers at Newbury described Thomas as 'a sugar baker living in St Thomas Apostle, a most violent ass', yet he himself had proudly adopted as his motto around this time 'Probus invider nemini' (Upright, envier of no one).[43]

It was not long after returning with his dying brother from Newbury that Thomas began work on his journal, in the course of which he provides valuable insights into his own political outlook. At an early stage in the journal he makes clear that he has a deep-seated antipathy to kings and lords in general, and to King Charles and the current peerage in particular, while stopping short of a principled advocacy of

[40] Lindley, pp. 278–9. Thomas Juxon's family connections, for example, included Presbyterians such as Richard Byfield and Maurice Gethin, a leading City Independent, Daniel Taylor, and the former Presbyterian turned Independent, Colonel Edmund Harvey: Lindley, pp. 70, 311; Greaves and Zaller, iii. 226–7; PRO, PROB 11/295/206 will of John Juxon. Daniel Williams was also apparently on intimate terms with Juxon and was to subsequently marry his widow: *DNB*, xxi. 387.

[41] PRO, SP19/1/42; CLRO, militia accounts: money lent for the support of City forces, accounts c.1643–1647/8, book 3, fo. 18. Thomas lent £26 13 4.

[42] BL, Harl. Ms. 986, fos. 19, 21; H. A. Dillon (ed.), 'On a Ms. list of officers of the London trained bands in 1643', *Archaeologia* 3 (1890), p. 138. Captain John Juxon died in the Allhallows, Bread Street, home of his brother-in-law, Maurice Gethin, where he had been nursed during his last days by his sister, Mrs Elizabeth Gethin. Thomas Juxon was also at his dying brother's side. John was buried in St Lawrence Pountney near his late parents on 16 October 1643 after a hero's funeral, with military honours provided by Colonel Harvey and his horse regiment: Lambeth Palace Library, VH 96/1508, will of John Juxon; Guild., Ms. 7670, fo. 119v; H. B. Wilson, *A history of the parish of St Lawrence Pountney, London* (1831), pp. 135–6; Burn, *Registrum ecclesiae parochialis*, p. 107.

[43] BL, Harl. Ms. 986, fo. 19; ibid., Sloane Ms. 2035B, fo. 27.

republicanism.[44] Commenting on the prince of Orange's 'designs towards sovereignty', Juxon declaimed against 'the great danger and snare in giving so much power and so absolute into one hand; withal that 'tis not safe to let the same man long in that charge, much less suffer it to be hereditary'.[45] Charles himself is portrayed as a scheming and devious king ('no prince ever used more dissimulation') who would stop at nothing to achieve his ends, and who was intent on complete victory while outwardly pretending to work for a negotiated settlement.[46] There is also an expression of moral antipathy to the queen's court in London as having been 'the greatest bawdy house in England'.[47] Juxon is equally scathing about the peerage, which is seen as enjoying a strong bond of common self-interest with the king.[48] On the other hand, he is most certainly not an advocate of a wider social dispersal of political rights. He deplores 'the unhappiness of a popularity, where things are transacted by multitudes, who are men taken out of them [sic] lump'. For him, the House of Commons was the representative body of the nation to which obedience is due by all, and he probably shared the sentiments he attributed to Cromwell about the need to submit to parliament and that 'The common people never were fit for government'.[49]

Although traditionally described as a political Independent, Juxon's political attitudes, like his religious convictions, are much more complex than such a simple party label would imply. He was certainly in favour of the 1644 campaign to reform Essex's army, describing the two radical activists from Westminster who were committed by the Lords for a verbal attack on that army as 'both gallant men'.[50] Two years later, he resolutely defended the political Independents in the Commons against the charge that they were opposed to peace and sound government: 'none drive less particular interests than they nor have served them everywhere more faithfully'.[51] At one point in the journal Juxon also writes as if he were personally acquainted with three of the leaders of political Independency, Vane, Wharton and St John.[52] Two Independent party leaders on common council, Colonel Thomas Player and Stephen Estwicke, are defended against the charge that they were religious Independents when they were 'only honest and ingenious men'.[53] Yet

[44] Below, pp. 29–32.
[45] Below, p. 92.
[46] Below, pp. 73, 98, 133, 144. This is a view of Charles I largely confirmed by recent research.
[47] Below, p. 93.
[48] Below, pp. 47, 68, 72.
[49] Below, pp. 102, 157–8.
[50] Below, p. 51.
[51] Below, p. 103.
[52] Below, p. 94.
[53] Below, p. 103.

despite this evidence of Independent political sympathies, Juxon never toed a rigid party line, for this would have run counter to both his convictions and his temperament. He provides a dispassionate analysis of the London mayoral election of 1646 in which the Independent candidate, John Warner, was defeated and the neo-royalist Sir John Gayre was chosen. In the circumstances, Juxon welcomed the result as avoiding a significant increase in party animosity between Independents and Presbyterians, and giving both parties an object lesson in the need to establish 'love and amity' between them.[54] But it is his remarks about the Presbyterian party leader, Sir Philip Stapilton, on the last page of his journal ('Thus died that brave and valiant wise Stapilton, to the grief of all his friends and his enemies too')[55] that finally confirms that Juxon was far from being locked into party loyalties.

By this stage, Juxon was one of the senior officers in the green regiment approved of by the Presbyterian London militia committee established in May 1647. His half-uncle and former partner, Matthew Sheppard, was colonel of that regiment and his lieutenant-colonel was the Presbyterian activist, John Lane.[56] Yet in the purge of militia officers following the army's march into London in August 1647, Juxon replaced Lane as the regiment's lieutenant-colonel under the leading City Independent, Owen Rowe, as colonel. A Presbyterian account of these purges bemoaned the fact that they 'have turned out the discreet and faithful Colonel Sheppard, and put in the Bull Rowe, as also honest and stout Lieutenant-Colonel Lane, and put that swearing phantastic fool Juxon in his place. I suppose the rest of the commanders of that regiment will not be commanded by a knave and a fool.'[57] Thus in spite of the fact that Juxon was not a rigid supporter of any party, he undoubtedly aroused exceptionally strong feelings of animosity in some of his political opponents – from the royalist dismissal of him as 'a most violent ass' to the Presbyterian denunciation of him as 'that swearing phantastic fool'.

Unfortunately, the journal ends with the army's march into London and the flight of the eleven members, and there is no surviving record of Juxon's attitude to, or possible role in, the subsequent events leading up to the king's trial and execution and the political revolution of 1648–49. His judgement on events may have been characteristically ambivalent: approving of the end of monarchy and the House of Lords but opposed to the army's intervention into the political arena to bring

---

[54] Below, p. 137.
[55] Below, p. 169.
[56] Nagel, 'The militia of London, 1641–49', appendix 4, p. 318; Lindley, pp. 377–8.
[57] Nagel, appendix 5, p. 319; Lindley, p. 388; *A pair of spectacles for the City* (4 Dec 1647), BL, E419/9, p. 9.

this about. Perhaps his belief in a providential God led him to share with other godly contemporaries a heightened belief in millenarianism. He would almost certainly have had little time for the Levellers and their ideas on religious and political freedom. Making one brief and final appearance on the English political stage in 1659, Juxon was elected MP for Helston, Cornwall, in Richard Cromwell's parliament. However, his parliamentary career appears to have been fairly non-descript.[58] At the Restoration, he became a leading figure among Irish adventurers seeking secure titles to the lands they had acquired in Ireland, and was resident in Dublin for a time busily engaged in that project.[59] However, he was back in London in 1669, if not sooner, when he was admitted to the court of assistants of the merchant taylors' company, and remained active in its deliberations until the spring of 1672.[60] By the latter date, he had remarried and he subsequently returned to Ireland to set up a new household with his second wife in Dublin.[61] Juxon died on 2 October 1672, and was buried on 14 October in St James's church, Dublin.[62]

The journal's provenance

Juxon's journal is deposited in Dr Williams's Library, 14 Gordon Square, London WC1H 0AG. The document measures five inches by seven inches, contains 121 folios and is bound in vellum covers which are worn and damaged, especially along the spine, and the edges of some of the enclosed pages are slightly frayed. The journal came into the library's possession on 25 March 1850 when the Rev. George Kenrick

---

[58] C 219/46/11; *CJ*, vii. 595, 600, 609, 622–3, 634, 637, 711–12; J. T. Rutt (ed.), *Diary of Thomas Burton* (4 vols., 1828), iii. 560; iv. 211.

[59] *CSPD Ireland, 1660–62*, pp. 101, 337. His 1672 will suggests he had been a resident of Dublin for some time. There is a reference to plate and other goods in Dublin; bequests were made to two Dublin parsons; his son William had been left there to be cured of his 'melancholy distemper'; and an earlier will made by Thomas Juxon had been lodged with an official of the exchequer in Dublin: below, appendices, pp. 188–91.

[60] He was elected fourth warden of the merchant taylors on 30 July 1669; was sworn a warden's substitute and an assistant of the company on 6 August 1669; was elected head or master warden on 12 July 1670; and was attending meetings of the court of assistants in April 1672: Guild., court minute books of the merchant taylors' company, vol. 10, pp. 245, 248, 321, 445–7.

[61] His will refers to a bequest to his new wife of all his plate and goods in Dublin 'and going thither', indicating that a move of household was in progress at the time the will was made: below, appendices, p. 189.

[62] National Library of Ireland (Genealogical Office), funeral entries, vol. 4, Ms. 67, fo. 178; ibid., vo. 11, Ms. 74, fo. 8. The design of Juxon's shield is laid out in the first entry. His widow was to marry Daniel Williams in 1675: *DNB*, xxi. 387.

(1792–1874), whose pencilled note is on folio 1, presented it on behalf of his brother, Samuel Kenrick of Handsworth (1790–1854).[63] Joseph Hunter, the antiquarian, had seen the journal by 1850 (perhaps before its presentation to the library on 25 March 1850) and was to subsequently transcribe the first 89 folios.[64] The journal was described and identified in the catalogue of Dr Williams's Library manuscripts drawn up by W. H. Black in 1858. George Yule appears to have been the first historian to consult the journal this century when researching his work on the Independents in the English Revolution.[65]

The journal probably came into the possession of the Kenrick family by a line of descent from Elizabeth Juxon, Thomas's daughter, but the precise route it took is somewhat conjectural. Elizabeth married her second husband John Wynne (d. 1714), a London barrister and one of the sons of William Wynne (1619–92), the builder of Wynne Hall. John Wynne was to bequeath much of his property to his niece, Sara Hamilton. The latter married as her second husband the Rev. John Kenrick (1683–1744), and the journal may have passed successively from father to son: from the Rev. John Kenrick to John Kenrick (1725–1803), from John to Timothy Kenrick of Exeter (1759–1804), and from Timothy to Samuel Kenrick of Handsworth whose brother George donated it to the library.[66] However, the journal may have passed more directly into the Kenrick family before Sara Hamilton's marriage to the Rev. John Kenrick. John Wynne predeceased his wife Elizabeth (Juxon's daughter) by eight years and it is unlikely that Elizabeth would have countenanced her father's manuscript passing into the possession of one of her late husband's nieces in her own lifetime. In her will made 8 March 1715, Elizabeth merely bequeathed to Sara Hamilton £20 for the purchase of a bed.[67] The main beneficiary of Elizabeth's will, and her sole executrix, was Mary Kenrick, the daughter of her cousin Rebecca Kenrick and granddaughter of Thomas Juxon's elder sister, Elizabeth,[68] and this seems to be a more likely route for the journal to reach the Kenrick family. There is no disputing the fact, however, that given the clearly close relations between Thomas Juxon

[63] Dr Williams's Library, the book of benefactors, fo. 183; a typescript note on provenance by John Creasey, the former librarian of Dr Williams's Library, inserted in the journal.

[64] BL, Add. Ms. 25,465. Hunter's transcript contains frequent errors, and several passages in the diary are omitted, especially towards the end of his transcript. A pencilled note at the end of the transcript (fo. 84) reads 'For continuation surplus 126 larger book top of page', but no such continuation of the transcript has been found.

[65] Communication from John Creasey, librarian of Dr Williams's Library.

[66] This is the route suggested in Creasey's typescript note.

[67] PRO, PROB 11/585/355 will of Mrs Elizabeth Wynne.

[68] Rebecca Gethin (Thomas Juxon's niece) had married Richard Kenrick on 17 May 1664 at St Peter Cornhill, London: International genealogical index, London.

and his family and Daniel Williams, the library that came to bear the latter's name is a most fitting eventual home for Juxon's journal.

The journal

Its format The manuscript is more accurately described as a journal rather than a diary in the conventional sense of a daily record of events, thoughts and reactions with a strong personal flavour. Except for the brief note about his marriage, there is nothing of a personal and private nature, nor do more mundane matters, such as his social calendar, feature at all. Juxon uses the first person singular just twice in the whole work (once when clarifying a statement and secondly when referring to his marriage), preferring instead to use the first person plural when not using impersonal forms of speech. His focus is almost exclusively on public affairs and political and military developments, and his perspective switches backwards and forwards between the City of London, the English parliament, Scotland and (to a much lesser degree) Ireland, and continental Europe.[69] It is a work of both description and analysis, showing developments within the different political arenas as interacting with one another under the watchful eye of a providential God, who could be expected to intervene to mould events when the need arose. In short, it is a major work of historical discourse in which periodic divine intervention is taken as axiomatic.

The narrative generally keeps to a chronological order, although Juxon's original text rarely provides consistently clear guidance as to dating. This can often be imprecise and has a tendency to leave it to the reader to furnish exact dates. There are at least twenty-nine dating errors in the journal, the vast majority giving the correct month but wrong day, and most of the latter are out by one day only. Juxon regularly halts his narrative, or sometimes inserts marginalia, to provide an analysis of the current situation, draw conclusions from events or developments, point up a moral, or record the beneficent intervention of God. He is quite consciously addressing an intelligent and, he assumes, sympathetic readership, and the text may well have been an initial draft of a work intended for eventual publication. This might explain his habit in the first thirty-nine folios of including reference numbers in the text immediately following mention of important declarations, letters, papers, speeches and the like.[70] The intention may

---

[69] The listing of royal birthdays at the start of the journal is completely out of character with the rest of the work. Perhaps it was the result of an earlier abandoned project to keep a commonplace book.

[70] Reference numbers are provided in eighteen instances, although the first seven have been crossed out.

have been to add later pertinent details from these sources, or possibly provide their text in appendices. Similarly, at four points in the journal there are significant blank sections which appear to be awaiting the addition of further text about Essex's 1644 setback in the west, the king's 1645 letter to the Lords, the Scots' 1646 letter to parliament concerning the 'unknown knight', and the March 1646 address of a parliamentary delegation to common council.[71] Furthermore, one written page of manuscript has been torn out of the journal.[72] This immediately follows a note about the interception by parliament of a letter from Edward Hyde in Jersey to the duke of Hamilton in Pendennis Castle, and perhaps originally contained further comment on that letter and its significance. There are a number of brief deletions and insertions in the journal, and at one point a passage of text is crossed out and a reworked text substituted.[73] One page of text is inexplicably in a different hand and, on another page, there are two marginal references in red ink.[74] A hand drawn in the margin occasionally points to a particular section of text.

There are three points at which Juxon goes over the same ground twice: the king's final escape from Oxford, the army officers' petition leading to the 'declaration of dislike', and the City's gaining of control over the militia.[75] Otherwise Juxon writes economically in plain, if at times somewhat compressed and ungainly, prose with the odd osten-tatious display of his knowledge of French and Latin and occasional displays of wit and gentle irony. He draws upon a Scottish term, for example, to mock the Scots' obsequiousness to their 'gend king', and in a similar vein refers to the 'twa kingdoms'. He also ridicules the obsession with social precedence that kept two princesses away from a wedding, 'such a hindrance is greatness to human society'.[76] A clearly well-informed royal response to the City remonstrance of May 1646 'seemed extreme luckily to favour' it, while Charles could not possibly 'desire the settlement of Presbytery out of love to it'.[77]

There are occasional factual and other errors in the journal apart from chronological slips. Juxon consistently confuses Guernsey with Jersey and mistakes Cardigan for Cardiff, the earl of Callander for the earl of Crawford and Lindsay, a mythical 'Lord St Leger' for Lord Sinclair, and, more surprisingly, Henry IV for Henry VIII.[78] He is wrong in his assertion

[71] Below, pp. 58, 96, 107, 111.
[72] Below, p. 127.
[73] Below, p. 89.
[74] Below, pp. 73–4, 75, 76.
[75] Below, pp. 118, 120, 152, 153, 154–5, 156.
[76] Below, pp. 81, 82, 117, 147.
[77] Below, p. 124.
[78] Below, pp. 105, 119, 120, 126, 134.

that the Independents were opposed to the execution of Sir John Hotham and in his estimate of the relative size of the opposing armies at Naseby.[79] He is also mistaken about the numbers of citizens subscribing the Presbyterian petition of March 1646 and the numbers of horse and foot desired by the Northern Association in April 1646.[80] The purported conversation between the countess of Bedford and the king which Juxon carefully quotes has the appearance of fanciful hearsay.[81] Yet such errors and uncorroborated reports are remarkably exceptional when set against the veracity and accuracy of the journal as a whole, and the obvious question arises: from where did Juxon derive his information?

Juxon would appear to have drawn upon a combination of public and private sources. One major source of information in the public domain was the constant stream of published material in the form of newsbooks, published letters, and printed accounts of battles and other key events. One general report of affairs begins 'For domestic news this week', and is followed shortly afterwards by 'We had also letters' introducing news about a military engagement.[82] Phrases such as 'there came news', 'there came news likewise', or simply 'news came', introduce factual reports of events or actions.[83] Cromwell's published letters furnished Juxon with details of the action taken against west country clubmen.[84] The surrender of Bristol in September 1645 was 'as by the printed relations', and details of the battle of Philiphaugh were clearly derived from a published source.[85] Other unpublished sources were of a semi-public nature, although some may eventually have reached the printing press. Juxon notes that parliament could rely on daily intelligence from Oxford, and he was apparently privy to some alarming fresh intelligence from royalist quarters which the parliamentary army committee hurriedly imparted to the London militia committee in April 1646.[86] A parliamentary agent, Monsieur Augier, provided regular intelligence from Paris on royalist intrigue in France, and Juxon apparently had some access to this correspondence.[87] There are also suggestions, conveyed by the use of the phrase ''tis said', that some information was gleaned from current reports heard on the streets or in major gathering places such as the palace of Westminster, the

[79] Below, pp. 71 & n. 186, 79–80 & n. 228.
[80] Below, pp. 108 & n. 353, 116 & n. 394. There are a further five instances of completely wrong or inaccurate statements: below, pp. 43 & n. 32, 118 & n. 401, 121 & n. 422, 153 & n. 581, 157 & n. 600.
[81] Below, p. 82 & n. 235.
[82] Below, pp. 93, 94.
[83] For example, below, pp. 99, 100.
[84] Below, p. 81.
[85] Below, pp. 84, 85 & n. 253.
[86] Below, p. 113.
[87] Below, pp. 119–20.

Guildhall or the Royal Exchange. As a Londoner Juxon could also observe what was being reported in Westminster and City-based committees. Finally, again as a London resident, he could personally witness events and report details about which other sources are silent.[88]

On a more private and conjectural level, Juxon had some important political contacts who could have furnished him with inside information. His uncle, Arthur Juxon, was a common councilman from 1643 to 1645, and Thomas himself was closely acquainted with the Somerset MP, John Harington, who sat in the House from July 1646 onwards. Although Arthur Juxon probably did not serve on common council in 1646–47 during those most eventful years in the City, his political contacts in the assembly would have been able to keep him and, through him, his nephew fully informed as to its political moods and major clashes. Thomas and his future wife, Elizabeth Carent, dined with Harington two days before he took his seat in parliament, and in the following August Harington sought his political advice. At the end of August, Harington conversed once again with Thomas and Elizabeth Carent prior to dining with the earl of Pembroke, and similar close contact between Harington and Thomas Juxon was to be maintained long after the period covered by the journal.[89] In addition, Thomas may have been personally acquainted with such leading Independent figures as Vane, St John and Lord Wharton.[90]

A final vital question that needs to be addressed is: when was the journal actually written? The answer is that it was almost certainly written after the events described, from notes taken at the time or from information gleaned subsequently. There are several pointers to this conclusion. Some of the chronological vagueness and the pattern of the errors in dating – especially how in many cases it is out by one day only – could be explained by the fact that it was not written on the day in question but afterwards. The blank sections may have been waiting for the addition of more text as the material was being organised for writing up. There are further clues in the text itself. There is Juxon's prescience with regard to the failure of Essex's expedition into the west in 1644, as well as his reference to the war ending where it began, with conflict between England and Scotland.[91] The reference to John Goodwin's contentious preaching in September 1644 fits into the chronological narrative, yet Juxon is also able to look ahead to

---

[88] For example, his report on the complicity of Alderman Bunce and some common councilmen in the invasion of the Houses in July 1647, or his account of Scots commissioners badgering MPs on 2 August 1647: below, pp. 162, 166.

[89] Stieg (ed.), *The diary of John Harington, MP*, pp. 29, 32, 34, 46, 61, 68.

[90] Below, p. 94 & n. 288.

[91] Below, pp. 56–7, 58, 61, 78.

Goodwin's sequestration from his living in May 1645.[92] The journal concludes in August 1647 with an account of Anthony Nicoll's confession, yet the first account of Nicoll's examination appears not to have been published until October 1647.[93] Juxon's reference to his own marriage to 'my dear wife',[94] rather than to his 'betrothed', also suggests that it was written up subsequently. The journal ends on the penultimate folio with the flight of the eleven members and the army in London. Could there possibly be a continuing volume taking matters through to the revolution of 1648–49 gathering dust in some private collection?

Its historical value There is much that is fresh and new in the journal which makes a significant contribution to an understanding of a complex period of political alignments and interrelated events. As a well-connected and well-informed London resident, Juxon is a privileged source when it comes to shedding light on the normally half-hidden world of City politics, and explaining the intricacies of its political complexion and alliances. Similarly, as a keen and intelligent observer of events, at a national as well as a London level, he provides a valuable perspective on a political and religious world that is on course for transformation. New and controversial tools of political analysis are sometimes employed by Juxon as he seeks to make sense of this changing world, but more often the recourse is to a more conventional godly explanation. Finally, a good deal of space and detail is devoted to the wider power struggles and key events taking place in continental Europe, which are subjected to a similar combination of secular and godly analysis.

City politics Two important London subjects are elucidated by the journal – the internal politics of common council, and the wider organisation and tactics of the Presbyterian alliance in the capital. The latter embraced the political Presbyterians at Westminster, grouped around Essex, Holles and Stapilton, whose Presbyterianism was founded more on political expediency than religious conviction; and the High Presbyterians of the City – London's Presbyterian ministers led from Sion College and their civic allies (the 'covenant-engaged citizens'), who were committed to a church settlement on the Scottish model.[95] Juxon is the main source of knowledge about the common council's political divisions and its internal debates, which the assembly's formal

[92] Below, p. 61 & n. 134.
[93] Below, pp. 169–70 & n. 649.
[94] Below, p. 150.
[95] The editors would like to thank Elliot Vernon for drawing their attention to the term 'covenant-engaged citizens' as the self-appellation of the High Presbyterian party in the City.

records were designed to conceal from view behind an outward show of civic harmony.[96] His analysis of the assembly's politics is grounded on the premise that majority opinion was decidedly more pragmatic than consistently partisan. Support for High Presbyterianism within common council was far from universal, and could never be taken for granted, as one of the votes on the controversial eldership ordinance of 20 October 1645 revealed, when, contrary to expectations, majority opinion was said to have endorsed Independent objections to allowing ministers the sole right to exclude parishioners from the communion.[97] Common council in early 1646, Juxon maintains, was a body within which a minority of party activists was able to impose its will on a silent and inactive majority. Thirty or forty supporters of High Presbyterianism were opposed outright by no more than five councillors, 'and the rest, who are the major part, are silent, as either not willing or not daring to appear; so a party carry on things there'.[98] However, faced with an unusually high level of attendance and the prospect of a headlong clash with parliament, as over the March 1646 petition, High Presbyterian councillors could lose the initiative and more moderate and conciliatory voices could prevail. Such an outcome convinced Juxon of 'the firm affection and inclination of the common council to the parliament, and that 'twas labour lost to attempt them'.[99] An attempt by militant Presbyterians a week later to revive the petition was defeated by the strong opposition of moderate councillors, and cordial relations were accordingly re-established between the City and parliament.[100]

Juxon is the main source of information for the little that is known

[96] Common council, the City of London's legislature, met in the Guildhall and was theoretically the representative body of all its freemen. Any freeman who was a ratepaying householder was eligible for election as a councillor and had to seek re-election each year. However, in practice councillors were usually drawn from among the more prosperous citizens and continued in office for successive years. Yet the common council elections of 1641 and, to a much lesser extent, those of 1642–46 proved controversial, as efforts were made to unseat political opponents. Common council had a total membership of about 237 councillors in the mid-seventeenth century but, like its national equivalent, the House of Commons, levels of attendance could vary considerably depending on the political climate and the issues raised. Common councils were usually called about five or six times a year, while the City's executive body, the court of the lord mayor and aldermen, normally sat twice a week and exercised a careful control over the former. The particular circumstances of the 1640s temporarily liberated common council from aldermanic control and led councillors to talk up the powers and privileges of their assembly, claiming that it was the representative body of the City. Juxon refers to common council in his journal as 'our representative body' and quotes examples of its presumption: below, pp. 102, 103, 122–3, 142.

[97] Below, pp. 89–90.

[98] Below, p. 106. In other words, Juxon is claiming that less than a fifth of the total membership of common council were openly and resolutely partisan.

[99] Below, pp. 109–10.

[100] Below, p. 111.

about the identities and activities of political Independents within common council. It is thanks to him that the seven Independent councillors who spoke out in the debate on the eldership ordinance of October 1645 are known.[101] Similarly, he is the sole source of information on Stephen Estwicke's prominence in the attack on the City's remonstrance of May 1646, as well as on the leading role of Robert Tichborne among the eleven members who insisted on recording their dissent to the remonstrance when it finally came to a vote. Yet on this, as on other occasions, the information given by the journal can be tantalisingly incomplete. Two of Tichborne's fellow dissenters are named, but the identities of the other eight are not revealed.[102] Likewise, it would be useful to know the identities of those councillors said to have played a part in the later petition of London Independents opposing the City's remonstrance, but no names are forthcoming.[103] The journal in April 1647 again notes Stephen Estwicke's leading role in resisting common council's attempts to force all members to retake the solemn league and covenant. It also fills in some of the detail about his violent expulsion from the assembly. Yet it is silent on the fact that John Brett, a fellow Independent councillor, had joined Estwicke in his recalcitrance.[104]

Some relatively rare details on debates within common council, or speeches to it, are to be found in the journal. There is illumination on the line of argument advanced by Independents against Presbyterian critics of the eldership ordinance of 20 October 1645;[105] the controversy sparked off on 11 February 1646 by the delivery of the letter from the Scottish parliament;[106] and the debate on the following 20 May over the City's remonstrance.[107] Furthermore, the journal is perhaps the only source for the content of the speech delivered by Samuel Browne, one of the parliamentary delegation to the assembly on 16 March 1646.[108]

The journal is essential reading for anyone seeking an insight into the organisation and tactics of the Presbyterian alliance in London. Juxon is at pains to stress the behind-the-scenes influence exerted by London ministers in this context, but perhaps some allowance should be made for his strong anticlericalism before fully subscribing to his clerical conspiracy theory. The City petition of 20 September 1645, complaining about the delay in settling Presbyterian church

---

[101] Below, p. 90.
[102] Below, pp. 122–23.
[103] Below, p. 125.
[104] Below, p. 156 & n. 596; CLRO, Jor. 40, fo. 215v.
[105] Below, p. 90.
[106] Below, p. 101; CLRO, Jor. 40, fos. 170–70v.
[107] Below, pp. 122–23 & n. 428; CLRO, Jor. 40, fos. 178v–8ov.
[108] Below, p. 109 & n. 361.

government, is described as having been 'fomented by the several ministers'.[109] London ministers are reported to have met together at Sion College to plan their attack on the Erastian nature of the eldership ordinance of 20 October 1645. They decided to work covertly through common council against the ordinance.[110] Presbyterian campaigning in the City continues during the following month, 'being stirred up and fomented by the ministers'.[111] The latter are again 'the contrivers' of the Presbyterian campaign to canvass popular support in the wardmotes during common council elections at the end of the year.[112] In early 1646, ministers are still exerting considerable pressure on common council to push them 'forwards and make them active'.[113] The passage of the measure appointing parliamentary commissioners to hear appeals against suspension from communion prompts ministers to send 'to their several agents in the City' to campaign against it.[114] Yet Juxon is also careful to record instances when the London clergy faced setbacks in their City campaigning; for example, they are reported to have failed to win the immediate endorsement of their objections to the 1645 eldership ordinance from the common council committee set up to confer with them.[115] Moreover, clericalist councillors were to have their hopes dashed when common council opposed granting ministers the sole right to exclude parishioners from the communion.[116]

There is also much valuable, and even previously unknown, information about the lay leadership of the Presbyterian alliance in the City, the tactics they adopted, and their wider political contacts. A Cheapside merchant, Lawrence Brinley, is identified as a key organiser of the City petition of 20 September 1645, copies of which had been printed and circulated in every parish for signature by all who had taken the covenant. As with other Presbyterian petitions, the plan was to gain common council endorsement of the petition prior to its presentation to parliament.[117] Juxon is particularly informative on the organisation of the City remonstrance of May 1646, and the high degree of coordination between City and parliamentary Presbyterians that lay behind it. He claims that the initiative for the remonstrance came from three leading figures in the earl of Essex's party – Sir Philip Stapilton, Lionel Copley and Edmund Harvey – and that after the text of the

[109] Below, p. 85.
[110] Below, p. 89.
[111] Below, p. 95.
[112] Below, p. 97.
[113] Below, p. 103.
[114] Below, p. 108.
[115] Below, pp. 89–90.
[116] Below, p. 90.
[117] Below, p. 85.

remonstrance had been approved by common council two prominent City Presbyterians, Captain John Jones and John Bellamy, sought Essex's advice on the timing of its presentation to parliament.[118] The journal is probably the sole source of information about a dinner attended by several peers and MPs, as well as some aldermen and other citizens, on 23 June 1646 at the home of another leading London Presbyterian, Thomas Browne, 'wherein the design is mutually carried on'.[119] The City's petition and engagement of 21 July 1647 is traced back to 'private meetings with all sort of persons' held in the city by the eleven impeached MPs.[120] In addition, some senior City figures are charged with complicity in the force upon the Houses of 26 July; Alderman James Bunce, along with some common councillors and others, are described as acting as an organising committee in the Palace Yard for the coercion of parliament.[121]

There is also some rarity value in Juxon's exposure of the political struggles that accompanied several City elections. He adds to other evidence about Presbyterian plans to use the common council elections of 1645 to canvass popular support in the wardmotes for another petition to parliament. At the same time, there were coordinated sermons in every ward urging electors 'not to choose men of erroneous opinions'. But most novel are his claims that the petition gained only limited support, for 'in several wards it was cried up, and in many not, so that nothing came of it'; an accompanying handbill campaign likewise did little.[122] The journal also confirms evidence from other sources that Independents fared badly in the common council elections of 1646, while candidates with royalist leanings did well. The explanation offered is that the ferocity of the Presbyterian campaign to unseat Independents and their supporters was such that even some Presbyterians fell victim and found themselves replaced by known royalists.[123] The surprise outcome of the mayoral election of September 1646, when the neo-royalist Sir John Gayre emerged as the victorious candidate, is also carefully explained by Juxon as the result of a three-way split in the parliamentarian vote produced by Independent/Presbyterian hostilities. The analysis is the occasion for one of the few contemporary exposures of political tensions and voting patterns within the City's electoral body of common hall.[124]

[118] Below, pp. 114, 123.
[119] Below, p. 128.
[120] Below, p. 161.
[121] Below, p. 162.
[122] Below, p. 97.
[123] Below, p. 144 & n. 546.
[124] Below, pp. 136–7 & nn. 510–14.

National politics In striving to make sense of the complex world of civil war politics, Juxon frequently resorts to the language of 'interest'. 'Seventeenth-century England', as Blair Worden has recently observed, 'saw a growing understanding of the extent to which politics is governed not by ethics or rights but by the "interests" of those who participate in it.'[125] The crown's perceived encroachment upon proprietorial interests during the early Stuart period probably did much to encourage this shift in outlook. Nevertheless, it was not until the early 1640s that the theory and language of interest became common currency among political commentators.[126] One of the most sophisticated exponents of this new political vocabulary was the civil war journalist, Marchamont Nedham.[127] Drawing upon a study of interest theory and the nation state by the Huguenot grandee, the duc de Rohan,[128] Nedham came to the view that the true or public interest could only be understood and served through the application of reason.[129] The surest way to reach a settlement, he argued, was if the various political groupings – royalists, Presbyterians, Independents etc. – abandoned all specious private ends and justifications and instead limited themselves to their rationally conceived or proper and 'peculiar' interests. Political stability, according to Nedham, did not demand that the parties sacrifice their particular objectives for the public good, as conventional wisdom dictated. Rather, it required the harmonisation of the parties' peculiar

---

[125] B. Worden, ' "Wit in a Roundhead": the dilemma of Marchamont Nedham', in S. D. Amussen and M. A. Kishlansky (eds.), *Political culture and cultural politics in early modern England: essays presented to David Underdown* (Manchester, 1995), p. 317. For the development and use of interest theory during the civil war period, see J. A. W. Gunn, *Politics and the public interest in the seventeenth century* (1969), ch. 1; M. A. Kishlansky, 'Ideology and politics in the parliamentary armies, 1645–9', in J. Morrill (ed.), *Reactions to the English Civil War* (1982), pp. 163–83; J. Scott, *Algernon Sidney and the English Republic 1623–1677* (Cambridge, 1988), pp. 207–8; R. Tuck, *Philosophy and government 1572–1651* (Cambridge, 1993), pp. 222–3, 228–40.

[126] Gunn, *Politics and public interest*, pp. xi, 1–3.

[127] The following paragraph draws heavily upon the work of Worden and Gunn: 'Wit in a Roundhead', pp. 317–19; *Politics and public interest*, pp. 47–8.

[128] The writings of the duc de Rohan influenced not only Nedham but also Algernon Sidney and a whole range of republican and Protestant theorists: Scott, *Algernon Sidney*, pp. 53, 76, 207; Gunn, *Politics and the public interest*, pp. 36–8, 48.

[129] Worden has argued that reason was 'central to the political creed' of the classical republicans of the Interregnum. They saw politics as essentially 'a conflict between reason on the one hand and passion and will on the other. Popular sovereignty answered to reason: the hereditary principle embodied passion and will': Worden, 'Classical republicanism and the Puritan Revolution', in H. Lloyd-Jones, V. Pearl and B. Worden, eds., *History and imagination* (1981), pp. 193–5. Juxon seems to have equated the royal interest, and perhaps 'greatness' generally, with irrationality (see below, pp. 23 n. 132, 29–30 & n. 188, 147), although whether he also shared the classical republicans' rationalist, Arminian leanings in religion is highly doubtful.

interests – a process of political compromise and accommodation which Nedham referred to as a 'union of interests'.

Juxon was thus employing a novel and indeed controversial mode of discourse,[130] although he rarely pursued the logic of interest into the Machiavellian territory sometimes explored by Nedham.[131] Juxon certainly applauded 'rational proceeding',[132] and was capable of taking a very dispassionate, Nedhamite view of politics; as at one point, for example, when commenting upon the Scots' alliance with the English Presbyterians: 'When the condition of the Scots is impartially considered, they had reason to apply themselves to the people and to make their party as strong as they could, else might the king and Independents have joined against them and they but left to shift for themselves.'[133] Similarly, he maintained that the parliamentarians' failure to prevail against the king was attributable in part to their propensity for being 'false to our own interests'.[134] These kind of pronouncements are reminiscent of the arguments used by Nedham in his more developed explications of interest theory.[135] And like Nedham in such works, Juxon eschewed the use of biblical quotations to make his point. But generally speaking, he employed the language of interest within the more conventional framework of the politics of virtue. The result is a curious mixture of high political analysis in sceptical, Machiavellian strain (although the Florentine never used the term 'interest') and the moral perspective on public events of the godly.[136] In common with many parliamentarian writers, Juxon interpreted the events of the civil war years as essentially a struggle between a public good, conceived in ethical and broadly puritan terms,[137] and selfish, private interests.[138]

[130] The novelty of the language of interest for Juxon is underlined by his occasional use of the Italianate forms 'interesse' or 'intresse'. See Tuck, *Philosophy and government*, p. 223.

[131] The language of interest has been described by J. Scott as a 'sceptical and potentially ... "morally ambivalent" form of analysis': Scott, *Algernon Sidney*, p. 207.

[132] Below, p. 83. He dismisses the king and his advisers at Oxford as 'these men of strong fancies but bad intellects': below, p. 43.

[133] Below, p. 147.

[134] Below, p. 74. Juxon at one point employed a similar line of argument with reference to the king: below, p. 79.

[135] For example, a tract attributed to Nedham, *Good English: or, certain reasons pointing out the safe way of settlement in this kingdom* (8 May 1648), BL, E 441/10.

[136] For this blend of the Machiavellian and the puritan among mid-seventeenth century English radicals, see B. Worden, 'Milton's republicanism and the tyranny of heaven', in G. Block, Q. Skinner and M. Viroli (eds.), *Machiavelli and republicanism* (Cambridge, 1990), pp. 230, 232.

[137] The struggle between private and public interest seems to be interpreted by Juxon in partly eschatological and providentialist terms as an aspect of God's 'extraordinary design' for the destruction of 'sensualities ... pomp, glory and greatness' and the setting up of a 'new monarchy': below, p. 89.

[138] Gunn, *Politics and public interest*, pp. 6–7, 38.

Thus at several points in his journal he implicitly contrasts the 'biased', 'particular', and self-serving interests of the king, the peerage, and the political factions in general, with the 'real happiness of the nation' and the 'common good'.[139] The difficulty in reaching a settlement, he argues, was because 'everyone almost has sought himself and driven particular interest ... But now that all must be gathered up into one head (viz. salus populi) 'tis hard, nay impossible, that each particular should preserve his pretensions, but relinquish for the public good; and men being corrupt, here lies the difficulty'.[140] Juxon, therefore, like many seventeenth-century radicals, clung to a rather traditional, moral view of what constituted the 'public good', while conceding that legal and constitutional forms could be overridden in the interests of the people.[141]

Unlike Nedham, Juxon rarely used the term 'interest' to refer to the political factions themselves.[142] In such cases he much preferred the more conventional and often pejorative label of 'party'.[143] He sometimes used the word party in its non-partisan sense, meaning simply a group or a part of the whole − thus he refers to 'the party of the Lords', 'the recorder and his party', 'the Lord Northumberland's party' etc.[144] But on several occasions, and particularly when referring to the royalists or the earl of Essex's supporters, his use of the term party carried more condemnatory overtones, being virtually synonymous with his most damning expression of political practice, 'faction' − by which he means the pursuit of selfish ends against the public good, or any group thus preoccupied.[145] For example, he refers to both 'the party at Oxford' and 'the faction at Oxford' in very similar contexts.[146] The growth of 'parties and factions' at Westminster, he opines, had 'extremely retarded the work'.[147] And he clearly regarded the leaders of the 'covenant-engaged' interest within common council as an especially 'violent' and

---

[139] Below, pp. 68, 72, 75, 76, 95, 98, 103, 116. He likewise contrasts 'bad and interested men' with the 'good and conscientious': below, p. 103. Juxon's belief that the pursuit of private interest and factional ends represented the greatest obstacle to the advancement of the common good was echoed by the New Model Army in the summer of 1647: Kishlansky, 'Ideology and politics', in Morrill (ed.), *Reactions to the English Civil War*, pp. 177–8.

[140] Below, p. 116.

[141] Gunn, *Politics and public interest*, pp. 38–9; Tuck, *Philosophy and government*, p. 223; J. G. A. Pocock, *The Machiavellian moment: Florentine political thought and the Atlantic republican tradition* (Princeton, 1975), p. 373.

[142] Juxon refers on two occasions to 'the Scots' interest', and once to 'the clergy interest': below, pp. 103, 110, 124.

[143] For a discussion of the various meanings which attached to the word 'party' during the 1640s, see Kishlansky, *New Model Army*, pp. 15–17.

[144] Below, pp. 43, 52, 57, 84, 147.

[145] Below, pp. 49, 95, 106, 113, 116, 135.

[146] Below, pp. 40, 45.

[147] Below, p. 70.

factious grouping, even though he generally labelled them a party.[148]

Juxon's preference for the terms 'faction' and 'party', rather than the more neutral 'interest', when describing partisan groups is revealing. His view of politics was influenced at a basic level by the doctrine prevalent just a few years earlier of an organic political structure. The importance he attached to unity, particularly among parliamentarians, reflected more than simply a pragmatic acceptance that a divided house cannot stand. Unity, for Juxon, was almost a moral requirement. Certainly he equated the wilful breaking of that unity for private, immoderate ends with factionalism and a repudiation of the common good.[149] Not even the parliamentary Independents, whose political objectives he generally approved of, escape his censure on this score.[150] Thus he castigated them for courting the ungodly party of the earl of Northumberland and deliberately squandering resources in Ireland merely to advance their 'faction'.[151] However, insofar as the Independents' aims were broadly consistent with defeating the king and 'salus populi etc.', their partisanship was less reprehensible in Juxon's view than that of the peerage or Essex's supporters. Juxon was at his most disdainful when highlighting what he regarded as the wilfulness of Essex's party (particularly in blocking the establishment of the New Model Army) and its factional manipulation of parliamentary proceedings in concert with the Scots.[152] The only true guardian of the public good, according to Juxon, was the 'honest' or 'godly party' – 'party' here being used in its neutral sense of group.[153] None of the nation's political constituents had driven 'less particular interests' than the godly party, or had served the commonweal more faithfully.[154] During the war, he observes, not one member of the godly party had deserted parliament or betrayed their trust.[155] Yet as the very term 'the godly party' suggests, there was a partisan dimension to Juxon's

[148] Below, pp. 106, 110, 111, 114, 119, 125, 144, 151, 153, 164.

[149] Below, pp. 116, 135, 137.

[150] In March 1645, Juxon comments that even though the younger Vane and Oliver St John favoured the Independent faction, they 'most sincerely do intend the real happiness of the nation'. Similarly, he implicitly contrasts the Independents with 'honest and ingenious men', and 'wise and good men': below, pp. 76, 103, 116, 117, 128, 135, 147.

[151] Below, p. 147.

[152] Below, pp. 67, 68, 72, 74, 75, 75–6, 79, 105–6, 113, 129, 139, 143.

[153] Below, pp. 56, 58, 103, 104, 114, 151. The meaning which Juxon attached to the term 'honest' in this context may well have derived directly, or at second hand, from Cicero and other classical writers, who equated it with what was 'utile', i.e. beneficial to human society and one's state, and the civic virtues of 'prudence, justice, temperance and fortitude': Tuck, *Philosophy and government*, pp. 7, 8. That Juxon seems to have used 'honest' and 'godly' interchangeably as political terms suggests that he saw the latter as being redolent of the same civic and humanistic virtues as the former.

[154] Below, p. 103.

[155] Below, p. 104.

conception of this group. Although occasionally he uses 'godly' or 'honest party' to apply to both the principal parliamentarian factions as distinct from the 'malignants' – that is, the royalists[156] – more often than not he associates the term with the parliamentary Independents, or other opponents of the Scots and Essex's faction.[157] He evidently perceives a close affinity between the 'honest party' and the Commons (which for most of the period covered by the journal was dominated by the war party and pro-New Model Army factions):[158] 'Now, and never till now, have they acted like the Commons of England and as such who (de jure) are to take care of the kingdom and revive there their almost obsolete maxim, salus populi etc.'[159] He also lauds the 'active' men in the New Model as champions of the 'godly party',[160] and when assessing Scottish politics he plumps for Argyle's hard-line covenanting faction as the only honest party in the kingdom.[161]

The journal reveals not only how Juxon thought about politics, but much about his political and ecclesiastical preferences, and it is interesting to note that these appear to feature the same mixture of the radical and the relatively conservative which he displayed in combining elements of interest theory and the politics of virtue. It is also evident that for all his disapproval of partisanship he was far from being a neutral observer of events. His highly critical stance towards the earl of Essex and his senior officers – the 'soldatesta faction' as he once refers to them[162] – was closely in tune with the views of the so-called 'war party' at Westminster and its allies in the City. Like the 'fiery spirits' in the Commons and the City radicals, he suspected that Essex aspired to be a latter-day Sulla.[163] Although he was scornful of Essex's martial abilities, at the same time he feared that the lord general intended to 'bring the parliament under the power of the army'.[164] Indeed, it seems that he was undecided where Essex's and Manchester's military incompetence ended and their machinations to advance their

---

[156] Below, pp. 137, 164.

[157] Below, pp. 61, 63, 103, 114, 151, 158. Although at one point he distinguishes between the 'honest party' in the Commons and the 'godly party' generally, he saw the former as defenders of the latter: below, p. 104.

[158] Below, pp. 75–6, 76, 77, 103, 104, 114.

[159] Below, p. 77.

[160] Below, pp. 80, 86, 104–5.

[161] Below, p. 135.

[162] Below, p. 49.

[163] From 1642, argues John Adamson, Essex was directing 'a political campaign ... to confer upon himself protectoral rank and power', or the 'unlimited commission of a Roman dictator': J. S. A. Adamson, 'The baronial context of the English Civil War', *Transactions of the Royal Historical Society*, 5th ser. 40, 1990, pp. 100, 108.

[164] Below, pp. 42–3, 46, 52, 55, 56, 58, 60, 63–5, 74.

fellow 'grandees' and restore the king on easy terms began.[165] Juxon's hostility towards Essex and his 'wicked' officers also extended, as has been seen, to the earl's political following at Westminster and in the City. On the other hand, he writes approvingly of the leaders of the war party – the younger Vane and Oliver St John[166] – and looks upon the religious Independents in the parliamentary armies as 'the most active and brave men' in defence of the people's liberties.[167]

Where he clearly diverged from the war party, or at least its leadership, was in his opposition to the establishment of the committee of both kingdoms.[168] He disliked this body for the same reason he had its predecessor 'the committee for destruction, I mean safety';[169] that is, because he believed that it would encroach too much upon the authority of the Commons. 'There wants nothing now but a dictator' was his pessimistic comment after the first ordinance for the committee had been passed.[170] He also feared that the 'grand council of state' would give too much power to the Lords in matters of war and peace. Nevertheless, he was forced to acknowledge that 'the state of things considered, 'twas absolutely necessary to be done'.[171] Moreover, his account of the committee's establishment, and particularly the opposition it aroused among those keen that 'his excellency [Essex] only should have the government and ordering of the army', suggests that he may have seen it as partly an anti-Essex measure.[172] This would perhaps explain his failure to sustain his criticism of the committee beyond early 1644.

Some of Juxon's most critical remarks were reserved for the Scots – which is perhaps hardly surprising given that they had very few genuine admirers in England, even among their parliamentarian allies. The Scots, in Juxon's view, were for the most part subtle, insinuating and greedy; a people raised on 'water and oatmeal', their loyalties fixed too much on their 'gend' (foolish) king, and possessed of a great desire to encroach upon the wealth, honour and power of their southern neighbour.[173] In other words, Juxon harboured most of the anti-Scots prejudices typical of the early Stuart English. His attitude towards Scottish intervention in English affairs was more complex, however, and underwent several changes during the period covered by the

[165] Below, pp. 63–5, 66, 72.
[166] Below, p. 76.
[167] Below, pp. 52, 68, 80, 86, 117.
[168] Below, pp. 46–7, 48.
[169] Below, p. 47.
[170] Below, p. 47.
[171] Below, p. 46.
[172] Below, p. 46.
[173] Below, pp. 62, 75, 78, 81, 82–3, 83–4, 87, 112, 115–16, 117. He occasionally took a more sympathetic view of the Scottish people's miseries: below, p. 88.

journal. In keeping with his war party leanings, Juxon welcomed the Scots' invasion of northern England early in 1644 and repeatedly excused their failure to make greater headway against the marquess of Newcastle's forces.[74] Significantly, Juxon's first harsh words about the Scots occurred at precisely the point at which the war party-covenanter alliance was beginning to break down. In the journal entries for October 1644, he expresses disgust at parliament's willingness to 'crouch' to Scottish demands for suspending the accommodation order: 'Thus the Scots encroach upon us, [and] having a firm footing will now draw the curtain'.[75] There then follows a lengthy aside on the Scots' cunning and duplicity.[76] His distrust of the Scots was heightened following their alliance with Essex and his faction early in 1645. Only when the plundering covenanter forces were destined to quit the kingdom, and their leaders had resisted the blandishments of the royalists and the French in delivering up the king to the English parliament, did Juxon resume a more friendly tone towards the Scots: 'The truth is, the Scots have discovered a very great constancy to their principles and engagements ... and filled their own kingdom with war and misery ... [which] must certainly draw from us a brotherly sense and assistance'.[77] At various points throughout the journal, however, he praised certain individual Scots, notably the marquess of Argyle and men associated with his 'honest' party in Scotland, such as Alexander Leslie, earl of Leven, and Archibald Johnston of Wariston.[78]

Juxon's dislike of Scottish intervention in English politics had several causes. One was his contempt for the Scots' concern to maintain the king's prerogatives. Another, and perhaps the most important, was his aversion to the Scots' clericalism and their desire for a 'covenanted uniformity' between the two kingdoms.[79] Similarly, he would have been disturbed at the covenanters' perceived willingness to don the bishops' mantle and persecute those who dissented from their views.[80] When it came to settling church discipline and polity, Juxon was very much an Erastian. Parliament, in his eyes, should have the last word on such matters.[81] And, although at one point in the journal he portrays parliament's ecclesiastical policy as the product of statecraft, a delicate political balancing act designed to placate the factions,[82] he evidently

---

[74] Below, pp. 44, 50. Juxon concedes that the Scots had come to parliament's aid 'in our necessity and have done us some good charges ...': below, p. 83.
[75] Below, p. 61.
[76] Below, pp. 61–2.
[77] Below, pp. 133, 146.
[78] Below, pp. 122, 126, 128, 135, 140, 145.
[79] Below, pp. 86, 87, 94, 99.
[80] Below, p. 62.
[81] Below, pp. 61, 86.
[82] Below, p. 86.

felt that the Commons' resistance to 'government *jure divino*' was a wise and indeed moral principle. For MPs to establish *jure divino* Presbyterianism was 'in effect to dissolve the parliament and lose their privileges quite'.[183] He seems to have welcomed parliament's settling Presbyterian discipline in such a way as 'not to give any coercive power to them [the clergy] ... that all may not be in a confusion, but that those that will may be settled, like the enjoining the directory'.[184] As these remarks suggest, Juxon was not concerned solely with the threat to English liberties posed by Scottish-style clericalism; he also regarded toleration by statute as 'opposite and destructive to any settlement of discipline'.[185] 'God in his providence', he claims, had prevented the religious Independents from obtaining statutory liberty of conscience 'and suffered authority to set up Presbytery'.[186] 'Confusion' and 'coercion' were both equally distasteful to Juxon, and he apparently felt that *jure humano* Presbyterianism, with *de facto* toleration for tender consciences, represented a godly middle course between these two evils.[187]

If Juxon was more or less in the mainstream of parliamentarian opinion on church government, when it came to settling the kingdom's divided civil polity he may well have favoured a more radical solution. Juxon was deeply antagonistic towards two of the three components of the ancient constitution – the king and the Lords. Indeed, he was hostile not just to Charles I and the English peerage, but to monarchs and lords in general: "Tis a miracle to see how the kings and lords are haunted with a malignity against Jesus Christ, as if his kingdom were incompatible with their tyranny, as indeed it is. Both cannot mutually flourish.'[188] Juxon's lengthy accounts of European affairs were partly

[183] Below, p. 106.

[184] Below, pp. 86, 87, 89–90, 95, 119.

[185] Below, pp. 95–6. It would reveal much about Juxon's thinking on this issue if his reaction were known to the Cromwell-Saye group's attempts to introduce a bill in October 1647 giving limited toleration to Independent congregations and moderate Anglicans: J. S. A. Adamson, 'The English nobility and the projected settlement of 1647', *Historical Journal*, 30 (1987), pp. 584–6; Adamson, 'Oliver Cromwell and the Long Parliament', in J. Morrill (ed.), *Oliver Cromwell and the English Revolution*, (1990), pp. 68–9.

[186] Below, p. 128.

[187] Those of the City aldermen who opposed the covenant-engaged faction committed to an erastian Presbyterian church which preserved the parochial system while allowing limited toleration: M. Mahony, 'The Presbyterian party in the Long Parliament, 2 July 1644–3 June 1647', (unpublished D.Phil. thesis, Oxford University, 1973), pp. 192–3.

[188] Below, p. 51. 'Greatness', according to Juxon, is 'a hindrance ... to human society' as well as being incompatible with Christ's kingdom: below, pp. 92, 147. Juxon, it seems, like Algernon Sidney and Milton, drew little distinction between monarchy and tyranny. Juxon and Sidney certainly perceived an increasing trend among continental princes to trample their people's interests in pursuit of dynastic and personal ambitions: Scott, *Algernon Sidney*, p. 196; Worden, 'Milton's republicanism', in Block, Skinner and Viroli (eds.), *Machiavelli and republicanism*, pp. 228–9.

intended to demonstrate the folly of princes and the imminent downfall of 'tyranny and monarchia'.[189] Like his radical contemporary, Sir Cheney Culpeper, he regarded the peerage as a 'private interest standing in the way of public good'.[190] If the greatest faction in the kingdom was the king and his 'junto', then the Lords were not far behind. It is striking that Juxon never makes any effort to distinguish between Essex's supporters in the Lords and peers such as Viscount Saye and Sele who were prominent figures in the Independent party.[191] Instead, he lumps all the parliamentarian nobility together under the label of 'the Lords and their party'[192] – a faction which he regarded as little better than a royalist fifth-column: 'But that our (what do you call them) Lords are designed with their master, it would not be imagined they should act as they do';[193] 'The king knows that the Lords are sure to him upon the interest of their peerage';[194] 'the Lords and their party ... certainly are agreed with the king and drive his interest, nor can do other';[195] 'The Lords and that party do much labour to hinder the army under the command of Sir Thomas Fairfax ... which appears whose interests they steer to, and how little they regard the real good of the nation, their peerage being their great idol'.[196] He has good words to say about only two English noblemen – the earls of Warwick and Northumberland[197] – and his praise of the latter early in 1645 may merely reflect the fact that the earl had been conspicuous in his support for the New Model Army.[198] Later in the journal Juxon criticises the Independents for courting 'the Lord Northumberland's party – whom

[189] Below, pp. 48, 92. Thus the prince of Orange, in attempting to achieve absolute power, 'comes too late upon the stage to act that part'.

[190] Juxon and Culpeper would probably have seen eye to eye on a broad range of religious as well as political issues. Their differences were more of degree than kind. Thus Culpeper, a religious Independent, seems to have attached greater importance than Juxon to the benefits of toleration and freedom of conscience: M. J. Braddick and M. Greengrass, eds., *The letters of Sir Cheney Culpeper, 1641–1657* (Camden Misc. xxxiii, 1996), pp. 137–48.

[191] The one exception to this rule occurs near the start of the journal when Juxon refers to 'the party of the Lords' who were enemies of the Scots: below, p. 43.

[192] Below, pp. 67, 68, 72, 74, 75, 187.

[193] Below, p. 47.

[194] Below, p. 68.

[195] Below, p. 72.

[196] Below, pp. 74, 75.

[197] Below, pp. 57, 76.

[198] For Northumberland's role in the creation of the New Model, see J. S. A. Adamson, 'Of armies and architecture: the employments of Robert Scawen', in I. Gentles, J. Morrill and B. Worden (eds.), *Soldiers, writers and statesmen of the English Revolution* (Cambridge, 1998), pp. 36–67. Juxon is complimentary about only one European nobleman, the duke d'Enghien, whom he describes as 'a most gallant prince, a true gentleman' and, although a Catholic, 'very favourable' to the Protestant interest: below, p. 145.

they know are not godly'.[199] His antipathy towards the king and peerage was strengthened by a millenarian conviction that God had marked their cause for destruction in anticipation of Christ's second coming.[200] 'When He destroys the old,' Juxon declares, 'He will set up a new monarchy and bring in the desire of nations.'[201]

Juxon's repeated denunciations of Charles and his nobility, and his belief that their tyranny was incompatible with the happiness of the kingdom, went well beyond the position of many contemporary writers that the two Houses were better able to determine the public interest than the king.[202] Juxon's comments suggest that he conceived of little possibility of a lasting and well-grounded peace in which the king was restored to his prerogative powers or his legislative veto. Whether at the same time he favoured removing the Lords' negative voice is a more difficult question. Juxon probably agreed with the statement he attributed to the New Model Army grandees that 'though the people were rationally the supreme power, yet the parliament legally was'.[203] But what exactly he means here is debatable. Did his reverence for the institution of the Commons as the ultimate guardian of the public interest[204] extend to a conviction that parliament's sovereignty was inherent in its elective nature?[205] To admit this is but a short step from labelling him a republican, which is even more problematic. Republicanism, as many historians have pointed out, is notoriously difficult to define.[206] Yet if he indeed believed that the king and the Lords should lose their veto, or even be cut out of the legislative trinity altogether, then it would be possible to argue that he had republican leanings in the narrow, constitutional sense of wishing to vest supreme

[199] Below, p. 147. Warwick is also criticised later for persuading Lord Robartes to desert the 'better party': below, p. 84.

[200] Below, pp. 89, 98, 121, 138, 145.

[201] Below, p. 89.

[202] Tuck, *Philosophy and government*, pp. 228–30, 234; Scott, *Algernon Sidney*, p. 209. Juxon thought single person rule and the hereditary principle to be detrimental to the interests of the Dutch. Whether he thought the same with regard to the English is open to question: below, p. 92.

[203] Below, p. 157.

[204] Below, pp. 56, 75–6, 77.

[205] In other words, did Juxon agree with the New Model Army soldiers when they declared in June 1647 'this we speak of in relation to the House of Commons, as being entrusted in the peoples' behalf for their interest in that great and supreme power of the commonwealth, namely the legislative power, with the power of final judgement'? (cited in Kishlansky, 'Ideology and politics', in Morrill (ed.), *Reactions to the English Civil War*, pp. 174–5).

[206] See D. Wootton, 'The republican tradition: from Commonwealth to common sense', in Wootton (ed.), *Republicanism, liberty and commercial society, 1649–1776* (Stanford, 1994), pp. 1–2; see also B. Worden, 'Marchamont Nedham and the beginnings of English republicanism, 1649–1656', in *ibid.*, pp. 45–6; Tuck, *Philosophy and government*, p. 222.

power solely in the people's elected representatives.[207] What can be said with a little more certainty is that Juxon would have been generally out of sympathy with the Levellers. Not only was he opposed to toleration by law, but he seems to have been against any widening of popular participation in parliamentary politics.[208] If Juxon's sometimes unwieldy synthesis of interest theory and proto-republican, or classical humanist, ideas was probably unusual among London's 'better sort' during the later 1640s, his contempt for the 'multitude' and levelling ideas was far otherwise.

In addition to providing important insights into the development of political thought during the 1640s, the journal contains a wealth of original material on key events and figures of the period. As a wealthy and well-connected London citizen, Juxon was ideally placed to observe the unfolding drama of civil war – much of which was played out in or near the City. A good deal of his information probably came from the vast array of 'printed relations'[209] which poured from the London presses during the 1640s. But he also had contacts within the common council, the Commons and the Westminster Assembly.[210] As a Londoner, he would likewise have had easy access to the lobbies of the Lords and the Commons, and, more importantly perhaps, to the Guildhall, which was the site not only of the common council, but also from 1646 of the army treasurers-at-war, and the committee of both Houses for the army.[211] It was perhaps at the Guildhall that Juxon became familiar with Oliver St. John and other leading parliament-men.[212] Juxon thus enjoyed a relatively privileged position among contemporary news-gatherers, and this is reflected in his journal. His comments on national and civic politics reveal hitherto unknown details about the careers of several important figures, and resurrect long forgotten incidents for which the journal seems to be the only extant source. For example, he provides a brief but colourful account of the first day's proceedings of the Oxford Parliament in January 1644, claiming that the debate

---

[207] Juxon is best described as a 'classical humanist' (to borrow Markku Peltonen's phrase) rather than a classical republican. Although not concerned specifically with constitutional forms, classical humanism, in its emphasis on 'civic consciousness', 'citizenship, public virtue and true nobility', provided many of the themes central to republican thinking during the 1640s and 1650s: M. Peltonen, *Classical humanism and republicanism in English political thought 1570–1640* (Cambridge, 1995), pp. 1–17, 311–12.

[208] Below, pp. 95–6, 102, 158. Tuck has identified a number of political Independents during the 1640s who endorsed 'the principle of election and the supremacy of an elective assembly, though one without any "vulgar" participation': Tuck, *Philosophy and government*, pp. 235–40, 247.

[209] Below, p. 84.

[210] Above, pp. 4, 7, 16.

[211] Below, pp. 112, 113.

[212] Below, p. 94.

between Sir John Culpepper and his opponents grew so heated that "twas believed they would have drawn' if the king had not arrived to break up the quarrel.[213] Shortly thereafter the journal contains another fascinating revelation – that Fleetwood and Harrison quit the earl of Essex's lifeguard for the Eastern Association army as a result of a bitter quarrel with 'Stapilton and that party' arising from efforts by the City radicals to circumvent Essex's authority as commander-in-chief.[214] The journal also provides fresh evidence concerning Lord Robartes's seemingly inexplicable defection to Essex's party in the summer of 1644.[215]

Juxon applies a fairly broad brush to the political events of his day, but on those few occasions when he narrows his focus to report on proceedings in the Commons the journal often provides a unique glimpse of what would otherwise be long lost debates and exchanges on the floor of the House. He records how a Commons' speech by Sir Arthur Hesilrige in September 1644 was vital in preventing John Glynne and his allies from punishing the radical City MP Isaac Penington for his negligence as lieutenant of the Tower of London.[216] More importantly, Juxon's summary of Cromwell's address to the Commons on 25 November 1644 reveals much more personal detail about the speaker than any other surviving account of this speech.[217] Juxon is also the only source to relate that the countess of Manchester invited Cromwell and the younger Vane over for supper the night before in an effort to take some of the heat out of their quarrel with her husband.[218] Apparently Manchester and his allies were feeling rather more vulnerable at this point than some historians have credited.[219] Certainly Juxon's claim that 'most men' in the City cried Cromwell up and Manchester down suggests widespread support among London's well-affected for the campaign to new model the armies.[220] Were it not for Juxon nothing would be known about important debates in the Commons on 20 February and 26 May 1646 concerning the City's links with the Scots.[221] On two occasions the journal even cites hitherto unknown utter-

[213] Below, p. 43.
[214] Below, pp. 151–2.
[215] Below, p. 84.
[216] Below, pp. 57–8.
[217] Below, p. 67. A. N. B. Cotton has speculated that Cromwell's relation of the 'effect and substance' of his narrative against Manchester was not a summary of the whole speech and probably excluded 'very important sections of it'. Juxon's own précis of Cromwell's words, which differs markedly from the printed summary, certainly supports this conclusion: A. N. B. Cotton, 'Cromwell and the self-denying ordinance', History, 62 (1977), pp. 217, 220.
[218] Below, p. 67.
[219] Cotton, 'Cromwell and the self-denying ordinance', pp. 211–31.
[220] Below, p. 67.
[221] Below, pp. 103–4, 124–5.

ances by the king: firstly to the countess of Bedford after his dash into the Eastern Association in August 1645;[222] and secondly to his council before he left Oxford in April 1646.[223] But given that Juxon probably lacked the kind of privileged access to royalist sources that he had where parliamentary and civic affairs were concerned, both of these speeches can be regarded either as apocryphal or of doubtful authenticity.

Although the journal does little to alter the conventional image of Charles I or Cromwell, it considerably magnifies the importance of another key political player of the period, the Yorkshire MP Sir Philip Stapilton. Juxon implies that it was Stapilton who was the leading figure in Essex's faction in the Commons (at least until the lord general's death in September 1646), not Denzil Holles, as most historians have assumed. Thus the journal refers to 'Stapilton and that party' and the 'Stapiltonian party'; Holles is rarely mentioned on his own and never accorded a factional following.[224] Essex's death and that of Stapilton, thought Juxon, 'were the ruin of their party'.[225] It seems likely that the survival of Holles's *Memoirs* has exaggerated his importance as a party leader relative to that of Stapilton. Certainly as a legal adviser to Essex and captain of his life-guard, Stapilton would have been on more intimate terms with the lord general than Holles was.[226] Moreover, unlike Holles, Stapilton was a member of the committee of both kingdoms – a position that would have given him significant influence at Westminster in his own right. On a more general level, Juxon provides firm evidence of what Valerie Pearl, Michael Mahony and other historians of civil war London have often surmised, but never satisfactorily substantiated, and that is the close collaboration between the Essex–Stapilton party at Westminster and the 'covenant-engaged' citizens in the City.[227]

Besides adding a wealth of fresh detail to the narrative of the 1640s, the journal offers a valuable new perspective on the political landscape of the period. Juxon is essential reading for anyone interested in the composition and evolution of parliamentary and civic political factions. His interpretation of the divisions at Westminster is broadly consistent with the view of David Underdown, Michael Mahony and several other recent historians that civil war parliamentary politics was based not upon a rigid two-party structure, but rather on the interaction

[222] Below, p. 82.

[223] Below, p. 120.

[224] Below, pp. 52, 84, 104, 154. It was Stapilton, claimed Juxon, who launched the attack in the Commons upon the New Model Army in July 1646: below, p. 131.

[225] Below, p. 169.

[226] V. F. Snow, *Essex the rebel: the life of Robert Devereux, the third earl of Essex 1591–1646* (Lincoln, Nebraska, 1970), pp. 203, 313.

[227] V. Pearl, 'London's counter-revolution', in G. E. Aylmer (ed.), *The Interregnum: the quest for settlement 1646–1660* (1972), pp. 35–6, 38; Mahony, 'The Presbyterian party in the Long Parliament', pp. 206–7, 224–8, 330–1.

between a number of bicameral alliances and interests.[228] Juxon saw
parliament and to a lesser extent its armies as being 'subdivided into
so many factions that the public can scarce prosper'.[229] When referring
to divisions within the parliamentarians' ranks he sometimes does so in
terms of a conflict between one or a combination of these factional
interests and the public good as represented by the will of parliament
or the desires of the 'honest', 'moderate', or 'godly party'.[230] He charts
the emergence during the winter of 1644–5 of a particularly potent
alliance of interests – 'the assembly, the Lords and the Scots', 'the
Presbyterian and lord general's and Scots' party', or the 'lord general's
party ... the Scots and Presbytery' – which formed in opposition to
new modelling the armies.[231] Ranged against this alliance was another
consisting of the 'Independent party' and anti-Essex officers, led by
Cromwell, to which inclined the younger Vane, Oliver St. John and
others of the 'moderate party'.[232] Over the course of the journal,
however, and particularly from early 1645 onwards, he makes more
frequent use of a dualistic model of parliamentary politics, often
employing the familiar dichotomy of Presbyterians (or 'the Scots' party')
and Independents.[233] Whether this reflected an increasing hom-
ogenisation within the two main alliances or was simply a convenient
short-hand is not made clear. Problems of interpretation are com-
pounded by Juxon's use of the terms 'Presbyterians', 'Independents'
etc. in reference to both political and religious groupings. In fact, he
appears to draw very little distinction between the two in the case of
either party.[234] Admittedly, on the majority of occasions when the
journal refers to 'Independents', it seems from the context that Juxon
largely has religious Independents (often army officers or citizens) in
mind.[235] But it is often difficult from mid-1645 to determine whether he
is referring to religious Independents, their political allies, or both.

[228] Mahony, 'The Presbyterian party in the Long Parliament', p. 15; D. Underdown,
Pride's Purge: politics in the Puritan Revolution (Oxford, 1971), esp. ch. 3; J. S. A. Adamson,
'Parliamentary management, men-of-business and the House of Lords, 1640–49', in C.
Jones (ed.), *A pillar of the constitution: the House of Lords in British politics, 1640–1784* (1989),
pp. 21–50.
[229] Below, pp. 72, 104.
[230] Below, pp. 56, 58, 63, 68, 70, 76, 80, 84, 104, 106. 'The Scots, the assembly, City,
Lords, Stapilton's party, and malignants, their interests all meet in one upon several
considerations against the godly party ...': below, p. 104.
[231] Below, pp. 68, 76, 79, 83.
[232] Below, pp. 61, 63, 75, 76.
[233] Below, pp. 70, 89, 95, 112, 116, 117, 120, 125, 132, 135, 137, 144.
[234] For examples of this confusion, or conflation, of meanings see below pp. 80, 86,
94, 95, 112, 117, 133, 139, 144.
[235] Below, pp. 40, 43, 61, 62, 70, 71, 72, 75, 79, 85, 86, 95, 103, 123, 125, 158. For
'Presbyterians' and 'Independents' etc. as largely political labels, see below, pp. 75, 76,
83, 88, 147.

The historian who has made most use of the journal in recent years
is Mark Kishlansky, who harnessed it very effectively to his thesis that
the breakdown of parliamentary unity and the emergence of party
politics did not occur until 1646–7.[236] The journal certainly supports
Kishlansky's contention that the self-denying ordinance was a non-
partisan device for resolving the conflicts among parliament's senior
officers, rather than (as some contemporaries and most historians have
maintained) a stratagem advanced by the war party for removing Essex
and his aristocratic allies from command.[237] Juxon was aware, however,
that the ordinance would strike most forcefully at 'the Lords and their
party' by placing the army in the hands of men fully accountable to
parliament.[238] And in general the journal lends weight to the more
established model of parliamentary political structure in the mid-1640s
in which a clash between two parties, or two factional alliances, was
the dominant theme by the winter of 1644–5 at the very latest.
Westminster, in Juxon's account, was consumed by factional rivalry
and the struggle between Presbyterian and Independent well before the
showdown between army and parliament in 1647.

The European context 'Foreign news is little welcome to the plebeian or
vulgar sort of people, because they do not comprehend how much the
present affairs of Christendom are interwoven and connected ... yet
the meanest capacity may gather good fruit from the results, and see
the evident hand of God in the actions and motions against the
Protestants' enemies'.[239] Like the author of *The military scribe*, Juxon
thought foreign news a fruitful source for discerning the workings of
Providence. This was implicit in his statement right at the beginning of
the journal when he declares that 'Th'affairs of Europe respecting the
Protestant party ... give great hopes that ere long the despised generation
shall flourish'.[240] It is also likely that he shared the newsbook writer's

---

[236] Kishlansky, *New Model Army*.

[237] Below, pp. 69–70, 77; Kishlansky, *New Model Army*, pp. 28–32. For the argument that
the self-denying ordinance was a weapon designed by the war party for use against Essex
and other aristocratic generals, see V. A. Rowe, *Sir Henry Vane the younger: a study in political
and administrative history* (1970), pp. 55–7: L. Kaplan, *Politics and religion during the English
Revolution: the Scots and the Long Parliament 1643–1645* (New York, 1976), pp. 85–9; Gentles,
pp. 6–10. Mahony and others have argued in a similar vein, although with more emphasis
on self-denial as a response of Cromwell and his allies to their vulnerability following the
formation of the Presbyterian-Scottish alliance: M. Mahony, 'The Savile affair and the
politics of the Long Parliament', *Parliamentary History*, 7 (1988), pp. 214–16; Cotton,
'Cromwell and the self-denying ordinance', pp. 211–31. Ashton's analysis of the self-denial
initiative is broadly in line with that of Kishlansky: R. Ashton, *The English Civil War:
conservatism and revolution 1603–1649* (1978), pp. 226–8.

[238] Below, pp. 69–70, 72.

[239] *The military scribe*, (27 Feb.–5 Mar. 1644), BL, E 35/21, p. 16.

[240] Below, p. 39.

opinion that this subject was of little interest to the vulgar sort. The space
and detail which he devotes to foreign affairs, his occasional inclusion of
quotations in French,[241] and the degree of knowledge of overseas events
and figures he assumes on the part of his intended readership, are further
confirmation that he was writing for a reasonably well-educated, well-
informed and thus (on the whole) well-to-do audience. He probably
acquired some of his information from newsbooks, particularly those such
as *The weekly accompt* or *The moderate intelligencer* which tended to dwell at
greater length than their rivals on European affairs. However, it is clear
that he had other, more arcane, sources at his disposal. His disclosures
concerning the Prince of Orange's bed-chamber politics,[242] for example,
or his account of the voting patterns in the Scottish parliament,[243] do not
appear in any of the newsbooks, and it is likely that he obtained material
more directly, via his contacts among the London mercantile community,
or simply through gossiping on the Royal Exchange.

Juxon seems to have prided himself on his ability to elucidate the
Byzantine workings of continental high politics. The picture he paints
of European affairs was one in which self-interested factions and rulers
ruthlessly vied for power by whatever means available.[244] Broadly
speaking, he organises his material around three main, and closely
connected, themes: the struggle between the 'Protestant party' and the
'Jesuited papist' faction, the rivalry of Habsburg versus Bourbon and
the host of lesser quarrels it subsumed, and the king's vain attempts to
work around these conflicts in order to secure military and financial
support against his domestic opponents.[245] When recounting foreign
news Juxon sometimes adopted the air of analytical detachment which
Machiavelli had made popular among writers on international relations.[246] Indeed, at one point he uses that most Machiavellian of phrases,
'reason of state', and acknowledges it as a valid warrant for princes,
even when it extended to the execution of dynastic rivals.[247] But
underlying reason of state and the 'pomp, glory and greatness' of
princes Juxon perceives a more powerful force at work – the unfolding
of God's great design of destroying the carnal and tyrannical monarchies
of man and establishing His 'new monarchy' that would 'bring in the
desire of nations'.[248] Closely linked in Juxon's mind with Christ's

---

[241] Below, pp. 78, 112, 136.
[242] Below, pp. 52, 92–3, 146–7.
[243] Below, pp. 135, 145.
[244] Below, pp. 45–6, 78, 88, 146–7.
[245] Below, pp. 45, 46, 47–8, 52, 88, 90–1, 106, 112, 129–30, 131–2, 136, 144–5, 146–7,
149, 153.
[246] Below, pp. 45, 46.
[247] Below, p. 72.
[248] Below, p. 89.

imminent second coming were the endeavours of Europe's peoples, the English included, to frustrate the absolutist tendencies of their rulers.[249] 'This seems to be clear', he wrote, 'that their governments are generally so tyrannous and insupportable that, besides God's design, they do bespeak their own ruin.'[250] The civil war in England was for Juxon just one theatre in a European-wide conflict between the forces of Anti-Christ and the 'despised generation' – a group which seems to have included not only the Protestant party but the oppressed peoples of Christendom in general.

Editorial decisions and practices

The main aim has been to provide a clear text of the journal with a view to making it as accessible as possible. Hence, abbreviations have been expanded and spelling, the use of capitals, punctuation and paragraph structure have generally been modernised. The major exceptions to this practice have been the retention of the original variant spellings of the word 'interest' as well as the latinised forms of some other words, and Juxon's deliberate use of the Scottish term 'twa' for 'two', where a particular significance is attached to the spelling. Translations have been provided in footnotes for passages in French or Latin in the text or appendices. The editors have also made insertions into the text enclosed within square brackets to help clarify the syntax or to provide essential information. Dates are in the 'old style' except that the new year it taken to begin on the 1 January. In order to ease chronological reference, dates given in the text are highlighted in bold type. Furthermore, footnotes are used to provide the precise dates of actions or events noted in the text and to correct faults in Juxon's own dating.

The notes and references to dates which Juxon periodically provides in the margins of the journal are distinguished from the rest of the text by being placed within angled brackets < >. Words crossed out, substituted or interlined in the journal are underlined and explained. Folio references to the original text are contained within square brackets. London is the place of publication of works cited in footnotes unless otherwise stated.

[249] Below, pp. 92, 132.
[250] Below, p. 92.

THE JOURNAL OF THOMAS JUXON

[fo. 1: blank]
[fo. 1v] <u>1646</u>
Prince Charles born 29th May and is now 16. Princess Maria born 4 November and is now 15. James duke of York born 14 October and now is 13. Princess Elizabeth born 28 December and now is 12. Henry duke of Gloucester born 8 July and now is 6. Henrietta Maria[1] born 16 June and now is 2.
[fo. 2] Anno domini <u>1643/4</u> stilo novo.[2]

Th'affairs of Europe respecting the Protestant party do seem to congratulate the new year and give great hopes that ere long the <u>great</u> [crossed out] despised generation shall flourish.

That what is worth our first notice was the business of Riley[3] etc. <**January 1st [1644]** was committed to the Tower> to have made their agreement with the king (id est the City only) and been neutral without any respect to the parliament or the Scots, without whom we cannot (by agreement of both the nations) treat, and so to have, if possible, hindered their coming, as will appear by their examination 1 [crossed out].

Count de Harcourt,[4] who calls himself prince, does not succeed in his factorship for the queen and the Catholic party. [fo. 2v] The Lord Goring,[5] having stayed the coming of the States ambassadors as long as he could, is now gone [ambassador] extraordinary for France to negotiate aid against the parliament, whom they entreat honourably.

The State ambassadors arrive here, viz. Joachimi, <u>Mein</u> Herr Burnell <u>and Mein Herr Reinswood: the first, the old agent, an honest man; 2nd, recorder of Amsterdam, a subtle man and great Arminian; the last, agent and both favourites of the prince</u> [underlined section inserted later] who were honourably received two days since. <**12 [January]**> Thursday,[6] the Houses of Parliament, the Scots commissioners and

---

[1] Henrietta Anne, youngest child of Charles I.

[2] Juxon does not employ the 'new style' (or Gregorian) calendar, in actual fact, but keeps to the 'old style' (or Julian) calendar. However, this edition of his journal takes the new year to begin on 1 January and not 25 March.

[3] Theophilus Riley, the scoutmaster general for the City of London who was involved in Sir Basil Brooke's plot in December–January 1643–44.

[4] Count de Harcourt, ambassador extraordinary from France, sent to mediate a peace in England.

[5] George, first Lord Goring, Charles's ambassador in Paris.

[6] Should read 18 January 1644.

assembly, with his excellency and many commanders, were feasted by the City at Merchant Taylors' Hall, having first had a sermon preached by Mr [Stephen] Marshall at Christ Church, and then walked to dinner, where the trained bands, on each side, made them a guard; the lord mayor <the Lords etc. were [on? – Ms. torn] foot after the which [t]hey did not [like? – Ms. torn] to follow [the? – Ms. torn] horse [heels? – Ms. torn] an omission [the? – Ms. torn]> sheriffs and aldermen riding before.[7] After dinner they had a psalm sung, and, which was very commendable, a committee was [fo. 3] appointed to take care of the remainders, the best whereof was sent to the Bristol people at Doctors' Commons, the rest to the several prisons. Thus that design which was intended for division gave this occasion for a brotherly meeting and so a counter-mine of their design.[8]

The party at Oxford are commendable in this: that they are indefatigable and restless, for at this time their design had several branches and held correspondency with several sorts of men. For Ogle, Smart's beau-fils,[9] being in prison, conceived some hopes of gaining the Independent party to the king;[10] [and] observing that the synod[11] was like to discontent them, therefore entertains discourse with Mr Nye[12] and Mr John Goodwin,[13] by the means of his keeper, that they would propose their desires and he would undertake to have them granted, but then he must be released and go to Oxford [fo. 3v] to negotiate.[14] The business being imparted to his excellency[15] and others, 'twas agreed they should go on and leave [given] to correspond, and Ogle to escape, yet the keeper had the wit to get a £100 off him for it. Being gone, a trusty man was sent from hence to manage the business,[16] and, though a mean man, yet had particular conference

[7] *LJ*, vi. 378. For a fuller account of this dinner at Merchant Taylors' Hall, see Baillie, ii. 134–5.

[8] Juxon's view of the impact of Riley's plot resembles that of Baillie who claimed that 'This accident, though invented for division, has made a firmer union of the whole party than ever': Baillie, ii. 134.

[9] Captain or Major Thomas Ogle – Peter Smart's son-in-law – was a prisoner in Winchester House.

[10] By the 'Independent party' Juxon is probably referring to the religious Independents. The political Independent faction did not emerge until 1645.

[11] The Westminster assembly of divines.

[12] Philip Nye, the Independent divine.

[13] Of St Stephen, Coleman Street, the leading London Independent divine.

[14] The fullest account of the Ogle plot can be found in B. M. Gardiner (ed.), 'A secret negotiation with Charles the first, 1643–1644', (Camden Misc. viii, 1883). See also Baillie, ii. 135–7.

[15] Both the earl of Essex and a leading member of his staff, Sir Gilbert Gerard, were evidently kept well-informed about the plot's progress: Gardiner (ed.), 'A secret negotiation with Charles the first', pp. 13–17, 27.

[16] This 'trusty man' was possibly the bearer whom Thomas Devenish, the keeper of Winchester House, entrusted with his letter to the earl of Bristol of 5 January 1644.

with the king, but especially with [the] earl of Bristol,[17] who much wondered they should not be for the king. But 'twas answered that they were constrained and could do no less, the king aiming at them in all his writings under the notion of Brownists etc. Bristol told him 'twas an unhappy mistake and never intended against them, but desired not to press upon it for then 'twould reflect on him.

In fine, liberty of conscience was promised them with preferment to particular men, and that he had consulted the primate of Ireland,[18] who was of opinion the temporal sword was not to be used to compel the conscience; and said he did not [fo. 4] like violent ways of neither side, which, when he saw the bishop of Canterbury to go, did believe 'twould spoil all. Told him that the Presbytery would be bitter against them, and if they would now appear for the king they might hinder the Scots coming, from whom they must expect no friendship.

This intercourse was for a good while thus carried on with great expectation from them. In the meantime, they deal with another Independent piece, Lieutenant-Colonel Moseley of Aylesbury,[19] to deliver up the town to the king, who, with leave, went to Oxford and treated with the king, and a sum promised him, besides preferment and balls of wild fire, given him by the king's own hand, to set the magazine and town on fire if it could not be taken, and particular letters to him under the king's own hand. The time **<Sunday the 21[January]>** for the delivery was set and Moseley had £200 in hand. They were extremely importunate to have it done before their new parliament did sit[20] [fo. 4v], that there might be something to encourage them and an assurance of what they intended. To this end, Rupert[21] had drawn his garrisons from Towcester and other parts to the number of 4,000 for the taking in the town, who were constrained to march 3 days and three nights in the hard frost and deep snow, in so much that they lost 500 upon their march that were not able to endure it. They within the town were prepared to salute them, but being come within 3 or 4 miles they had notice of it and drew away enraged.

Devenish claimed that the bearer was 'in some measure made privy into the design in general, as one who hereafter good use may be made of, his interest in that sort of people [the religious Independents] being greater than his outward condition promiseth': Gardiner (ed.), 'A secret negotiation with Charles the first', p. 27.

[17] John Digby, first earl of Bristol.

[18] James Ussher.

[19] Lieutenant-Colonel John Moseley, an officer in the parliamentary garrison at Aylesbury.

[20] The Oxford parliament which first sat on 22 January 1644.

[21] Prince Rupert, Charles's nephew (son of his sister Elizabeth and her husband, Frederick V, the Elector Palatine), commander of the king's horse.

And to complete this work, at the same time the Lord Lovelace[22] sends a servant with a letter to Sir Henry Vane junior,[23] wherein desires to have a trusty agent sent to him; [and] for that he had matters of extreme consequence to impart, safe convoy should be granted. Sir Henry, being sensible it might be a temptation to his hurt, acquainted the solicitor,[24] Mr Speaker, Sir Arthur Hesilrige and Mr Browne[25] with it, [fo. 5] and, for the more security, the Scots commissioners. 'Twas agreed that (by virtue of an order of the Commons in Riley's plot for the better discovering of it by all ways and means possible) he should continue to correspond; therefore returns an answer that he would send him one Mr Wall,[26] a true brother and one in whom he might confide, desiring to use him with respect. This letter was showed to all the forenamed persons, and Mr Speaker had a copy of it signed by himself that 'twas vera.

Mr Wall went and met the Lord Lovelace at Maidenhead, stayed that night and had some hours conference with him in which he seemed to be ingenious. Several things were proposed to us and from us. Mr Wall desired le[ave?] to give in writing under his hand what he proposed to be for the better satisfaction of his party (for under that notion they went); he [Lovelace] refused, but Wall, for his memory, put the heads in writing. [fo. 5v] Next day returned [and] presented his brevet to them that employed him; 'twas reported to the House and approved. But in the interim, these gentlemen opposing the coming of my Lord Holland[27] into the House, the lord [i.e. Essex], to be revenged, would have had these 5 persons accused of treason for treating with the enemy,[28] as, they pretended, contrary to an ordinance of parliament; but could not be found. Then my lord general commanded Dorislaus,[29] his advocate, to examine Mr Wall and others in it, pretending 'twas against the laws of war, which the Houses did extremely resent – that they should accuse any of their members without acquainting them first with it, which they called the accusing of the five members; nay, that my lord general should seem to exercise a power over the members was to bring the parliament under the power of the army.

[22] Lord John Lovelace, one of several peers who had left the Westminster parliament to join the king at Oxford in August 1643.

[23] Sir Henry Vane junior, a leading war party figure.

[24] Oliver St John.

[25] William Lenthall, Sir Arthur Hesilrige and Samuel Browne, MP for Dartmouth (Devon) in the Long Parliament.

[26] Moses Wall, the earl of Warwick's chaplain.

[27] Henry Rich, first earl of Holland, younger brother of Robert Rich, second earl of Warwick, and a leader of the peace party in the Lords.

[28] *LJ*, vi. 381, 391.

[29] Isaac Dorislaus, advocate-general of Essex's army.

They their malice appeared; Stapilton[30] and Glynne[31] [inserted] was deep in it. His excellency said that Vane was always against the recruiting of his army, as if that obliged him to prosecute the business. [fo. 6] But they were quickly weary of the business. The Scots commissioners were sensible of it, and took to themselves, having an equal hand in it with Sir Henry. They plainly saw the party of the Lords etc. that thus pursued the business were not great friends of theirs, but had better assurance of Vane and the rest.

But here we may, by the way, observe the industry of the king's party, and how at the same time treated with the Independent ministers and officers and parliament men, and also had a concurrence with the citizens. The plot was well laid, though upon mistaken grounds, but it pleased God to fool them, these men of strong fancies but bad intellects.

<22 [January]> Monday, the anti-parliament at Oxford began, where the king came and made a speech to the Lords and then to the Commons in their House, though unusual.[32] In the Commons there was a gentleman that first spake and said the way to restore peace and happiness was to enquire the cause of their troubles.[33] [fo. 6v] That 'twas his opinion the papists should be first removed the court, then the army, and till [then? – Ms. torn] they could not expect to prosper. But 'twas quickly replied that the motion was against reason, in respect they had showed themselves as good subjects as any others and had ventured their lives and estates [more? – Ms. torn] than any. This grew to bandying on both sides, in so much that 'twas believed they would have drawn. Notice whereof was given to the king; he came and then quieted the business, but rejourned the House. And about this time, as the king sought to draw the Independents to him upon pretence of giving liberty of conscience, there was pressed in the common council[34] that the parliament might be petitioned to for the establishing of [church] government and to prevent gathering of churches and private meetings. By this means to disengage the same persons also, and, if possible, to do something in defence of themselves.

An Apology[35] of Mr Goodwin, Nye etc. 2 [crossed out]. The Scots

---

[30] Sir Philip Stapilton, captain of Essex's life-guard.

[31] John Glynne, recorder of London.

[32] Gardiner, i. 299; Rushworth, v. 560–61; Clarendon, iii. 293–4. The king addressed both Houses in Christ Church Hall and not separately, as Juxon claims.

[33] The 'gentleman that first spake' was evidently Sir John Culpepper: *The kingdom's weekly intelligencer* (23–30 January 1644), BL, E30/19, pp. 314–15; *Mercurius, etc.* (31 January–6 February 1644), BL, E31/18, pp. 9–10.

[34] On 22 January 1644: CLRO, Jor. 40, fo. 86.

[35] *The Apologeticall Narration* published by five Independent clergy at the end of 1643 in response to a November 1643 petition of London ministers to the assembly of divines

government clear 4 [crossed out]. [fo. 7] **<26 [January]>** News now came of the Scots being near Alnwick, which was very welcome 3 [crossed out]. That they came not sooner was from the ill weather, and then the wind being contrary could not advance sooner, having shipped their great guns. The snow did stem this service. There [i.e. at Alnwick], the enemy could not drive away their cattle nor fire their stacks of corn, as was intended. <A declaration of both kingdoms [6 crossed out]> A Scots declaration of their coming[36] 5 [crossed out] [words underlined inserted later].

<3 [February 1644]> News came this day of a defeat given to the Lord Byron by Sir Thomas Fairfax and Sir William Brereton upon the Friday before.[37] Upon th'approach of our army the enemy drew off from the town, ran'gned their army in battaiglio, we the same. Upon the first charge of our horse on the right of theirs, which was through and through, we retouted[?] them, and made them forsake the field, leaving the foot to our mercy, with th'artillery and bagage to us. Most of them remained our prisoners and many of [them] officers of quality. Many foot took the covenant.[38]

[fo. 7v] **<1 February>** Upon the Sunday last there came a trumpet from General Ruthven,[39] with a pacquet from him and the prince, duke of York,[40] Prince Robert and the rest of the lords and gentlemen of the conclave at Oxford, to his excellency, which [imparted? – Ms. torn] that they desired him to appoint commissioners, and they would do the same, to treat, if it were possible, to put an end to these distractions.[41] He returned for answer, by a trumpet, the covenant and declaration of both kingdoms.

Sir Edward Dering[42] came now in and did submit to the parliament, who have dealt favourably with him.

<2 February> The States ambassadors went for Oxford, not having had any visible conference with the parliament.

There came now certain news that the Danes had gathered about 7,000 horse and foot in Jutland to oppose the Swedes, with whom [fo.

---

opposing the gathering of churches. It brought to an end the earlier reticence of the Independent clergy by openly stating their differences with the Presbyterians: Tolmie, *The triumph of the saints*, pp. 95–6.

[36] Rushworth, v. 487–94.

[37] The battle of Nantwich, 25 January 1644, at which the northern parliamentarian commanders, Sir Thomas Fairfax and Sir William Brereton, defeated John Lord Byron, general of the king's forces in North Wales and the Marches.

[38] The solemn league and covenant of 1643.

[39] Patrick Ruthven, earl of Forth and Brentford.

[40] James, duke of York, the second son of Charles I.

[41] Rushworth, v. 566–7.

[42] Sir Edward Dering, a Kent baronet and MP; a political moderate who was the first to accept parliament's terms for a pardon at the beginning of 1644.

8] they had a battaiglia. The Swedes did wholly rout and surprise th'army, as well horse as foot, baggage and artillery. Their field marshal fled for Zeeland. They only stripped the Boares and sent them home; the rest generally took pay. So that the country is theirs. Besides, Gustav Horn is coming from Sweden with an army of 20,000 to fall upon Denmark, and Torstensson,[43] having recruited, will return into Germany. In the meantime, the state of Denmark have called an assembly and deputed some to the crown of Sweden for agreeing. In Italy they are pretty weary of blows. The pope has had the worst and labours a peace. The French, if they leave, will entertain their refuse and be with a great army in Italy in the spring.

[fo. 8v] The king, in pursuit of the cessation in Ireland,[44] has not only disaffected the English army that was sent over by the parliament and paid by the adventures [sic], and brought over to fight against their masters as the rest do against the Phesitiarii,[45] but also has brought over 1,500 Irish of the natives and commanded by the Lord Muskerry and O'Neill[46] with others, who have in their keeping the city and castle of Bristol, and the old garrison commanded out.

This week the count de Harcourt returned for France, his voyage being unsuccessful. 'Twas made believe that at his coming things would be in a readiness and both party [sic] willing, and that the king would allow them to be a parliament, but found it contrary. [fo. 9] The king (as Digby in his to [Sir Henry] de Vic[47]) has said this for a foundation of what he does: that he will never acknowledge the parliament for a parliament, which if he grants, he does not only approve of what they did before, but also since he left them, and so consequently null whatever he has said or writ against them; and besides, 'twould overthrow the anti-parliament at Oxford, and wither the expectations from it.

If they deny it to be a free or the parliament then the Houses would not treat. If they did, 'twould be under the capacity of rebels, which they neither could nor would do or suffer. He [i.e. Harcourt] refuses to call them a parliament and must not, because he's but an agent for the faction at Oxford and therefore to follow order. Being last at Oxford, wrote to the parliament and directed his letter to [crossed out]

---

[43] Lennart Torstensson, commander of the Swedish army in Germany.

[44] The cessation was agreed on 15 September 1643: Rushworth, v. 548–53.

[45] 'Phesitiarii' appears to be the full form of the word intended by Juxon but its meaning is a complete puzzle.

[46] Donough MacCarty, Viscount Muskerry, and Turlough[?] O'Neill: see Rushworth, v. 548.

[47] English resident at Brussels; the letter concerned was of 27 December 1643: LJ, vi. 368.

A Maisr [fo. 9v] A Messieurs Grey de Wark[48] and Lenthall, not owning them for anything [though? – Ms. torn] the speakers of both Houses, but 'twas excused – his secretary, being a stranger, was not well acquainted with their titles <yet might have learnt better at Oxford> And therefore, to be even with him, the parliament would not own him for an ambassador, so his work was at an end. Yet was not well-pleased that he should be sent for to be made a fool of, for he quickly found how squares went at court, where the Spanish faction ruled all, and Don Cottington[49] came not to visit him at all; which Harcourt ill resented and found himself in some danger to gratify the Spaniard while he thought himself pursuing his own interest[50] only, id est that of France.

[fo.10] There has been several debates about a council of state,[51] which at first the Lords propounded to the Commons, nominated their men and the Commons and Scots that should be joined in, and sent it to the Commons with an earnest desire to pass it, peradventure upon supposition that the king might come in, and then they only to be of his council. But now the Lords and some others that were left out laboured much to have an addition of lords, as Pembroke, Salisbury, etc.,[52] and if not that then to have none at all, alleging that secrecy is the life of an army, and it could not be amongst so many; that 'twas most proper his excellency only should have the government and ordering of the army, and to this he was willing.[53] But the state of things considered, 'twas absolutely necessary to be done, and that General Leslie would not willingly be commanded by Lord of Essex, specially his officers being so bad.

[fo. 10v] <11 [February]> At last it was concluded for 3 months, and to consult, debate and determine and [order? – Ms. torn].[54] <Their names> Earl of Northumberland, earl of Essex, earl of Warwick, earl of Manchester, Lord Wharton and Lord Robartes, Lord Saye. Commons: Sir Gilbert Gerard, Sir William Waller, Sir Arthur Hesilrige,

[48] William, Lord Grey of Wark, speaker of the House of Lords.

[49] Francis, first Lord Cottington.

[50] Lit. intresse.

[51] The committee of both kingdoms.

[52] Philip Herbert, fourth earl of Pembroke, and William Cecil, second earl of Salisbury, peace lords and allies of Essex.

[53] Juxon supports the view that the setting up of the committee of both kingdoms was an anti-Essex move. For analysis of the political make-up of the committee, see V. Pearl, 'Oliver St John and the "middle group" in the Long Parliament: August 1643–May 1644', *English Historical Review*, 81 (1966), pp. 508–14; L. Mulligan, 'Peace negotiations, politics and the committee of both kingdoms', *Historical Journal*, 12 (1969), pp. 4–5; Kaplan, *Politics and religion during the English Revolution*, pp. 18–24.

[54] The ordinance of 16 February 1644 setting up the committee of both kingdoms: Firth and Rait, i. 381–2.

Sir William Armyne, Sir Henry Vane senior and junior, Sir Philip Stapilton, Mr Crew, Mr Browne, Mr Recorder, Mr Solicitor, Mr Wallop, Mr Pierrepont, Colonel Cromwell. For the Scots: Lord Maitland, Lord Loudoun, Sir Archibald Johnston, Mr Barclay. By this means the close committee[55] is nulled and all things are to be agitated by this council. There wants nothing now but a dictator.

The Holland ambassadors coming to Oxford, the king would have assigned them a house, but they refused it upon the same terms as they did the same from the parliament, viz. [fo.11] not to be engaged to either side. A day of audience appointed them wherein they only gave the king some compliments (for, as themselves said, they knew not what else to say), which liked the king so ill that he told them if that were all they came for they might return again; which they took for an answer and were ten miles on their way when the king sent for to have them return back, and then told them he intended not that for an answer to them.

<7 [crossed out]> Earl of Forth,[56] general to the king, sent a letter to his excellency full of compliments, but in sum, desired to have safe conduct for 2 gentlemen from Oxford to bring some propositions. He sent it to the Houses. They, finding it not to take notice of them, would not of it, [and] sent it back. So, 'twas referred to the council of state.[57]

[fo. 11v] But that our (what do you call them) Lords are designed with their master, it would not be imagined they should act as they do. The grand council of state – whose ligament is secrecy, and therefore were all the members of it by an oath to [swear? – Ms. torn] it – when it came to the Lords they refuse it [to? – Ms. torn] mean their House <they claim this privilege as annexed to their peerage>, and upon this consideration: that they would have the liberty to come at their pleasure and hear their debates, that so Oxford might be furnished with the news, as they did at the committee for (destruction), I mean safety.

'Tis most credibly reported that this last Xmas, in the holidays, there came very [inserted] a great black eagle <with fired eyes> into the room where the duke of Saxe was at dinner; that it set upon one of the chairs of state for 3 days and nights, vomiting streams of fire a little before he vanished away.

The Swedes go on in Jutland; General Horn is come with a great army into Schonen. [fo. 12] This sudden falling upon Denmark does trouble France, especially since [Colonel] Guebriant['s] defeat. Hereby, that [sic] are forced to contribute the greatest part of their forces not

---

[55] The committee of safety.

[56] Patrick Ruthven (see note 39 above).

[57] i.e. the committee of both kingdoms. The parliamentary diarist Sir Simonds D'Ewes also used the term 'council of state' when referring to this committee: BL, Harl. Ms. 166, fos. 9, 12v, 13v.

only to recruit the foresaid army but yet more, because the emperor will now, by the absence of the Swedes, domineer in Germany and for the Spanish party there. They condole this a[s] the mutilation of a considerable member. Yet the common people of that kingdom rejoice at it, surely out of a natural abhoring tyranny and monarchia; so also does our people. And though the prince of Orange does favour Denmark, yet the Hanseatic towns the contrary.

Since our council of estates was established the transactions of state are with little noise. Sir Richard Grenville, brother to Sir Bernard, who had been a commander for us in Ireland, upon his return here took the covenant and was entertained, being a brave soldier, [fo.12v] and honoured with the charge of being lieutenant <28th[February]> general of the horse to Sir William Waller;[58] fairly rode to the king when the [sic] went down towards his charge, carrying £1,200 with him.

The Scots are come over the Tyne at [Hexham? – Ms. torn] and afterwards took Sunderland.

<March [1644]> Rákóczi[59] is entered Hungaria with a great army, and beaten Humanei [word circled] the Hungarian Palatinate forces. The great Turk will second him. 'Tis now certainly known that the king of Denmark and prince of Orange were resolved to join in an assistance of the king against the parliament, but 'tis now prevented. The Swedes have sent to his excellency that there might be an amity between the parliament and them, and that they would assist them with ships etc.

<7 [March]> The States ambassadors returned from Oxford, and write a letter to the speakers of both Houses that they had something to offer to them towards a treaty. [fo. 13] 'Tis therefore moved in the Commons' House that as they have always been forward, so now also to show their readiness. Therefore, did there pass a vote, <15 [March]> which was after delivered to the Lords, that something might be agreed on by the grand council of state as a ground for a firm and lasting peace; and in regard the commissioners of Scotland had instructions to that purpose, that they [i.e. the Scots] might thereby have something to work upon 'twas referred to the aforesaid grand council of state.

Grenville was proclaimed traitor, rogue and skellum, and the proclamation hung upon a gibbet in the Palace Yard and at th'Exchange.

While the parliament are thinking upon propositions, and the king seems to be forward, they [i.e. the Houses] at Oxford do proclaim the parliament, the earl of Essex and all that adhere to him and assist him

---

[58] Sir William Waller, Essex's rival for command of the parliamentary forces.
[59] György Rákóczi, prince of Transylvania.

with [inserted] the Scots army, traitors.[60] Thus does God seem to dislike always our inclining to accommodate with them [fo. 13v] whom God will have no peace with, and by this does, as it were, clearly show their design for ruin.

<21 [March]> It pleased God now to send us bad news, for whereas Sir John Meldrum,[61] with a great body, had lain before Newark and were in a great possibility of gaining of it, Prince Robert comes unexpected, with forces from Yorkshire joining to him. At which time our commanders were ready to fall by th'ears; the Lord Willoughby with Colonel King, whom earl [of] Manchester had given the command of that country to under him. My lord would not obey him, no more the other officers.[62]

And so Robert came up to the trenches, having there beat a party of our horse who went before to charge them over a bridge; 2 regiments of foot were commanded to attend that service and secure their retreat over the bridge, but at their return found none, and so were enforced to shift for themselves, by which means, unawares, came to their trenches. Then were propositions agreed on to leave all fire-arms and ammunition, and to march away with sword and colours etc. [fo. 14], but having them in their power left them not so much as their clothes.

'Twas too much confidence on our side that kept back relief; and then some say the soldatesta faction[63] would not let Sir John have the honour of the reduction, being too honest for them. This did much amaze us, being contrary to expectation, and advantage them by reputation.

<10 [April 1644]> It pleased God now this Saturday to give us a reviving from Sir William Waller, and while we were mourning our tears were wiped away.[64] Sir Ralph [Hopton] had the advantage in number, being 12,000; and we, but 8,000, had the advantage of a hill and a wood, which he gained and had routed Balfour's horse, but our reserve recovered it and then both gave fresh charges. 'Twas well fought on both sides, but it pleased God to give us the day, which, when they observed, drew away their artillery. We pursued them and routed their whole foot; lost about 40, they 500 with many prisoners. Colonel Thomson[65] of horse [inserted] lost a leg, yet so far from being

---

[60] On 12 March 1644: Rushworth, v. 565.

[61] Sir John Meldrum, the Scottish commander of the parliamentary forces in Nottinghamshire.

[62] For the quarrel between Colonel King and Lord Willoughby, see C. Holmes, 'Colonel King and Lincolnshire politics, 1642–46', *Historical Journal*, 16 (1973).

[63] Juxon seems to be referring here to the cadre of senior officers associated with Essex, which included Lord Willoughby.

[64] The battle of Cheriton, Hampshire, on 29 March 1644. News of the victory reached Westminster on 1 April: *CJ*, iii. 443.

[65] George Thomson, colonial trader and brother of Maurice Thomson.

discouraged that he said he had another leg to lose for Jesus Christ. The word on our side was (God for us), which the enemy also had; then was ours Christ save us.

[fo. 14v] Upon this defeat, the king is persuaded again to set up his standard, which was done at Marlborough,[66] hoping thereby to draw in the country, who, though force was added to this act, yet prevailed it not, for few fish came into the net.

Our counsels were conform to this, therefore a general rendezvous was appointed to be at Aylesbury upon the 19th present for all the forces on this side [of the] Trent to march thither. This made the king's party apprehend Oxford and their other garrisons that were drawn out to be in danger; did therefore quickly return again, and the queen for Bristol.

It now pleased God to raise us up again by the surprisal of Selby by the Lord Fairfax[67]etc., with [John] Belasyse, the governor of York, and many more officers of quality, and 1,500 foot with other provisions; the most of them were of the garrison of York. [fo. 15] Which unexpected and sudden accident enforced Newcastle[68] to retreat thither (having no other place left) lest Fairfax prevented him. This fell out extremely well for the Scots, who were straitened in their quarters <the Scots were come by Boroughbridge on the West Riding most providently>, and in the pursuit Newcastle vii and modis[69] lost 4,000 of his. Yet in the Scots' march southward at this time they endured the greatest hardship, for their marches were very long, and the country cleared of all manner of provisions. Now did the Scots and English [crossed out] Fairfax's horse join, and an inter-vieu of each other's forces. Newcastle sends away his horse to join with Rupert, [and] remains with the remnant of infantry in York (about 5,000). The Scots and Fairfaxian forces surround York. Rupert gathers a great force, especial of horse and dragoons, in all about 10,000, to relieve the marquess.

In the interim, Lord Manchester with an army [fo. 15v] of 12,000 horse and foot marches into Lincolnshire, sets down before Lincoln, and within few days (having quickly gained the lower town) storms the close,[70] in which were lost of ours about 40 and three officers; on theirs about 80, 800 prisoners, as many arms, 120 horse, their artillery etc., with many high and low officers and the gentry of the county.

This encouraged our new soldiers, and so reduced the whole county to our devotion. The army now are free to wait on Rupert, having

---

[66] On 10 April 1644.

[67] On 11 April 1644.

[68] William Cavendish, first marquess of Newcastle, commander of royalist forces in the north.

[69] i.e. ways and means. What exactly Juxon means by this phrase is not clear.

[70] On 6 May 1644.

joined their horse with the Scots and Fairfaxian; in all, 8,000 horse and dragooners designed to attend the plunderer, who stood off for Shropshire expecting the Irishes landing.

Poor, yet valiant, Lyme, having been strongly surrounded, made several sallies with advantage, [and] was relieved by our ships since with 300 men and ammunition, and can hold out.[71]

[fo. 16] The king of Persia is now departed this world and so is the queen of Poland – [an] alleged Jesuitess and the great disturber of that kingdom; the hope of that faction. 'Tis a miracle to see how the kings and lords are haunted with a malignity against Jesus Christ, as if his kingdom were incompatible with their tyranny, as indeed it is. Both cannot mutually flourish.

<May 13 [1644]> There was now a great rumour of the king's coming to London only with a small train, and 'twas feared of the wisest, having in it the greatest hopes for him, if nicely managed.

<[marginal note running down the above page] The king was at Reading and offered to deliver up himself to the lord general if he would let his army be his security and also engage his honour to conduct him to the parliament, where he would endeavour an accommodation; if it could not, then to be brought back to the place where he was. But the parliament, hearing of this, sent an express to the lord general by no means to entertain him, or any message, without their consent, not knowing what to do with him [i.e. the king]. Upon this, was their Aulicus's dream of the king coming to London.[72]>

My lord general went from hence [crossed out] The king dismisses his new parliament at Oxford into their several counties to raise money. Major Taylor[73] and one Mr Ball[74] of Westminster, both gallant men, were committed by the Lords; the cause really was there were some of our citizens, either out of pride or malice, offered to undertake the payment of 25,000 foot and 6,000 horse for six months, and to let his excellency and Sir William Waller have their proportions.[75] The rest to be for the guard of the City, and so the trained bands and auxiliaries to rest, [fo. 16v] but this upon condition: that all taxes (the excise excepted), with that for the army, should cease. When it came to be debated, the gentlemen above assured the projectors that out of the prisons they could not have them, but must be constrained to take

---

[71] Essex relieved Lyme on 15 June 1644.

[72] Juxon is referring here to the pamphlet by Francis Cheynell, *Aulicus his dream, of the king's sudden coming to London* (15 May 1644), BL, E47/22.

[73] Silvanus Taylor, sergeant-major in the Westminster regiment of Sir James Harrington.

[74] William Ball, a gentleman from St Dunstan in the West.

[75] *CJ*, iii. 458, 462, 466; *LJ*, vi. 498, 504, 506, 527, 531, 538; CLRO, Jor. 40, fo. 94; Lindley, pp. 320–22.

them and such as were not residents within the line,[76] and then they would have none but rogues and such as were not fit to be trusted; and should they employ them, 'twere to put a sword into madmen's hands that would cut their throats.[77]

This did so vex the others [i.e. the projectors] – seeing themselves deluded (for indeed all inhabitants were already listed in the trained bands or auxiliaries, and they pretended to have a third number these excepted) – they reported that they said to put trust in my lord general and his officers was to put a sword into madmen's hands. Upon this, Stapilton[78] and that party, with Copley,[79] took occasion to quarrel with [Charles] Fleetwood and [Thomas] Harrison – two gentlemen that had from the beginning served my lord in his lifeguard and other charges and done extreme good service – for being forward to reform the army, [and] were counted enemies and endeavour to commit them. Dorislaus came so far as to examine Mrs Kendall, a citizen's wife,[80] what Harrison discoursed of when at supper with her. Thus daring do they grow, and if we should once come to be under the power of the army, which they desire, we see what we are to expect. In th'end they were ashamed and suffered it to die.

[fo. 17] News came about this time that the young prince of Orange had, nolens volens,[81] come into the princess's chamber and lay with her, and in the morning bid her if she would now to go to her father again, for the truth is they intended to serve the prince a Spanish trick; pretended the match for to serve their ends. Which being done, resolved to fetch her away, not intending the prince should have her; intended to divorce them. When our queen heard they had lain together [she] did extremely rail at the prince and the lady that had her in custody, but the prince of Orange intended not his son should be made artaillie:[82]

---

[76] The London lines of communication.

[77] The precise words Taylor and Ball were accused of uttering were 'that the adding of greater or other forces unto the lord general's army was but to put a sword into their hands to cut our own throats with it, or to go with it to the king': HLRO, main papers, 25 April 1644, examinations of witnesses concerning the speeches against the lord general. This alleged observation was made on 18 April at a meeting of the City's militia committee at Coopers' Hall.

[78] i.e. Sir Philip Stapilton, captain of Essex's lifeguard. Juxon appears to be the only source for this quarrel between 'Stapilton and that party' and Fleetwood and Harrison, although the fact that such a falling out did occur would certainly help to explain the two men's decision in the spring of 1644 to quit Essex's lifeguard and join the Eastern Association army: C. Holmes, *The Eastern Association in the English Civil War* (Cambridge, 1974), pp. 172, 201.

[79] Lionel Copley, commissary general, a leading member of Essex's party.

[80] Probably the wife of the City merchant, William Kendall, a member of the London sequestration committee.

[81] Willy-nilly.

[82] Scottish form of artillery (*O.E.D.*). The meaning here is obscure.

salus salutem etc.[83] God crosses the king's counsels every way.

About this time[84] Colonel Behre,[85] who had been plundering in Warwickshire, affronted Colonel [John] Middleton and the Scots nation, and was so far from having reason that Behre was made commissary of the horse to my lord general. There was great quarrelling about it and were both committed for a time.[86] Middleton was after made lieutenant-general of the horse to Sir William Waller.

During this time the committee of estates [i.e. the committee of both kingdoms] sent to Colonel Harvey[87] to go along with Sir William Waller, but he utterly refused it, though they sent to him again and again and used him with great respect and civility; nay, was offered to be sergeant-major-general to Waller. Non-obstante[88] all this, and an order of the House with a full concurrence of the militia and several days deliberation, yet told them that he would rather carry a musket under his excellency than have any charge under Waller, [fo. 17v] saying that he was an unfortunate man and that he had a commission before him to command the counties that he then did. 'Tis true he had a commission pro tempore for the expedition to Gloucester, but no longer. He carried himself extreme insolently to them, and the committee expiring 'twas referred to my lord general, who ordered that so many horse as were in his regiment should be sent to Waller in lieu of them <that was the first time they were affronted; an ill precedent>.[89]

<15 May 1644> My lord general now goes to his army, where, when they come to Newbridge and Islip, 'twas rainy weather and the waters very high. The business was disputed several days with equal loss. Colonel Harvey had they [sic] convoy of ammunition and stayed 3 or 4 days longer than he should, which put them to uncertain counsels; being arrived (his excellency was exceedingly displeased at his stay).

[fo. 18] They resolved on the Monday to fall on the town, but there

---

[83] The original classical phrase is conjectural. Two possibilities are that it may be a contraction of 'una salus victis nullam sperare salutem' ('the only safety for the conquered is not to hope for safety') or a reference to another phrase meaning 'good fortune [i.e. the goddess of good fortune, Salus] grants well being [salutem] to the virtuous'.

[84] The beginning of May 1644.

[85] Hans Behre, a Dutchman with his own troop of Dutch mercenaries.

[86] *The declaration of Commissary-General Behre against divers slanders and lies spread abroad against him* (1 May 1644), BL, 669 f. 10/3; *Observations on the declaration of Commissary-General Behre* [2 May 1644], BL, 669 f. 10/4; *CJ*, iii. 478, 488.

[87] Edmund Harvey, a London silkman, whom Marchamont Nedham claimed in 1648 was 'once a most furious Presbyter' but, as a result of his purchase of church lands, had been 'drawn over to the Independents'. Clement Walker later described Harvey as one who had turned from 'a furious Presbyter to a Bedlam Independent': *Mercurius pragmaticus* (22–29 August 1648), BL, E461/19; Clement Walker, *History of Independency*, pt. II, p. 13.

[88] Notwithstanding.

[89] *CSPD, 1644*, pp. 83, 92, 103, 136, 150, 176, 200; *CJ*, iii. 488, 490, 493.

was timely notice given, which caused the king that night at eleven (have [sic] put the city in a posture) to depart with ten coaches and a party of six thousand horse and foot, without any intelligence of it to my lord [i.e. Essex]. Waller (being then quartered at Witney) hearing of them, resolved to pursue them, who were already at Burford with their army (which was 12 miles) ere we were awake. Waller gave notice to his excellency that he would pursue, and did so effectually that the king was up at 3 o'clock cutting and slashing them to horse, and so went away for Evesham. The world wondered how such a party with artillery and baggage could move invisibly and without interruption 12 miles before our intelligence.

[fo. 18v] During this time the Commons sent up to the Lords for the continuing of the committee of estates, which they continued to refuse <unless Pembroke and Salisbury might be added> till at last Mr [William] Strode, at a conference, told them the Commons were resolved to adhere to their votes, and withal desired a concurrence for the disabling the deserters[90] of either House to return and vote. In conclusion, were constrained to pass a dormant ordinance that came from the Lords, but with an exuberance of power more than they thought fit to pass it with, but now were constrained to in respect of their strait, which nettled the Lords.[91]

Whilst the army were near Oxford the Holland ambassadors came to his excellency to know if he desired peace, and so in order to that propounded to treat, but he would not entertain any discourse with them till the committee of parliament were present. [fo. 19] And then told them 'twas that they all desired and laboured for, but if they intended any such thing were to address themselves to the parliament, by whom he was commanded not to entertain any treaties without their order. They [sic] ambassadors came away for London as soon as the king left Oxford. We have no obligation to them; they have their instructions from the prince of Orange and must serve the interests[92] of Oxford.

Prince Rupert, having gathered a body of 10,000 horse and foot, finding it difficult to relieve York, make [sic] a diversion into Lancashire (which people had timely notice of it and ordered to join their forces with the earl of Denbigh,[93] but would not come out of their own country, pretending they had 30,000 at 24 hours warning and that he durst not come there). He caused them to draw off from Lathom House

[90] i.e. Holland, Bedford, Portland, Conway, Clare, and Lovelace from the House of Lords.

[91] The committee of both kingdoms was eventually re-appointed on 22 May 1644: *CJ*, iii. 481, 483, 485–6, 489–94, 496–8, 500–501, 503–4; *LJ*, vi. 541–3, 548–9, 551, 553–4, 556–7, 559, 562–4.

[92] Lit. intrestes.

[93] Basil Fielding, second earl of Denbigh.

into Bolton, which he assaulted and, with 500 lost, took it and put them to execution.[94] [fo. 19v] Having tyrannised, Bashaw-like,[95] and raised a great army of horse and foot, comes into Yorkshire, upon which the besiegers resolved to draw off, and did before he approached them, resolving to fight with them, and accordingly did as in (10) is fully related <2nd July 1644>.[96] This victory was a critical blow, and yet 'tis not believed by the malignants. 'Tis since certain that there hath been buried 4,000 and more, besides a great number wounded. 'Tis certified and confirmed that the marquess of Newcastle, with many others of quality, are arrived at Hambrough [i.e. Hamburg] from Scarborough, where they confirm the news; and the rather to excuse their flying, had the wind not favoured them a day or two, they had perished for want of provisions, for they carried none with them. They blame Prince Robert's rashness.

[fo. 20] Sir William Waller followed the king <and by this did hinder him from joining with Prince Rupert, which was the design and therefore of good consequence to prevent>, who led his foot a long dance, and at last they came near. The king drew away, [and] Waller, thinking to give him a touch in his rear at parting, sent a party to fall on, who were so confident that their word was 'victory' – too soon. But the king's horse did so handsomely charge them that they retreated and left 11 drakes.[97] Yet our horse did gallantly and freed our foot, who else would have further suffered; [we] lost 100 and odd.[98] Great thanks was for this at Oxford and Prince Robert's beating the Scots etc. army.

In the interim, [the] lord general goes on in the west, but they come not in as was expected [and] their design is wholly broke. For they waited till we had received some blow in the north, as Lord Essex did after that before Newark; [and] though before was contented to have his army reformed, but now told them if they would make use of him they must let him choose his own officers and such as he could trust.

[fo. 20v] Sergeant Glanville,[99] sometime the speaker in the Commons' House, came to the parliament from Oxford and the like the earl of Leicester.[100]

Browne[101] is now made major-general, and to please him his

[94] Clarendon, iii. 371–4; *An exact relation of the massacre at Bolton, May 28, by Prince Rupert* (28 May 1644), BL, E7/1.
[95] Bashaw or Pasha, a high-ranking Turkish officer or commander.
[96] The battle of Marston Moor.
[97] A drake is a small cannon.
[98] The battle of Cropredy Bridge on 29 June 1644.
[99] Sir John Glanville, Commons' speaker in the Short Parliament.
[100] Robert Sidney, second earl of Leicester.
[101] Richard Browne, the London coal-merchant.

commission is in words very large, but yet in th'end tells him he must be subject to the commands of the parliament, committee of both kingdoms, or my lord general. In order to that, have commanded him to join with Sir William Waller, but that does not please him and therefore does snuff at it, [and] the business is retarded. In fine, Sir William Waller is commanded <u>with</u> [crossed out] on another design, leaving Browne in his quarters at Abingdon.

The States ambassadors had an audience in both Houses.[102] The Lords in their robes and the House hung etc. At their approach the Lords rose and put off their hats then sat down. At the Commons' House they only put off their hats but did not rise. Their speech is (11). [fo. 21] Being ended they withdrew, expecting they should [have] been sent for in again, and thanks returned in most ample manner, and withal took it not so well that (as the Lords) they did not rise to them. But 'twas, for their satisfaction, intimated they [i.e. the Commons] were the fathers of the kingdom and therefore might take more upon them; and besides, the States ambassadors arrived in December last and were till now ere they would acknowledge them a parliament. They might therefore very justly take a little time to return them an answer; especially in a business of this nature and being devotionaries of the king.

<**13 [July?]**> The manifesto of Denmark and queen of Sweden.

Captain [Richard] Swanley, being with a squadron of our ships on the coasts of Pembrokeshire, where he performed brave service; met with a barque coming from Ireland with soldiers, in which were some 50 of the natives, whom he sent to swim to their own country.

[fo. 21v] My lord general advances into the west and so to Plymouth to relieve that port that was besieged, which was done with success.[103] The counsels were divided whether he should advance or no. Stapilton, Balfour and that crew were for the negative; Field Marshall Robartes,[104] General-Major [Philip] Skippon and that party for the affirmative. High words passed on both sides, but 'twas carried for the last, though we cannot see by what general rule he should quit his retreat Plymouth and draw himself into a barren and enemy country and where he could expect nothing. Stapilton obtains leave to come to London, where Harvey and Copley are, and all extremely bent against the good party, and complain of the council <u>and my lord's present condition</u> [inserted] as desperate.

---

[102] On 12 July 1644: *CJ*, iii. 559–60; *LJ*, vi. 628–9.

[103] Essex's presence in the west caused the temporary lifting of the blockage of Plymouth in July 1644: Rushworth, v. 690.

[104] John, Lord Robartes of Truro, later first earl of Radnor.

The king draws after with his whole force and enquarters near Essex; endeavours to straiten and necessitate him [fo. 22] and, in fine, bring him to his mercy, which he would certainly do but that we have a good lord admiral to friend.[105] The king raised a sconce below Fowey to prevent our ships coming up that river, but it only puts them a point farther. The king now grows confident either of weakness or willingness to render, [and] therefore undertakes to send a letter to Essex by the Lord Beauchamp,[106] son to the marquess of Hertford and his excellency's nephew (14).[107] There was also a letter from Prince Maurice and from the officers of the army, except Wilmot,[108] for which he's accused; his apology (16).[109] His excellency returned answer to the last that he believed what they did was by order from, and consent of, his majesty. He had no such order from the parliament to treat in any business and therefore desired them to receive it from a satisfaction.[110] The world look upon this act of the king as [a] great piece of unworthiness and folly; to appear in a business of this nature without being pre-assured of the other side. [fo. 22v] The king sends forth a declaration to all Christian persons inciting them to take part (17).[111]

<August 26> The prince elector[112] arrives here and is lodged in Whitehall, but the parliament did not (at least seemed not) so clearly resent it, and voted a strange welcome: to have given him 14 days time to stay and then to be gone, but 'twas afterward moderated and sent (18).

My lord general [crossed out].

The Lord [Connor] Maguire and [Hugh] MacMahon, two Irish lords and the principal in that rebellion, with a great steel saw got through the door of their chamber and made an escape;[113] for which the House of Commons, though Alderman [Isaac] Penington, the lieutenant, were in no great fault, yet they voted him out and would have fined him might the recorder[114] and his party had their will. But

[105] The earl of Warwick, who supplied Essex's army on its march into the west.

[106] Henry Seymour, Lord Beauchamp, eldest son of William Seymour, first marquess of Hertford.

[107] On 6 August 1644: Clarendon, iii. 394–5; Rushworth, v. 691–2.

[108] Henry, first Baron Wilmot of Adderbury, Oxfordshire, lieutenant-general of the horse, who sent a private letter of his own to Essex.

[109] On 9 August 1644: Clarendon, iii. 396–8; Rushworth, v. 692–3, 696–7; *The accusation given by his majesty against the Lord Wilmot: together with the Lord Wilmot's declaration of his innocency* (12 August 1644), BL, E7/27.

[110] On 10 August 1644: Clarendon, iii. 398; Rushworth, v. 693.

[111] This was the so-called 'one and all' campaign which Charles launched with a royal proclamation at Chard on 30 September 1644: Rushworth, v. 715–6; J. L. Malcolm, *Caesar's due: loyalty and King Charles, 1642–46* (1983), pp. 201–2.

[112] Charles Lewis, Elector Palatine, nephew of Charles I.

[113] On 17 August 1644.

[114] John Glynne.

Sir Arthur Hesilrige put them in mind of their obligation to him for his good service and so 'twas moderated. But it continued that the City should present another or, if they will, him to them, which the honest party do desire.[115] [fo. 23] <19 September> While 'twas thus in dispute it pleased God they were found and returned to their old lodging, and so hope 'twill end the business.

The prince elector gives to parliament the reasons and motives of his coming (19).

There came some time past a manifesto from the Lord Inchiquin[116] and other commanders in the south of Ireland, wherein they declare themselves for the parliament, as also letters to the king to the same purpose (20). And as a testimony of his reality sends a letter of his resolution to Colonel [Henry] O'Brien, his brother, governor of Wareham, near Poole, who presently surrenders the place and was shipped for Ireland to his brother.[117]

My lord general having committed an error in these concoctions goes on to multiply them.

[bottom third of the page is blank]

[fo. 23v] [first two-thirds of the page is blank]

Upon this success[118] the king sends a letter to the parliament seeming to desire peace (21).[119]

[The] lord general comes to Southampton [and] disposes of his own regiment into the Isle of Wight, upon which there are some jealousies, and that partly in respect of the conduct of [fo. 24] our affairs in Cornwall. In particular, there was taken of our officers at the Lord Mohun's house[120] Colonel Butler[121] of my lord general's regiment, and Colonel Aldrich[122] of Aylesbury and others. Butler was quickly let to gain his exchange upon his parole, who was to be Sir John Digby taken at Grafton – a man so considerable that my lord general desired the parliament, when they were moved to his exchange, not to do it; but now no man but this. Coming back, he brought with him propositions

---

[115] Juxon appears to be the only source for Hesilrige's speech in defence of Penington. D'Ewes noted that Penington 'found so many friends that in the issue the House declined the passing of any censure upon him for the present': BL, Harl. Ms. 166, fos. 110–110v.

[116] Murrough O'Brien, sixth Baron Inchiquin and future first earl of Inchiquin. He declared for parliament on 17 July 1644 and was made president of Munster by the committee of both kingdoms in January 1645: CSPD, 1644, p. 357; CSPD, 1644–45, pp. 271–2.

[117] Wareham surrendered to the parliament on 10 August 1644: Rushworth, v. 697.

[118] The surrender of Essex's foot at Lostwithiel on 2 September 1644.

[119] On 8 September 1644: Rushworth, v. 712.

[120] The house of Warwick, second Baron Mohun of Okehampton, at Boconnoc, Cornwall, was seized by royalist forces on 14 August 1644.

[121] John Butler, colonel of Essex's own regiment of foot.

[122] Colonel Edward Aldrich, parliamentary governor of Aylesbury.

from the king, gave them to Colonel [Thomas] Tyrrell,[123] he to Stapilton, and so were they dispersed into the army without acquainting the parliament and contrary to the articles [crossed out] ordinances [inserted] of war. After this, Butler was several times in the king's quarters, and after both Aldrich and he being, with their regiments, commanded to several ports of importance, basely quitted them and run away, which was to the loss of [crossed out] which produced our so great loss there.[124] There was one Colonel [John] Weare, a Cornish gentleman, who pretended to raise a regiment for the parliament and having done betrayed it to the king, which added to this unhappy loss.

[fo. 24v] The parliament now endeavour to make the best of their loss and the best use. Do therefore command Lord Manchester, who was come about Reading, to advance and join to Sir William Waller. And now this causes a great dispute, for Manchester will not come under Waller, no, nor command him, but that my lord general be over all. His lordship fears [crossed out] In the interim, he does fall out with Cromwell and all that party and violently sets himself against them, being firm to the Scots and their church discipline.[125]

<October 1 [1644]> At the same time there's a command for 5 regiments – trained bands at Hamlets, Westminster, Southwark, the red and blue of London – to make ready to march to join with the Lord Manchester, who resolves not to march ere they come. At the same time, there was a design by Sir Henry Vane and the solicitor etc. to put Skippon over the London brigade and to join to him the remainder of my lord general's, but it could not be attained, nor would Skippon accept of it.[126] [fo. 25] And at the same time would they have had Colonel Cromwell (because Lord Manchester would not join and march according to order) to have commanded his army, but it could not be. In conclusion, Sir James Harrington[127] was in chief over the London brigade, lord general he took the field, and all to meet at their rendezvous and he to head them. And 'twas computed [the] lord general [had] 2,500 horse and as many foot, Waller 4,500 horse and dragooners, Lord Manchester 3,000 horse and 5,000 foot, the London brigade 4,500 foot; in all, 10,000 horse and 12,000 foot.

---

[123] Thomas Tyrrell, a colonel of foot in Essex's army and later MP for Aylesbury and Buckinghamshire.

[124] For details of this controversy see Rushworth, v. 702–3, 710–11; *CJ*, iii. 641, 645; BL, Harl. Ms. 166, fos. 125v–126; HLRO, main papers, 3 December 1644.

[125] *CJ*, iii. 620–21, 635–6; *LJ*, vi. 699, 700, 712; Bruce, pp. 27–41.

[126] The initiative for placing Skippon in command over the London brigade came from the brigade officers. St John (the solicitor) reported their request from the committee of both kingdoms to the Commons, which rejected it: Rowe, pp. 49–50; Baillie, ii. 235; *CJ*, iii. 651, 653, 655; BL, Harl. Ms. 166, fo. 128v.

[127] Sir James Harrington was colonel of the Westminster militia, a 'parochial Independent' and a later supporter of Pride's purge.

The parliament not being hitherto able to reform the lord general's army, though have done their utmost, being very sensible of the mischiefs that arise to us <u>from</u> [inserted] such wicked officers, and now having them in London, command them not to stir <u>beyond</u> [inserted] of the line of communication without order from them.[128] They are Sir Philip Stapilton, Colonel Behre, Quarter Master General [John] Dalbier, Commissary Copley, Colonel Harvey, Dorislaus, Colonel Aldrich and Colonel Tyrrell.

[fo. 25v] The king's resolution is to adventure another battaigle, believing if we lose this 'twill be our last if he then to ship away for beyond sea the persons excepted by the parliament, and himself (imagining he may when he will) to come to the parliament. The king had now the opportunity, if he would, to have gone for Oxford and avoided fighting, but he resolves to fight. Therefore, comes up for <**26 October**> Newbury and draws up his army between the town and Donnington Castle in a place of advantage, resolving if we would fight to assault him. Which (after we had faced him all Saturday) we did upon the sabbath day evening, and with much difficulty gained 8 pieces of canon and slew about 80, then routed and destroyed a body of horse led by the earl of Cleveland,[129] who was taken prisoner. The night drew on, and the king having ambuscado[130] the avenues into Newbury into which he retired, we could not pursue. That night he leaved [sic] his artillery and baggage into Donnington Castle and marched away at midnight through the town and over the river.[131]

<[marginal note to the above account] This speaks the war to continue yet longer, which indeed it must do till it have devoured the causes of it.

We had wounded and slain near 1,000 men. The horse and foot of my lord general were drawn within musket shot of the enemy's canon, and had not their chief officers, viz. Balfour, [and] were fain to charge without order. Had they been 2nded with but 500 horse, might have ruined the king's [continues in the margin of fo. 26] army, who ran away both horse and foot seeing the resolution of our men, that did not fear their canons. God seems not to favour the great officers; certainly [we] were ill served by them>

[fo. 26] News now came of the taking of Newcastle by assault by the Scots under the command of Leslie.[132] The governor and many others

---

[128] Juxon appears to be referring here to the Commons orders of 27 and 30 September 1644 relating to the examination of Butler, Tyrrell etc. by the commissioners for martial law and the committee for reforming the lord general's army: *CJ*, iii. 641, 645.

[129] Thomas Wentworth, first earl of Cleveland.

[130] Placed troops in ambush.

[131] Rushworth, v. 720–32; Clarendon, iii. 432–8.

[132] On 19 October 1644: *CJ*, iii. 676.

recoured[133] into Tynemouth Castle, where they stood upon dispute, but were, in fine, compelled to surrender that too.

About this time Mr Thomas [crossed out] John [inserted] Goodwin, minister of Coleman Street, having preached that the parliament had no power to command any way of government in the Church to enforce it upon the consciences of men, for which he was convened before a committee of parliament,[134] who examined the business (Mr Prynne being most fierce and bitter against him, as formerly against Colonel Fiennes)[135] and, in fine, was by the parliament suspended.[136]

Upon our defeat in Cornwall the parliament made an order and sent it to the assembly, which was to authorise them to choose a committee for the accommodating the differences between the Independents and Presbyterians.[137] This was much stomached at by the Scots and our rigid Presbyters, and delayed. The moderate party inclined much to the Independents. In fine, upon the taking of Newcastle there's a letter sent to the committee of both kingdoms from the committee there.[138] [fo. 26v] The parliament crouch so far as to send, by several of the Lords with the mace, this letter to the assembly and also superseded their former order for an accommodation, ordering them not to proceed in it.[139] Thus the Scots encroach upon us, [and] having a firm footing will now draw the curtain. They have the great officers in my lord general's, Sir William Waller's and Manchester's army, are powerful in the committee of both kingdoms and in the parliament and assembly. The judgements of men are diverse on them. Some say they resent the loss of a king by the crown of England and that nothing can repair them but a republic. Others that they professed to come in now: 1. for the gospel; 2. for the maintaining their king; 3. for their own liberties; that the king and they understand each other well enough, and when they have insinuated and have power will declare for him, and then they say the quarrel will in th'end be

---

[133] Recovered.

[134] *Theomachia: being the substance of two sermons preached upon occasion of the late defeat in the west, 12 September 1644*, BL, E12/1. Goodwin was not summoned before the committee of plundered ministers until May 1645: BL, Add. Ms, 15,669 fos. 66, 68v, 74.

[135] W. Prynne, *A full reply to certain brief observations [by John Goodwin] on Master Prynne's twelve questions about Church government* [19 October 1644], BL, E257/7; *Articles of impeachment and accusation exhibited in parliament against Colonel Nathaniel Fiennes ... by Clement Walker and William Prynne* (15 November 1643), BL, E78/3.

[136] Goodwin was sequestered from the living on 22 May 1645: BL, Add. Ms. 15,669, fo. 75v.

[137] The accommodation order of 13 September 1644: *CJ*, iii. 626.

[138] The letter sent from the Scots commissioners at Newcastle on 23 October 1644: *CJ*, iii. 684; *LJ*, vii. 43–4.

[139] *LJ*, vii. 43; *CJ*, iii. 684.

between the 2 nations. Their great interest,[140] some say, is their Presbytery, and will as much persecute the Independents as the bishops them.

<[marginal note to the above paragraph] They that think the king and they do correspond: 'tis first from that part of the cause of their coming, viz. for his preservation. Then, that they have hindered us from being too violent, which else should have been, and that he excepted not against them to bring propositions to this – answer: that they have this peculiar, to be politique and pretend fair, though we find the contrary. Then, we had declared we could not make peace or treat without them, and though they should temporise with him, yet he'll not trust them but wait to be revenged, for they have given him greater cause than this nation – we stand for our own. That [they] had whatever they could desire, and no cause to seek a war, though some say if we had not sent for them they would have come and rather than fail for the king,[141] resolving to make a purchase here and fish – besides, they have executed several lords and king's friends. Then, their God their Presbytery, which they must not desert nor the king admit, being that which above all fetters the civil power. Then, they did set the Swede on Denmark to divert him from us, which is not of little advantage to us, and to him the contrary. And last, the hatred that's to them, being looked upon as the first stirrers, and having shown us the way. If he court them 'tis to devour them, though it may be [they] have the favour to be last>

[fo. 27] The prince elector was admitted a member of th'assembly, where he does daily come and sit to hear their disputes.

<**Monday 4 November [1644]**> This week did the earls of Pembroke and Warwick come into the assembly and chide the Independents for retarding the work of reformation.[142] This week the propositions[143] were finished and my lord general despatched away a trumpet for a safe convoy.

The king returned to Woodstock and so to Oxford, rallying his forces, with whom the earl of Northampton[144] and Gerard[145] out of

---

[140] Lit. intress.

[141] The syntax here is unclear.

[142] Warwick, Pembroke and four members of the Commons attended the Westminster assembly on 7 November 1644 with a request from both Houses to hasten its work on reforming church government. When the Independent ministers in the assembly then entered their dissents to the assembly's resolution to send up such work as had already been completed, 'My Lord of Pembroke was exceeding urgent and smart against all those, that should go about to hinder the work of the church': John Lightfoot, *The journal of the proceedings of the assembly of divines* (ed.), J. R. Pitman (1824), p. 323.

[143] The Uxbridge propositions.

[144] James Compton, third earl of Northampton.

[145] Sir Charles Gerard, general of south Wales.

Wales join, and so to Wallingford, plundering the county of Buckingham. 'Twas certainly known he intended to fetch his artillery etc. from Donnington Castle, and a letter to the castle to the same purpose was intercepted by us. We, upon this news, marched (from Abingdon and thereabouts, where our army was drawn) towards Newbury, the enemy being at Wallingford. The horse were forced to quarter at the greater distance for want of forage. News came on the Friday night that the king was upon his march and would relieve the castle the next day, being about 7,000 horse and foot.

Orders were given for our horse to hasten to the headquarter [sic], which was at Newbury. [fo. 27v] A council of war called whether or no we should fight him ere he came, or after, or not at all. The honest party, Skippon and Cromwell etc., were for the affirmative, but Lord Manchester and Crawford,[146] his major-general, whom he follows with Balfour etc., were against it. That they should not hazard the loss of Newbury but preserve it for a winter quarter, that the place was not advantageous. And Lord Manchester gave his reason that if they fought and beat the king he yet would be king, but if he beat them they should lose their army, nay their estates, and it may be their heads too.

<9 November> In fine, they [sic] king's party advanced about 2 o'clock in the afternoon. We had raised up breast-works to secure the town of Newbury. The king's foot skirmished with us and fell on very desperately while the horse advanced, and having horses ready drew out their artillery from the castle [and] some say £900 money with the great seal [inserted]. Our horse were all drawn beyond the river and town in a sure place.[147] The greatest part of the king's party drew away that night, leaving 2,500 horse and foot, with their artillery, not far off. The next day the army was drawn forth and Cromwell importuned to follow them, but 'twas not assented to. [fo. 28] So the king's whole party did safely come to Wallingford on the Sunday night. This was the greatest affront that ever we received, being 14,000 and the king but 7,000; his being first routed then harassed up and down, and we had timely notice of it also. The fault is chiefly laid upon the Lord Manchester and Crawford and Balfour.

Thus has all this year been shamefully lost. The king when we came near Oxford in the spring and might have either kept him there or at least from recruiting and gathering an army. But my lord general disobeying the orders of the House [and] going into the west when he should have followed the king, which was upon design to ruin and

---

[146] Lawrence Crawford, a Scot and religious Presbyterian, was major-general of Manchester's Eastern Association army.

[147] Rushworth, v. 730–31; *LJ*, vii. 61.

disappoint Waller, which it did, for the king beat him and took away his artillery.[148] And then hoping by this to raise himself a considerable army and engage that part of England to him and so to force us to a treaty and agreement with the king. But it proved contrary, for the king followed him into the west and then into Cornwall (where we hoped to have freed the marquess of Hamilton, who was prisoner at Pendennis), and by Sir Jacob Astley's counsel chose rather to straiten and necessitate us than fight, which had been our best, but his worst, play had it been first done when the king came there.

[fo. 28v] The king having thus shamefully dismantled our army by the neglect and treachery of our great officers (those who since are confined to London), who desired not so soon an end of the war, or at least with so much disadvantage to the king's [sic], [and] therefore furnished him against the treaty. And now, having laboured to draw all our forces together to stop him in the west, we yet lost that opportunity, suffering him to come to Winchester without a blow, though we were much superior in horse as well as foot, for he was not above 10,000 in both, and we 20,000. And this was Lord Manchester's fault, who would not advance from Reading till the London brigade came <And ever since has been getting petitions from the association[149] to recall him, for he came and tarries against his will, and so it prospers> The king drives his design on to hinder our conjunction, which though he could not effect, yet might, without any let, have gone to Oxford, but chose rather to give us battle, knowing if he were beaten yet the articles should be the same and his peace not the further, but if he beat the parliament he had his design and ends.

Therefore does he choose Newbury, where he had the castle of Donnington to friend, and resolves if we will fight it shall be upon disadvantage. [fo. 29] And then finding himself too weak, secures his artillery and baggage in Donnington Castle, hazards some few foot and horse, and retreats in the night with the rest towards Marlborough. In 14 days recruits, tells us he'll come and relieve Donnington, which he does before our faces, then draws away to Marlborough to amuse us. Pretends strongly that he'll relieve Basing, to prevent which we draw away thither, and he presently falls into the town of Newbury, securing the river and all that tract of ground betwixt it and Oxford for his garrisons this winter.

Thus has he obtained all his ends this summer, which had been extreme wisely managed by him. We are too much upon the defensive and let him, though inconsiderable to us, give us the law and make us

[148] At Cropredy Bridge.
[149] The Eastern Association.

follow his motions, though it be our part, especially having so many advantages, which as 'tis advantageous to him, doing only what he has designed, so the contrary to us.

The fundamental cause is so interwoven that it can scarce be prevented, at least altogether, for monarchy is more fit [crossed out] has [inserted] the advantage in conquering and obtaining by armies, and a republic of maintaining and assuring a conquest,[150] and therefore [fo. 29v] the prince of Orange's compliment to our queen when she was there had reason. He told her that the state of England was like to continue troublesome; for as the king would never want a party to adhere to him, so the parliament were not fit to manage a war. We prosecute the war with respect and in order to an accord; the king drives to a conquest using all means to the extremity.

Upon this great affront my lord general's officers here in town, with himself, take the advantage to complain against them that keep them here; they being the only men to conduct an army, the rest novices and incapable, and by this means would get themselves again into credit. And though Waller were for fighting and Balfour not, yet they endeavour to render him the cause of it and ascribe it to his infortunateness. And, to say the truth, the wiser sort of men do not believe him so fit for the conduct of an army. Though in this particular it past by the major part of the votes at the council.[151] Some are of an opinion that many of my lord general's officers are resolved to do nothing worthy till he returns. [fo. 30] And therefore 'tis resolved that with all speed he go down to head the army, otherwise it will certainly dissolve.

The propositions being ready to go, the parliament hastens the assembly[152] to given [sic] them some draft of the government which is most evangelical to present with the other things. Therefore 'tis voted: 1. that a Presbytery is according to the Word; 2. that it is to consist of presbyters and elders; 3. that many churches may be under one presbytery. To which there's 7 dissent, and enter it − Mr Thomas Goodwin, Mr Nye, Mr [William] Bridges, Mr [Jeremiah] Burroughs, Mr [William] Greenhill, Mr [William] Carter[153] − and petition the House to have liberty to bring in their reasons into the assembly, which is granted and done by them.

There came that week a stinging petition from the committee at Knole in Kent,[154] who desire a recruit of the members of parliament,

---

[150] Juxon may well be glossing Machiavelli here. *The Prince* is the likeliest source.
[151] Juxon appears to be the only source for this vote on Waller in the committee of both kingdoms.
[152] On 7 November 1644: *CJ*, iii. 691; *LJ*, vii. 52.
[153] The seventh was Sidrach Simpson who was not listed by Juxon; *LJ*, vii. 70.
[154] On 14 November 1644: *CJ*, iii. 695–6.

execution of justice upon delinquents, and that their lands may be sold in their comt.[i.e. county] and they'll pay them the money for it, that they may be put into a posture of war; and, seeing our own nation are treacherous and [fo. 30v] will not make an end of the war, that the Scots may be called up more southerly (which is already done for they're come to Nottingham); and if the House do not assent to them they're resolved to stand upon their guards, for they have 20,000 men in a readiness and are resolved neither to give nor take quarter off the enemy.

<18 [November]> Monday, news came that upon the king's intending to relieve Basing House we drew away from Newbury thither, but stayed not. Nay, they that had all this summer besieged it, and were now in a great possibility to take it in, were commanded away from it by Lord Manchester, Sir William Waller and Sir William Balfour, to their extreme grief.

So that our great army being [crossed out] is now [inserted] shamefully beaten and cudgelled out of the field into their winter quarter; nay, into our own quarters, whereas we should have lived upon them – to our great dishonour and discouragement, not having done any considerable action.

[fo. 31] <20 [November]> This day our commissioners, with the propositions, went towards his majesty, viz. earl of Denbigh, Lord Maynard, Mr Pierrepont, Denzil Holles, Mr Whitelocke and the Lord Wenman; for the Scots, Lord Maitland and Mr Barclay.[155] The [sic] found his majesty at Oxford.

The king has now eased General Forth of his place, and has made Prince Charles generalissimo, and Prince Robert lieutenant-general, of all his armies, and Hopton general of the artillery in the Lord Percy's[156] place. The Prince Charles is [crossed out].

<22 [November]> This day MacMahon, one of the two Irish rebels that got out of the Tower, having been tried and condemned by a jury at the king's bench, was executed at Tyburn as a traitor, i.e. hanged and quartered.

Sir Arthur Hesilrige and Sir William Waller having made report to the House of Commons of the defeat at Donnington Castle, but not to the full contentment of the House, Cromwell was by them commanded to give a relation, which he did from the defeat before Newark to that day, and that with so much clearness and ingenuity that the Houses rested satisfied therewith.[157]

---

[155] Basil Fielding, second earl of Denbigh; William, Lord Maynard; William Pierrepont; Bulstrode Whitelocke; Thomas, Lord Wenman; John, Lord Maitland; and Robert Barclay.

[156] Henry, Lord Percy.

[157] For Cromwell's speech in the Commons on 25 November 1644, see Bruce, pp. 78–95; Abbott, *Writings and speeches*, i. 302–11; Rushworth, v. 732.

<[marginal note to the paragraph above] The night before, the countess of Manchester did invite Cromwell and Sir Henry Vane to supper, and told him at the table that her lord did exceedingly honour and respect him etc. Cromwell answered, 'I wish I could see it etc.'>

He laid the whole blame, or the greatest part, on Lord Manchester. He did confess his judgement was for Independency, [fo. 31v] and so were most of them under his command; and it might be some were Anabaptist, but he told them 'twas not for that that he chose them, but because they were honest and gallant men; men that were faithful in their duties and would fight. And whereas there was a report that he and they had a design to be the head of a party and to carry on their desires by force, he did solemnly protest that 'twas by command and from the authority of that House that he first took up arms, and 'twas for the preservation of them and the kingdom with their liberties; which, if it should please God, to bless with success. And that they had once hated the queen in point of discipline,[158] [and] did not doubt but as God had given them hearts to be active for Him, so, if they could not submit, He would give them to be passive; but they were resolved never to take up arms for their religion.[159] This rung [underlined and 'rang he' written above] throughout the City and about, and most men cried him up and Manchester down.

Lord Manchester now coming to town, he does, by way of recrimination, accuse Cromwell in the House of Lords.[160] My lord general (for that he might be near the House, takes a lodging close to the Lords' House) and he, with the rest, do engage to defend Manchester; and, that he might carry his business, does interest the Scots and the assembly, [fo. 32] and upon these ground: first, says that 'twas Cromwell that on the Friday night did refuse to send for his horse when 'twas his judgement and desire of the rest; and if he [Manchester] were unwilling to fight it was the next day, when it could not be but without extreme disadvantage, the horse not being come up; that the particular words[161] were spoken by Sir Arthur Hesilrige, and he only said he was of his opinion. But further, says that Cromwell has said he hoped to see the day when there should not be a lord in England; then, that he would as soon fight to beat out the Scots as against the king; again, that the assembly was a company of persecutors, and that he would raise such a party as might make the parliament grant their desires etc. This was

---

[158] i.e. her Catholicism.

[159] In the printed accounts of this speech Cromwell makes no reference to his religious preferences or to his motives in taking up arms.

[160] *LJ*, vii. 73, 76, 79–80; Rushworth, v. 733–6.

[161] i.e. 'that if they fought and beat the king he yet would be king, but if he beat them they should lose their army, nay their estates, and it may be their heads too': above, p. 63.

the substance of his accusation, by which he has engaged the assembly, the Lords and the Scots; and that so far that the Scots have sent to have satisfaction from him [Cromwell] or they'll not fight a stroke. The design is to bring in his [Manchester's] charge first, and not by way of recrimination, partly hoping thereby to escape and to disable him [Cromwell] from being a witness; and 'tis endeavoured to turn the stream of all upon him and his party, for they say, 'ruin him, for he's the head, and you ruin all'.[162]

[fo. 32v] **<Saturday 3 November>**[163] But in the interim, our commissioners return for [sic] Oxford, having been most unworthily used and reviled. The propositions were publicly read in Christ Church; the prince and Prince Rupert and Maurice etc. were there. All that they had for answer was (for they were not, nor had, any power to treat, only to return his answer to them) that he would not desert the Church, his crown, nor friends, and when they should send a safe convoy he would send a more particular answer.

The Lords have condescended to it but the Commons not, and 'tis said upon this ground: that at [sic] Oxford and the king does cry up Independency and could willing [sic] let them enjoy their conscience, but he's afraid they will intermeddle in matters of state and that they talk of the kingdom of Christ. There was also an intimation from him that if they would send any to treat for them safe conduct should be granted. And if it come to this, that that party [the Independents] lay down arms, then has the king his ends, for he knows they are the men that fight most cordially and are those that he cannot vitiate nor draw off. Now if we shall cause them to the same, or make them leave the kingdom, shall therein serve the king's interests[164] most really. [fo. 33] The generality of men that are not in that way; as they are loose in religion, so in their resolution. The king knows that the Lords are sure to him upon the interest[165] of their peerage; and for the Commons, they're so low in their spirits and biased with their particular interests[166] and relations, that they'll do almost anything. For an instance, one Captain Grenfeild[167] of horse, a gentleman of Berkshire county, was snapped [i.e. captured] by Wallingford garrison, comes up to get his exchange, and none must serve but Endymion Porter's son that was

---

[162] Baillie, early in December 1644, was convinced that if Cromwell could be removed from the army then it would 'break the power of that potent faction [i.e. the Independents]': Baillie, ii. 245. For the attempts by Essex's party to bring charges against Cromwell, see BL, Add. Ms. 37,343, fos. 343v–46; R. Spalding (ed.), *The diary of Bulstrode Whitelocke 1605–1675* (1990), pp. 160–1.
[163] Should read 30 November: *CJ*, iii. 710–11.
[164] Lit. intrestes.
[165] Lit. intrest.
[166] Lit. intrests.
[167] Greenvile: *CJ*, iii. 711.

taken at the battle near York,[168] who commanded as major-general and a papist. This, because my Lord Essex had passed his word for it, though extremely unreasonable, was carried in the House by 20 for the affirmative, by which 'tis plain how much they are fallen and submit.[169]

The Lords will not pass the bill for executing the archbishop of Canterbury, and say they're not satisfied. The Commons offer, if they please to say wherein, to do it.[170]

The Commons, upon debate, do fling out the accusation of Manchester contra Cromwell as that which is against the privileges of the House, and resolve to stand to him.[171]

<7 December [1644]> Sir John Hotham was this day condemned for that having been an officer under the parliament had traitorously deserted his trust and adhered to the enemy, for which he was to have his head cut off. He only replied that there was another tribunal. [fo. 33v] **<9 [December)>** Monday, there came a letter signed by Rupert to my Lord General Essex in his majesty's name, to desire a safe conduct for the duke of Richmond and the earl of Southampton[172] to the Lords and Commons assembled in the parliament of England at Westminster and the commissioners of Scotland, to bring the king's answer to the propositions sent by our commissioners.

<[marginal note to the paragraph above] 'Tis said that when our commissioners were at Oxford our Prince Charles made some overtures to them which did much startle the king>

The House of Commons did this day[173] pass a vote, having for several hours debated it, that no member of either House of parliament shall, during this war, enjoy or execute any office or command, military or civil, which hath been granted or conferred on any member of either House, or by any authority derived from either House, and that an ordinance be brought in accordingly.[174] This vote, though upon the face seem to confound all our armies and militia, yet indeed is the way to lay a good foundation for them. It stills all differences between lord general and Waller, and between Lord Manchester and Cromwell. It puts the war in such hands as they [the two Houses] may not be afraid to q[uaerere],[175] and such as shall not dispute or cross their commands,

---

[168] Endymion Porter's eldest son, George Porter, was captured at Marston Moor.

[169] The vote in Essex's favour over the exchange was 93 to 52: *CJ*, iii. 711.

[170] *LJ*, vii. 111; *CJ*, iii. 734; ibid., iv. 2, 7, 10. The Lords passed the ordinance for Laud's attainder on 4 January 1645: *LJ*, vii. 125–7.

[171] Juxon seems to be referring to the Commons resolutions of 4 December 1645: Gardiner, ii. 88–9.

[172] James Stuart, first duke of Richmond and fourth duke of Lennox; Thomas Wriothesley, fourth earl of Southampton.

[173] 9 December 1644: *CJ*, iii. 718.

[174] *CJ*, iii. 718; Rushworth, vi. 4–5.

[175] i.e. to question.

and from whom, with less danger, they may demand reason. For the other, besides that they were of the parliament, and if punished might lessen the House, of which there's no need; so also they had friends in the Houses, and so drew into parties and factions, which extremely retarded the work. And then, several places made them not care how long it lasted, but now will envy others and grudge their happiness and so endeavour a speedy end. 'Tis a very strange piece of providence, and being but now so divided that wise men knew not what to say or do, or could see to the end of it.[176]

[fo. 34] **<14 [December]>** The duke of Lennox[177] and earl of Southampton came to town and had Somerset House assigned them for their lodging. **<16 [December]>** The parliament vote that, without leave, none of their members should visit them, but the Lords quickly voted them to go that would; earl [of] Warwick feasted them [inserted].

The Commons had a long debate whether the earl [of] Essex and lord admiral should be excepted in their vote. 'Twas carried negative, and but by 7 voices,[178] which does not a little vex Lord Essex and the rest of them.

<17 [December]> The king's message was presented in the Painted Chamber,[179] there being appointed a committee of Lords and Commons, with the commissioners of Scotland, to receive it.

Wednesday there was a particular fast kept by the two Houses only. The next day the Commons' House sat late and, in the conclusion, voted for treaty.[180] The next night [there] came from the king, to the two lords here, new instructions.

'Tis laboured that a vote may pass that none may bear office in the armies or otherwise that will not take the covenant of both kingdoms; by which the other side think to gall the Independents.[181] 'Tis firmly believed the king will endeavour an accommodation, and that the Independents shall have liberty of conscience, that he may, by that, obtain the same for the papists. And the judgement of the 1st is that they [the Catholics] should not be troubled for their religion simply,

[176] For a similar comment see Baillie, ii. 247.

[177] Above note 172.

[178] On 17 December 1644: *CJ*, iii. 726. The tellers for the yeas (93 votes) were Denzil Holles and Sir Philip Stapilton; for the noes (100 votes), Sir Henry Vane junior and Sir John Evelyn of Wiltshire.

[179] His answer to the propositions of both Houses which had been brought by Richmond and Southampton: *CJ*, iii. 725–6; *LJ*, vii. 103–4.

[180] The fast was held on 18 December and the vote taken on 19 December: *CJ*, iii. 729.

[181] *CJ*, iii. 726, 728. The attempt to have a proviso to this effect added to the self-denying ordinance was rejected on 19 December 1644.

provided they may be hedged in from being mischievous to the state.

[fo. 34v] There was this week news of a design to betray Lynn, Reading <The party that had falsely accused was hanged> and Plymouth to the king, as also Stafford. But it has pleased God to prevent them all.

An agent from the crown of Sweden, who has been in Scotland, arrived here this week.

<**24 [December]**> Sir Alexander Carew[182] was beheaded at Tower Hill, [and] died very resolutely. He was condemned for endeavouring to betray St Nicholas Island, near Plymouth.

The lords from Oxford returned this day. The ambassadors of Holland have taken their leave of us and are gone to Oxford for the same purpose. The lords from the king return, having only made some little way towards the treaty.

There's much labouring by the Lords to save Sir John Hotham,[183] and yet the Commons remain firm to their resolutions. Sir John was to die Tuesday the last December, and being in his way came a reprieve from the Lords, which the lieutenant of the Tower accepted of. The next day his son came,[184] and after a short speech (in which he wholly denied to have had any design of treason against the parliament) did with great resolution receive the stroke. <**1 January [1645]**> The next day came the father,[185] who prayed a long while and at last, but with more discomposedness than his son, died. 'Twas an addition to his trouble that the captain died first, it being his turn, and then had hopes his son might have been spared. [fo. 35] There was not so general a contentment in the people, as many thought the father had somewhat hard measure, he having done the parliament so good service. The Independents would not have had him died;[186] the Lords

---

[182] Sir Alexander Carew was second-in-command of the garrison at Plymouth and had attempted to surrender the garrison to Prince Maurice. He was executed on 23 December 1644.

[183] Sir John Hotham, governor of Hull, was sentenced to death on 7 December for having secretly corresponded with the royalist commander in the north, the earl of Newcastle.

[184] Captain John Hotham, who was also sentenced to death for his role in the same secret correspondence with Newcastle. He was executed on 1 January 1645, the day before his father's execution.

[185] Sir John Hotham was executed on 2 January 1645.

[186] Juxon is mistaken here. According to Clarendon, Sir John Hotham had many friends among the 'Presbyterian party' at Westminster, but their efforts to secure him a reprieve were thwarted by 'divers of the Independents, his mortal enemies, he having uttered some speeches against Cromwell and the Independents'. On 30 December 1644 the Commons divided on the question of whether to concur with the Lords in sparing Sir John Hotham's life; the political Presbyterians Sir Philip Stapilton and Sir John Coke were tellers for the yeas, but lost the division to the political Independents Sir John Evelyn of Wiltshire and Oliver Cromwell: *Clarendon state papers*, ii. 184; *CJ*, iv. 4.

and party were discontented at it and railed at the council of war for cruel etc. But God over-ruled and so had ordered it.

There's now great labouring towards a treaty, especially the Lords and their party, who certainly are agreed with the king and drive his interest,[187] nor can do other. And therefore demur upon the ordinance for the taking of the members from employment, that so we must either agree or, if not, the armies shall be in such hand [sic] as are true to their party. In the meantime, the king's forces have fair play without interruption, and draw towards Sussex, whom, to oppose, the committee of both kingdoms have commanded Lord Essex and Manchester, but they'll not stir.

The bill for the archbishop of Canterbury's death is passed,[188] and the same day that the directory for worship (in opposition to his litany) was finished, and the same day that he gave the king the counsel against the 5 members. **<10th [January] Friday>** And was executed at Tower Hill, dying in a most calm and composed manner. The sun presently (it being a close day before and after) burst forth as soon as the blow was given, and retired again. His last speech (25). [fo. 35v] Some say the king will do as much for the marquess of Hamilton,[189] which in reason of state he may, being the next heir, or, as some say [inserted], the true heir [inserted] to the crown of Scotland.

<13th [January]> The Commons went up with a resolution to the Lords to pass this great ordinance,[190] but instead of it give reasons [against]; yet the malignants laugh at them, and say they are enough flexible in what concerns the king, but when it comes to their own particulars are stiff.

The Lords have hitherto managed the war with respect to the king; and so as to enfeeble us, and resolve if we will not agree as is intended between Oxford and them, they will keep the sword in their own power if they can. The treaty will be on the parliament's part. The Lords and their party much desire it before extremities have forced us to decline our ceremonies to them, and before they be too much lessened. The Independents desire it, hoping t'obtain that liberty from the king which the Presbytery will not allow. And the Scots like not our conduct of affairs, which is so much left to providence as if we had not heads, and they see us exceeding facile and irresolved; apt to betray one another, and subdivided into so many factions that the public can scarse prosper. Then, they may too much expose themselves to a foreign enemy, drawing away so great forces from home. [fo. 36] And last,

---

[187] Lit. intresses.
[188] On 4 January 1645.
[189] James Hamilton, third marquess and first duke of Hamilton.
[190] i.e. the self-denying ordinance.

the general weariness of the whole kingdom and the oppression of all men in places of authority. And then, we manage not this war for continuance; for there is no discipline in the armies, nor any certain way for maintenance. Nor is it desired lest this then encourage the soldiers to spin it out, when there's a certain spring of money.

'Tis the king's best game to treat, at last [sic] to show his willingness, and delude the people – the same reason the parliament – then he may beguile us by it. And his greatest advantage is by agreement, though on low terms. He may do more on us by the nearness of his presence and warmth of favours than [by] arms. He has places and other means t'oblige, especially seeing almost all the gentry are necessitous and ready to be hired. His nobility and gentry that are not of the junto party[191] do abhor their masters, and are much reduced in their estates, and yet not the favourites. Besides the disadvantages on that side and their great poverty, and [crossed out] depend only upon foreign aids. Ireland cannot much more serve them, at least if we will hold them in employment.

<20th [January]>[192] The House of Commons have voted Sir Thomas Fairfax for general, Major-General Skippon for the foot, and Middleton for the horse; twelve regiments of foot, eleven of horse, and one of dragooners, to consist of 14,000 foot and 6,000 horse.[193]

[fo. 36v] <29 [January]> This Wednesday the commissioners from the king and the parliament met at Uxbridge, each taking for their lodgings the right side of the way as they came into the town. That day was spent in visits and civilities. The principal things are: 1. religion; 2. militia; 3. Ireland. The king, for religion, will have an elective presbytery and a moderator, under the name of a bishop, to be also elective. For Ireland, he's resolved not to discontinue the cessation; no, not after the expiration of the time he has now granted it them for, though by act of parliament he promised to do nothing in that business without them.

<17th [February]> The treaty ended on Saturday.[194]

In this interim of time, Goring surprises Weymouth[195] <Melcombe Regis not> through the negligence of the soldiers and treachery of the

[191] By 'junto party' Juxon was probably referring to what Clarendon termed simply the 'junto'; that is, the inner ring of royalists at court which determined policy: see I. Roy, 'George Digby, royalist intrigue and the collapse of the cause', in I. Gentles, J. Morrill and B. Worden (eds.), *Soldiers, writers and statesmen of the English Revolution* (Cambridge, 1998), p. 75.
[192] The following, down to the bottom of folio 36v, is in a different hand.
[193] The vote was taken on 21 January 1645: *CJ*, iv. 26.
[194] The treaty of Uxbridge ended on Saturday, 22 February 1645.
[195] On 11 February 1645.

town. Sir William Waller is, upon this, commanded towards the west, with the horse of lord general and Lord Manchester. Colonel Graves[196] command the first, but basely refused and said he would not go with such a rogue as he was (and so came away plundering the country, having reduced themselves for [sic] 1,500 to 600). They went from Croydon to Wikham [High Wycombe?] and thereabouts, still plundering as they went and committing [fo. 37] the greatest disorders upon the earth, and daringly send propositions to the House to have their pay and then that my lord general may continue to command them – to his great dishonour, who takes no care to quiet them.

The Dutch ambassadors, being come from Oxford, make their address to the House.

The news came of the surprisal of Shrewsbury by storm,[197] Prince Maurice having drawn out the greatest part of the garrison to relieve Chester, which he did; but at that time we were even with him.

The Lords and that party do much labour to hinder the army under the command of Sir Thomas Fairfax, knowing that the war will neither be carried on to their, nor the king's, interests[198] by this; for 'tis plain they intend so to drain the Commons and City that they shall be never able to nourish rebellion or faction, and the king has not so much prevailed by his force or policy as by our respective and indifferent manage [sic] of things, and being false to our own interests.[199]

<15th [February]> The Lord Maguire was this Thursday executed as a traitor at Tyburn [inserted].[200]

The news now came of the regaining of Weymouth,[201] which, with the circumstances, is admirable. Waller though ready and willing to relieve it, yet neither lord general's nor Cromwell's horse would go with him. [fo. 37v] He then shipped away 300 of his foot for Weymouth, but the wind came cross and were driven into the Isle of Wight; there stayed till the work was done.

The enemy was resolved to gain Melcombe, it being of infinite concernment to his majesty's affairs in reference to the total gaining of the west and for the Frenches. We fell in upon the town of Weymouth and surprised Chapel fort, but were repulsed to the drawbridge with great hazard of losing all. But it pleased God, the governor gave a fresh onset and beat them quite out of the line, and so remained that night, during which time their scouts discovering a body of the country

---

[196] Richard Graves was a colonel of horse under Essex and became a staunch Presbyterian.
[197] On 22 February 1645.
[198] Lit. intresses.
[199] Lit. intresses.
[200] He was executed on 20 February 1645.
[201] On 28 February 1645.

people gathered on a hill (with clubs etc. to defend themselves from their plunderings), imagined them to be Sir William Waller, and so reported it to their general, which struck them into such a panic fear that they all fled away in the night; left the invincible north fort with all things in complete order, which might have cost us many a man. This whole business, the juncture of times and things and things [sic] considered, makes it a most visible hand of providence and a good omen for this year.

There's strange tuginge ['tugging' written above] about the list of the new army which Sir Thomas Fairfax has put in. And herein the Scots do join with Stapilton, Holles, etc. to alter it that it may go their way and their countrymen preferred, to which the Lords, Lord Essex especially, adhere; not that they love the Scots, but in revenge and despite to the other party.

[fo. 38] The Lords have not only refused to pass the list, as the Commons had done and as Sir Thomas put it in, but, contrary to their own ordinance, undertake to nominate and cast out about 50 not only Independents but such as were good, putting in most vilde[202] persons of their own [crossed out] both nations; which appears whose interests[203] they steer to, and how little they regard the real good of the nation, their peerage being their great idol.[204] The Houses send [to the City] to desire that £80,000 may be advanced for the present upon the ordinance for this army, which is assented to provided the list may pass.

Our brethren[205] the Scots do utterly refuse to be mustered and say 'tis not in the articles. They brought so many into England, and till you pay them all their arrears will not muster, though they are not above a 1/4 part; besides that, they pay not the common soldier and have wholly plundered wherever they come, carrying all into Scotland, both cattle and other things. They have withdrawn their intimacy from Sir Henry Vane etc. and are adhered to [the] lord general, Stapilton etc.; partly in opposition to the Independents and to balance the other party.[206]

The Lord [sic] at last, by one voice, do pass the ordinance for the list as it was presented; but 1st the Commons told them that if they

---

[202] Vile.

[203] Lit. intresses.

[204] *CJ*, iv. 26, 31, 63–6, 73, 75–7, 81, 83; *LJ*, vii. 259, 262, 264, 266–8, 272–4, 276–7; BL, Add. Ms. 31,116, fos. 198–98v; HLRO, main papers, 10 March 1645, fos. 145–8.

[205] The words 'our brethren' are written in red ink in the margin to the left of the words 'our brethren' in black ink in the body of the text.

[206] The breakdown in the alliance between the Vane-St John group and the Scots only seems to have become common knowledge late in February 1645: D. Underdown, *Pride's purge: politics in the Puritan Revolution* (1971), p. 67.

refused in this, which was for the apparent good of the kingdom, they must be forced to assume their own power and do it without them.[207] This very much weakens the Presbyterian and lord general's and Scots' party.

[fo. 38v] **<ult. martii [1645]>** Monday. This day the commission of Sir Thomas Fairfax was again set upon, but passed not the Lords, where 13 to 9 lords, Essex, Warwick and Manchester etc., were for the negative.[208] The Commons again pressed them to it. In my lord general's [commission] there was some touch to have a care of the king's person, and now they would have had it put in that, if the king were there in person, he should not fight. But it was at last the next day concluded that if the king were there he should only send to him to desire him to withdraw.

Wednesday, the Lords Essex, Manchester and Denbigh laid down their commissions, having opposed the other to the last.[209]

<[marginal note in red ink] **March 31 1645>** (Our directory came forth some days since)

Thus it pleases God (though with the greatest opposition) our business goes on, and the Commons have only herein showed themselves and appeared considerable, and the Lords, by much striving, have fared the worse. The Independent party will by this bear up, and the Scots and Presbyterian abate. Yet 'tis said the [sic] Sir Henry Vane the younger and the solicitor, though they favour the Independents, yet are the men the [sic] most sincerely do intend the real happiness of the nation. The earl [of] Northumberland does more and more appear truly noble.[210] He is to be governor to the duke and Princess Elizabeth, and they are [crossed out] he is to be allowed from the parliament £10,000 per annum as well for that as in regard of his extreme losses. Sir Henry Vane etc. have procured of the puritans £100,000, for which they have the ordinance for Sir Thomas Fairfax's army.[211]

[fo. 39] The States ambassadors are returned from Oxford and are upon the going home. This certainly said, that they did every meal send the king (they being at Oxford) two bottles of wine for his own

---

[207] The Lords passed the list on 18 March 1645: *LJ*, vii. 268, 272–7; Gardiner, ii. 187; BL, Harl. Ms. 166, fo. 184v.

[208] *LJ*, vii. 289–98; *CJ*, iv. 94–5. Fairfax's commission passed the Lords on 1 April 1645. Gentles estimates the vote as 11 to 9: Gentles, pp. 22, 452–3 n. 132.

[209] On 2 April 1645: *LJ*, vii. 299; *CJ*, iv. 96–7.

[210] Northumberland and his 'gentleman-servant', Robert Scawen, were instrumental in the creation of the New Model Army: J. Adamson, 'Of armies and architecture: the employments of Robert Scawen', in Gentles, Morrill and Worden (eds.), *Soldiers, writers and statesmen of the English Revolution*, pp. 45–8.

[211] This is a reference to an ordinance of 31 March 1645 for a loan of £80,000 from Londoners: Firth and Rait, i. 656–60. Several leading godly citizens acted as treasurers at war for the money.

table. And the soldiers there refused to march without money; the king was fain to persuaded [sic] and promise them money and the next day gave them 2s a man. Thus has he reduced himself to the scorn of the Hollanders and humours of base vermin by deserting his best friends. Though Prince Robert, with all their possible assistance, went resolved to regain Shrewsbury at last [crossed out] least, yet Brereton having drawn into a body, and at last [sic] 2,000 commanded musketeers of our brethren joining with him, the princes retreat to Worcester. In the interim, Waller and Cromwell etc. are not idle in [the] west but beat up their quarters and drive them together, that they may resolve on something. Sir Thomas Fairfax has 1,000 new levied horse sent to him to Windsor, and will appear for diversion speedily.

There passed now, but with much ado and no marvel, (that self denying) vote of excluding the members of both Houses from places either military or civil <And that all places not military or judicial shall be farmed, the profits pro publico>during the sitting of the parliament.[212] And herein have they clearly vindicated themselves that they do not seek themselves, or desire the continuance of the war for their particular advantages. Now, and never till now, have they acted like the Commons of England and as such who (de jure) are to take care of the kingdom and revive there their almost obsolete maxim, salus populi etc.[213]

[fo. 39v] <8th April [1645]> The earl of Warwick gave in his commission for admiral (30).[214]

The Swedish agent here received an answer to the queen of Swedes to our parliament, wherein she desires an eternal league of friendship, offensive and defensive, for religion, contra all mortals. We return the same expressions and desire there may be commissioners appointed to treat of the expedients. The States ambassadors also took their leave and went away upon Tuesday the 26th ditto; they gave in a paper to the Commons (31).

<ditto 14th> The Kentish people did again, upon the pretence of refusing to be impressed and pay any more taxes, rise about Dartford, but were by the vigilance of Colonel Blount[215] quickly suppressed; the chief of them taken and since the most active hanged.

<21st [April]> The garrison of Newark surprised Nottingham bridge. The king was ready to have gone for the Isle of Ely from Oxford with a strong party of horse and so fallen into the association, but it pleased God was happily prevented by Cromwell and forced to draw in again. After which he routed and beat 3 regiments of their

---

[212] On 3 April 1645: *LJ*, vii. 302–3.
[213] Salus populi suprema lex ('let the good of the people be the chief law').
[214] He resigned on 9 April: *LJ*, vii. 311.
[215] Thomas Blount of Wricklesmarsh, Kent.

horse, took 400 of them, summoned Bletchingdon House, in which was Colonel Francis Windebank[216] governor, and has it delivered.[217] But the governor, being come to Oxford, was called to a council of war for it and condemned to die.

The king sets out a proclamation to all that will come in by the last of May [that] they shall be pardoned.

[fo. 40] The Scots are now desired to advance, but not to the good liking of all; there be sad stories of their demeanour in the north parts. Besides their debothedness [i.e. debauchedness], they are extremely cavalierish and drink healths to the king's officers and to the confusion of the roundheads; and indeed, do only mind their own particulars but not the cause, and our parliament seem either to want hearts or power to demand reason of them. This, with their grievous taxes upon the country and false musters, will wholly bring <**May 5th**> us out of line with them and so into jealousies, which will not be omitted, but fomented, to a division, and, in fine, to make the war end with them, where it did begin.

The Prince Edward, <u>one</u> [inserted] of the Prince Elector's brothers, has married at Paris Mademoiselle Anna, fille de duke de Mantua; elle a dans ce royaume dix mille livres sterling de rente <u>this</u> [crossed out] Elle est aussi forte Catholique mais non pas brouillant.[218] This will assist the French design by taking off this prince from minding his own interests,[219] but surrendering them to the crown of France to obtain a peaceable enjoyment of his lady and her dowry.

The king now, as well as the parliament, is drawing into the field. Cromwell and Browne are to join. Browne appears and is peremptory to him; are disunited. Browne is to lie before Oxford. Sir Thomas goes to relieve Taunton with the first forces raised, but being commanded back sends a party and 'tis done.[220] He returns without delay (having almost tired his men) to Reading. [fo. 40v] Colonel [Edward] Massey is made major-general of the west.[221] The king seeming to go towards the north, the Scots army that was coming retreat.

Our armies, or rather counsels, seem to be divided – some for following the king, others for the siege of Oxford; though in the beginning of a year, rather soon in the field and hinder the enemy's

[216] Second son of Sir Francis Windebank, former secretary of state.

[217] On 24 April 1645.

[218] 'Miss Anna, daughter of the duke of Mantua; she has in that kingdom a private income of ten thousand pounds sterling a year. She is also a strong Catholic but not a troublesome one'.

[219] Lit. intresses.

[220] On 11 May 1645.

[221] Colonel Edward Massey, formerly the parliamentary governor of Gloucester, was appointed major-general of the Western Association forces by ordinance on 24 May 1645.

conjunction is best. But they that could not hinder this New Model would crush it in the bud, and indeed the king's interest[222] lies to do it, because he's to seek friends and correspondence and then knows these will not be so soon baffled. The malignants work that way, and [the] lord general's party in revenge; the Scots and Presbytery because they're [i.e. the New Model Army] Independents.

Colonel [Sir Charles] Gerard defeats Major-General [Rowland] Laugharne in Pembrokeshire[223] [inserted] and so comes freely to the king, who this year recruits from Worcester side; lying all this while there, and the rather to hinder us from assisting Wales.

The Scots army, without [the] Yorkshire and Shropshire horse, are to follow the king.

<24 May [1645]> There came a manifesto from the Scots commissioners about the motion of their army etc.[224]

<30 [May]> About this time the king took in Leicester by storm; used the people extreme cruelly.[225] This a a [sic] great disadvantage and the loss of a county, especially at this time of the year, which makes the king in the best posture. The fault in part is laid on Colonel [Bartholomew] Vermuyden, who had a great party of horse and did not interrupt the king as he might. <[marginal note to the above paragraph] 300 lost by us in it, sorely[?] ill fortified and manned and all for to save; the counties[?] are generally ignorant>[226]

[fo. 41] Since what with this and dissuasions by my Lord Manchester, and [the] lord general [having] laid down his commission, so that one and other way all our old soldiers etc. have left, the Scots especially; and this not only in scorn to Sir Thomas but to ruin the army and make us intreat their help again, in so much as many say [the] lord general must into the field. Colonel Cromwell is sent down to secure the associated counties and raise what forces he can.

<June [1645]> Sir Thomas draws off from Oxford, leaves Browne, marches to join with Cromwell, and the king labours to hinder it. Cromwell is desired by Sir Thomas and the horse officers to command the horse; 'tis agreed by the Commons, but the contrary party were not willing; yet 'twas done and both joined their forces.[227]

Taunton was no sooner relieved [than] be [sic] re-besieged, and with all that party in it, to which Massey is to march and relieve them.

<14th [June]> The king's army was greater far than the parliament's

---

[222] Lit. intrest.
[223] By mid-May 1645.
[224] *LJ*, vii. 390–92.
[225] Leicester was taken on 31 May 1645.
[226] Juxon's meaning is not clear here.
[227] *CJ*, iv. 169–70; *LJ*, vii. 421; Rushworth, vi. 39.

(engaged and fought the 14th June on Saturday), as by the relation and letters.[228]

<18th [June]> And to complete the victory, Leicester was summoned and taken in after 24 hours before it, by accord.

The king had all the reason in the world to fight. The parliament had now disobliged th'old officers and all the Presbyterian party (and so the assembly), laying them aside, which was not done without must [sic] discontent. And now [the king] intended to try the Independents, who were most raw and inexperienced; and if that he could have given them a blow now at the beginning of the year, together with their loss of Leicester, and beating from Oxford [fo. 41v], it would not only have rendered him master of the field but, with the reputation of it, have brought in many towns and left him free to have gone into th'association, but might have hindered them from recruiting again. Besides, 'twould have set all together by th'ears at homes [sic] and brought the parliament trouble enough, as may appear by a petition upon the loss of Leicester, to have an account of the last treaty at Uxbridge (which, to say the truth, have failed to inform the world of, whereas the king had presently a declaration set forth to abuse the world and made great use of it, and the more from the parliament's silence).

There were certainly many that were not very well pleased with this victory. But herein did God vindicate His honour; this army being looked upon with scorn as wholly inexpert, and the grandees imagining themselves the only men. This put an honour upon and engage the parliament and kingdom to favour that party who were most active in the service, and so shows that God looks not as man, but by the despised subdues the mighty, [and] will honour the humble not the proud. This changed the scene strangely and startled the king's party everywhere.

<July 15th [1645]> A parliament assembled in Scotland, to which we sent our commissioners: earl [of] Rutland, Lord Wharton, Sir Henry Vane senior, Sir William Armyne, Captain [Thomas] Hatcher, Mr [Robert] Goodwin.[229]

[fo. 42] **<1 July>** Sir Thomas Fairfax, having a little refreshed his men, marched with his body into the west to join with Colonel Massey, and both to relieve Taunton, now besieged by Goring etc., with 10,000 men, [who], upon the approach of our men, drew off. This is the 2nd

---

[228] The reference is to the battle of Naseby, fought on 14 June 1645. Juxon is wrong about the relative size of the armies; parliament's army at Naseby was nearly double the strength of the king's forces: Gardiner, ii. 247; Gentles, p. 55.

[229] These commissioners were sent to the Scottish parliament primarily in order to negotiate the removal of Scottish garrisons from Carlisle and other northern English towns in the Scots' hands. The ordinance appointing the commissioners was read in the Commons on 12 July, and in the Lords on 28 July: *CJ*, iv. 206; *LJ*, vii. 514–15.

time Taunton was relieved by him. Goring was sent for to come to the king before the battaigle [i.e. Naseby], but he excused in regard of the great hopes of taking in Taunton (we intercepted his letter); thus put him in great disfavour with the king.

<10 [July]> Sir Thomas fights with Goring against his will near Bridgewater; beats him to purpose and <23rd [July]> presently storms and takes Bridgewater, which was an extreme strong and rich place, many officers etc. This is of very great consequence and taken beyond expectation and without great loss.

The city of Carlisle was at last surrendered into the hands of the Scots (having lain long before it), though the governor would not without it might have a Scots [crossed out] an English [inserted] garrison; and though the articles were so concluded, yet our brethren would not observe it, which occasioned much discontent and gave jealousies of them [inserted].[230]

After he had beat [crossed out].

At last Scarborough Castle was surrendered.[231] [Sir Hugh]Cholmley obtained to go into Holland.

<August [1645]> The clubmen in Dorsetshire, Wiltshire etc., grew at last, having often appeared in bodies to declare against the parliament. And though fair means were used to reduce them yet 'twould not do, [fo. 42v] <3rd August> but were in th'end constrained to cudgel them, which Colonel Cromwell did to some tune, as by his letters.

There as [sic] now some discourses, or rather intentions, of renewing propositions for to send to his majesty, and the rather in regard of the good successes of the parliament.[232] This has its rise from the Scots, who dote much on their gend[233] king. <6th [August]> Their army is now set down before Hereford. The king comes out of Wales with 2,000 horse and makes his course by Newark, there adds 1,000 more, comes to Huntingdon and plunders it to purpose, so also St Ives (and so alarms Cambridge that the scholars come running away 6 upon a horse, in great confusion); stays not but comes to Bedford and Onbourne[Woburn?] and does the like, and indeed it fell most heavily

[230] The Scots' garrisoning of Carlisle after its surrender on 28 June 1645 was conceived by the Commons to contravene the terms of the solemn league and covenant and generated considerable ill-feeling at Westminster towards the Scots: *CSPD, 1644–45*, p. 619; Baillie, ii. 301; H. W. Meikle (ed.), *Correspondence of the Scots commissioners in London 1644–1646* (Edinburgh, 1917), p. 92; [William Fiennes, Viscount Saye and Sele], *Vindiciae veritatis, or an answer to a discourse intitled Truth it's Manifest* (12 September 1654), BL, E811/2, pp. 115–19.
[231] On 25 July 1645.
[232] On 18 August 1645 parliament agreed to draw up new peace proposals.
[233] Foolish, simple (Scottish term).

upon his own friends that longed to see him there and would not stir.[234] They were so plundered, beaten and abused that he has lost more friends than in any voyage a good while. Those that stood at the doors and bid them welcome [inserted] and rode out to meet them fared no better.

He came into the countess of Bedford's, set him down, and told the lady, 'Madam, you have seen [me] in a better condition than now and may do again'. She replied that he might quickly be if he would go to his parliament. 'What to do?' said he, 'they would cut off my head if I were there'. 'No', said she, 'sir, they would be certainly very glad of your coming and use you with all respect and honour'. He swore a great oath he would not trust them.[235]

[fo. 43] Sherborne Castle is taken at dicretione[discretion?] and in it Sir Lewis Dyve,[236] with many officers and soldiers etc. The plunder was the soldiers', the castle was to be demolished. 'Twas a strong piece and of importance; was stormed. Some weeks since, the strong castle of Pomfret [Pontefract] was taken by the parliament's forces with a [inserted] great booty in it; in a word, all th'artillery and arms etc.[237]

The king, after his plundering voyage, returns to Oxford with about 2,000 horse, tired and tattered. There is great blame laid upon David Leslie,[238] who was commanded, with their horse, being 2,000, and Poyntz's[239] and Rosseter's[240] as many, of all which he had the command, to follow the king, which had he done [the king] could not had time to plunder, nor ever have got his jades to Oxford.

Leslie, when they all met, commands Poyntz to attend Yorkshire, and Rosseter the association, or rather Lincolnshire, and he would wait on the king. Being then 10 miles from him lay still one night, and then the king marched 20 miles farther the next day. Received a letter from the chancellor of Scotland to march presently thitherwards in regard of their last great defeat,[241] which he did, leaving the king and not commanding the aforesaid colonels to follow. This he did only from a single letter, when he had neither order from either parliaments, committee of both kingdoms, commissioners in London or armies, but to the contrary, to follow. [fo. 43v] And thus left their gend king to

[234] For the king's plundering 'voyage' in August 1645 through Huntingdonshire, see Gardiner, ii. 290–1, 302.

[235] No corroborating evidence for this purported exchange has been found and Juxon may be reporting fanciful hearsay.

[236] It was taken on 15 August 1645; Sir Lewis Dyve was governor of Sherborne.

[237] Pontefract was taken on 21 July 1645.

[238] Lieutenant-General David Leslie, commander of the Scots' horse.

[239] Sydenham Poyntz, commander of the Northern Association army.

[240] Edward Rosseter, who commanded a detachment of the New Model Army based in the Eastern Association.

[241] Montrose's victory at Kilsyth on 15 August 1645.

take bad courses and plunder, which he did more than ever, and had reason, coming from the hungry mountains. But this gave ill symptoms of them, as if they would not hurt that party if could choose. David Leslie presently marched with 4,000 horse and 2,000 dragoons towards Scotland.

Sir Thomas Fairfax stays not at Sherborne but, having given order about it, sends away the same day part of his horse towards Bath to drive in their parties, which was happily done and that city taken.[242] The army marches directly towards Bristol rather than to Exeter, that no enemies might be behind them.

The first thing attempted was Portshutt [Portishead] point, which was presently taken,[243] and by that means our ships that lay without came up. This is rational proceeding. The king stays not in Oxford but away towards Worcester and so to relieve Hereford, which at his approach the Scots quit, having been there above 3 weeks and not intrenched. The king was about 3,000 tired horse only; they 9,000 foot, 2,000 horse. Marched away to the general amazement of the world, not acquainting our commissioners with their design.[244] General Leslie has since published his reasons. They march home; [they] who had came in with but 2,000 galloways, have now, with David Leslie, 5,000; here, 2,000 and 4,000 baggage horses. With plunder this is well increased, and in that they principally aimed at.

[fo. 44] One of them told a friend at their first coming he wondered they [i.e. the English], being so rich and happy a people, did not make a peace, for, said he, 'could we [i.e. the Scots] have been worse than we were would never have taken up arms'. They send to the parliament, from Scotland, that they desired not to withdraw their brotherly assistance, but desired us to send them fresh men of ours to them, which the parliament thought unreasonable and thereto returned that if they would draw out their garrisons in York[shire?] and north etc. would send to have men raised to supply, which would be the soonest done. They have 8 garrisons in those parts. They leave the kingdom with almost a general content to it.

They came in, 'tis true, in our necessity and have done us some good charges, but have been well paid, carried it always very high, and were the support of the Presbyterian party, thinking to have carried all before them. They [crossed out] To them adhered the synod, lord general and all that discontented party not out of love but for ends. But 'twill not do; they, as well as others that thought to have saved us, have missed and God only will be He. They certainly would have had

---

[242] On 30 July 1645.
[243] On 28 August 1645.
[244] The siege of Hereford was raised on 1 September 1645.

a good accord for the king if victorious. And truly, the unexpected miseries that are happened in their kingdom occasions strange thoughts to know the cause − I mean in reason.

But that which seems a miracle is that Lord Robartes − who was ever taken for a dependent or strongly inclining and with whom Sir Philip Stapilton and his party could never agree being now returned [crossed out], but 'twas supported by the better party[245] − [fo. 44v] being now returned from Plymouth as if his interest[246] should be [crossed out] were altered, changes his party and adheres most firmly to the Scots, lord general and his party, with a strange and bitter spirit to his friends. But they that know the cause say he remembers the Cornwall business and how far he was the occasion of their drawing thither, and that Sir Philip intend and swore to be revenged and bring it to a council of war; had n'other way to save himself but by adhering to his enemies, in which the earl [of] Warwick helped him. The man is strongly for the peerage.[247]

Poyntz is command to follow the king towards Wales.

Sir Thomas intend to fall in upon Bristol, having 5,000 stout men from Somerset and Gloucestershire; cordial which vexed Rupert [to] the heart. This business had a conclusion, and [was] taken, as by the printed relations. Which how advantageous, all [perso?]ns judge; for if at the losing of it [i.e. Bristol] we thought the kingdom lost and the enemy in gaining it the kingdom gained, which shall we now think, being recovered. Prince Rupert was at the taking it and he surrendered it.[248]

The House of Commons the same morning the news came took into consideration Nat Fiennes, and considering that when he held it there was no old soldiers [i.e. veterans] in it, nor Prince Rupert, had but 800 foot <killed them 1,200 men>, the city not fortified as now, nor any army in appearance to succour; whereas the prince and many others were in it, the town much more fortified, [fo. 45] had in it near 5,000 men, two armies both in 60 miles each side, [and] we lost not 300 men. This gave them reason to judge him clear of cowardice and so was voted into the House again with great joy.[249]

<15th [September 1645]> Monday. Came the articles agreed

---

[245] For the war party's backing of Lord Robartes prior to his *volte-face* in the autumn of 1644, see BL, Harl. Ms. 166, fos. 36v, 37; Clarendon, iii. 387.

[246] Lit. inter[e]st.

[247] Juxon appears to be the only source to claim that Robartes switched allegiance out of fear of retribution by Stapilton (and Essex), or that Warwick was instrumental in his conversion. For Robartes and his role in encouraging Essex to march into Cornwall, see Clarendon, iii. 386–7; [Saye], *Vindiciae veritatis*, pp. 49–50.

[248] Bristol was surrendered on 11 September 1645.

[249] On 12 September 1645: *CJ*, iv. 273.

upon at Bristol with a gallant letter by the general to Prince Rupert. The parliament voted Major-General Skippon governor; since which they have attempted and now taken Berkeley Castle upon surrender,[250] which is another addition of comfort to the city of Bristol and clears all Gloucestershire. News came that the horse under David Leslie and Middleton came unexpected and fell upon Montrose's headquarters, consisting of 2,000 foot and 1,000 horse, which were of his best men.[251] Cut off most of his foot and took the horse, except 200 [he] himself escaped with. Took several persons of quality, amongst the rest one [Sir Robert] Spottiswood that the king had made secretary in the place of Lord Lanark,[252] whom this lord took and with him the signet and the letters and papers from the king to Montrose, where it appears he was created duke of Fife – where St Andrew lies buried – generalissimo of the armies and viceroy of Scotland. There were some of our English that did very gallantly in the action.[253]

Upon the sad news of Scotland formerly,[254] Sir Thomas Fairfax and the chief officers sent a letter to General Leslie to condole the miseries of their country, assuring them that, the affairs of this kingdom permitting, the parliament commanding, and they desiring it, would [fo. 45v] to hazard their lives for the restitution of their kingdom, and not only so but were resolved never to lay down arms while there was found in the three kingdoms a man to hold up a sword against the parliament.

This week was buried Mr William Strode,[255] one of the five members; Mr Hampden, Mr Pym, and he being dead.

The latter end of this week was a petition printed [and] sent into every parish for to be subscribed by all that had taken the covenant, and that their qualities should be also set down; and brought [in by] Mr Lawrence Brinley. 'Twas to press the parliament to establish that form of [church] government presented to them by th'assembly. This was fomented by the several ministers and intended after to be presented to the common council for consent and so to the parliament.[256] 'Twas intended against the Independents. The House of Commons had notice of it and voted it to be scandalous and contain many untruths; sent to

---

[250] On 26 September 1645.

[251] The battle of Philiphaugh, 13 September 1645.

[252] William Hamilton, first earl of Lanark.

[253] 'The good service of some English in Commissary General Middleton's regiment is much spoken of': *Montrose totally routed at Twidale [Philiphaugh] by Lieutenant-General Leslie* (13 September 1645), BL, E301/19, p. 6.

[254] i.e. Montrose's victory at Kilsyth on 15 August 1645.

[255] On 22 September, having died on 9 September.

[256] *To the right honourable Lords and Commons assembled in parliament, the humble petition of [blank]* (20 September 1645), BL, 669 f. 10/37 (Ms. note 'sent to Mr George Thomason to get hands to it about 20 September', Fortescue, i. 397); BL, Add. Ms. 31,116, fo. 240.

the lord mayor to call a common council, which was done Saturday night and order given to suppress it.[257]

<22nd [September]> The Scots maintain their government by maintaining their general assemblies, in which they have the greatest peers and hold it forth as jure divino, and from whence there is no appeal. This they labour for in England, and by this the ministers, being the great party, carry it, and by their power there keep themselves in credit with their parishes. [fo. 46] The parliament of England seems not to intend the holding out of any government jure divino, for that were to set them <the several parties for discipline> together by the ears, but intend to keep the reins in their own hands. And yet will settle the Presbytery (but so as not to give any coercive power to them), and this that all may not be in a confusion, but that those that will may be settled, like the enjoining the directory. If [crossed out] They are obliged to a neutrality in this because both parties are too considerable to be disobliged. The Presbyterians are great and have the Scots to them, and the Independents have done too good service to be so ill rewarded as not to have their liberty (but banished, which will follow by consequence), when that [sic] have done so much for our liberties.

The Devizes is since, by Sir Thomas Fairfax, taken in, and Laycock House in Somerset, also Berkeley Castle,[258] which render the country clear by Colonel Rainborowe. To the first the Scots obtained a 2nd defeat of the forces under Montrose; forced him into Douglas Castle with 10 men, so that not only the gross of the army remains but David Leslie returns.

<26> There came news that Major-General Poyntz fought with the king near Chester being [crossed out].

[fo. 46v] <26 [September]> The forces of Cheshire fell upon and took in the suburbs of Chester, and kept them, i.e. one part of them. The king drew to relieve it with a body of 5,000 horse and dragooners, being his choice and last in those parts. Poyntz, having without rest marched 300 miles, came at last, though much weary, being about 2,500 horse, fell upon the king's forces; was disordered, but was relieved by Colonel [Michael] Jones, who had gained the suburbs, and, in fine, gave the king and [sic] very great and sad overthrow, having killed three hundred, besides persons of quality, and taken 1,200, besides arms and a very great number of brave officers and of remark, indeed the best that were left him.[259] The king escaped with a body of horse, resolving to attempt once more the relieving Chester.

[257] On 20 September 1645: *CJ*, iv. 280.
[258] On 23, 24 and 26 September 1645.
[259] The battle of Rowton Heath, 24 September 1645.

There was a petition pretended from Plymouth, but believed from the west country gentlemen here, to have Sir Thomas go and relieve that town, not being able to hold out this winter. 'Twas concluded he should and is gone.[260] By this means will hinder them [the royalists] from their contributions and disturb them in their only quarter that now rests to them.

Winchester with the castle were taken in by Cromwell by composition; 600 took arms under us. Bishop [Walter] Curl, bishop of Winchester, was in it.[261]

[fo. 47] The Scots were, seeing they desired not to march home, commanded to lie before Newark, having done nothing this summer. But for answer the commissioners put in their paper that they desired the discipline of the Church might be established according to their platform, that we would send propositions to the king, pay them £60,000 and their arrears, arms etc., and then [they] would do as the season of the year would permit.[262] This did not relish with any but their own party and does presage worse disputes. They care not to have the war ended, nor are willing to return to water and oatmeal. They had gathered so much plunder they would not advance till it were well disposed of, and are therefore gone to Newcastle. The parliament are resolved, in point of discipline, never to condiscend that the general assembly shall have the last and determining voice, for they like not to be under the clergy.

<4th October [1645]> Alderman Adams chosen mayor.[263]

Our forces marching towards Langport House, near Salisbury, they in it quitted it before we came. 'Tis said the Scots army will not come to Newark, but stay about Durham because the parliament have appointed commissioners to examine upon oath what has by the Scots been taken from them <they will, if they can, hinder this>; which done, wise men say we shall not owe them much.[264]

[fo. 47v] Basing House being undertaken by Colonel Dalbier, he fortified a quarter and made his approaches, but wanted men. Cromwell came to him and the [sic] fell to batter, and <13th [October]> after to make breaches, at last to storm,[265] which was done and most of them put to the sword; the marquess[266] and Sir R[obert] Peake, the governor, excepted. The House being partly battered and burnt was after, by

[260] LJ, viii. 6–8; CJ, iv. 355; CLRO, Jor. 40, fos. 144v–45.
[261] On 5 October 1645.
[262] LJ, vii. 619–22, 630–31; CJ, iv. 283.
[263] Alderman Thomas Adams, lord mayor of London 1645–46.
[264] LJ, vii. 691, 694; CJ, iv. 339–40.
[265] Basing House was stormed on 14 October 1645.
[266] John Paulet, fifth marquess of Winchester.

order, razed to the ground. There came also news of the taking of Chepstow upon the Welsh side of Severn.[267]

There was a letter sent from the king to General Leslie, which he sent up to the commissioners; it [im]parted as much as his to my lord general when in the west. There have been great debates about sending home the Scots army. They say, if they return then the Independent party will swagger; if not, must endure their plunderings, which are insupportable. The northern counties are very sensible of them and extremely enraged.[268]

The Scots press much the sending of articles [crossed out] propositions to the king, which certainly is that their people seem not to be satisfied with them nor us, as having not done our utmost to persuade him. And then they consider their own country, which at best is very poor and now much ruined and not able to support the people. And though Montrose be worsted and forced to fly to the Highlanders who are for him, yet there, may continue to vex them, for they're not able to follow him. [fo. 48] And then their being here, as 'tis uncertain how short so with great discontent and in a manner upon charity, [and] may, in the interim, lose all their own country etc.

'Tis said that there's an ambassador gone from Spain into Ireland and one going from France, both of them thirsting to devour that kingdom. The Spaniards labour much a peace with Holland in reference to Flanders, and then, having but the French to deal with, will do well enough. But 'tis believed nothing can be done without the French concurrence, especially considering the prince of Orange his particular inclination to the French. The king of Denmark offers to come in person and interpose here [inserted]

<20 October> There came news (after the beating of the two princes into Belvoir Castle going to the king) that there went a strong party of horse under the command of Lord Digby, [Sir Marmaduke] Langdale etc. to relieve Skipton Castle; surprised 1,000 of our foot, but being closely pursued by the Yorkshire horse under Colonel [John] Lambert, were totally routed and beaten, being near 2,000, in which was Digby's coach and papers our foot recovered.[269]

God seems to follow with strange and constant success, insomuch as some say of this year, and of Fairfax and Cromwell, that it fares with

---

[267] Chepstow surrendered on 10 October 1645.

[268] The first debate in the Commons on whether to send home the Scots army occurred in October 1645 following receipt of letters from Yorkshire bemoaning the 'infinite oppressions and extortions' of the Scottish forces in the region: *CSPD, 1645–47*, pp. 183, 189; Bodleian Library, Ms. Nalson IV, fos. 187, 212–13, 214, 244.

[269] The battle of Sherburn in Elmet, 16 October 1645: *LJ*, vii. 666; *CJ*, iv. 316, 320, 324; *The Lord George Digby's cabinet* (26 March 1646), BL, E329/15.

them as with the king of Sweden.[270] The Presbyterians do apply it that way and grieve it's done by those hands. The Independents glory and believe by them to oblige to a liberty.

[fo. 48v] There has been this year, considering the time, now more dry weather than has almost been known, by which our armies have had the freedom to march, especially into the west, which else could not have been done.

God makes all things concur when He will; and yet to consider how generally people make carnal conclusions, and believe they are redeemed to engage more deeply in the world and sensualities, is an argument He has not done with us. For certainly He has not made this sad and bloody work without some extraordinary design. He has not let out our corrupt blood that we might lick it up again. He has not defaced and profaned all our pomp, glory and greatness, past almost a possibility of repair, that we should now give out ourselves and project for them again. When He destroys the old, He will set up a new monarchy and bring in the desire of nations.

<25th [October]> The town and castle of Monmouth was taken in[271] having [sic] before Chepstow, and by this means all that county was reduced; upon which the county of Cardiff came into the parliament and so all south Wales.

The ministers of London that are of the assembly, with the triers, caused at [sic] committee to be chosen of aldermen and commons, presenting to them several objections against the insufficiency of the ordinance for the choice of elders etc., which indeed was the result of a meeting at Sion College.[272] [fo. 49] And would have persuaded the common council to present the same to the parliament as from themselves, and they not to be seen in it. It had several debates, especially one. [crossed out]

The ordinance for the choice of elders came forth, wherein every classis in London was appointed 3 ministers and 6 others or triers to try those that should be made elders in every parish etc.[273] But the ministers were not well pleased with it, therefore met at Sion College and found the parliament had put as many more laymen as clergy, which showed what they intended; and besides, had not given power enough to them. Therefore endeavoured at a common council [that] a committee might be chosen to consider of the needful, which was done.[274] There, they presented many objections<or questions to the

[270] i.e. Gustavus Adolphus.
[271] On 24 October 1645.
[272] The headquarters of clerical Presbyterianism in London.
[273] The ordinance of 20 October 1645: Firth and Rait, i. 793–7.
[274] The City committee to confer with ministers about the eldership: CLRO, Jor. 40, fos. 148–48v.

parliament>, which would have had them set their hands to, but 'twas refused and referred to a common council, where it had a long debate. Aldermen [Thomas] Andrews, [John] Fowke, Colonel [Rowland] Wilson [junior], [Robert] Tichborne, [Samuel] Moyer, Francis Allen, and [Richard] Waring held it for the negative, alleging that it had been long and seriously debated in parliament, that ordinance, and 'twas not judged fit to allow them more power. If the ministers desired anything they should deliver it under their hands as their desires, and if 'twere judged fit they would join with them, but by no means to make it their sole act, which was the desire of the ministers; and so the court were resolved and th'other disappointed. The parliament this week, by a vote, granted liberty of conscience to those of Barmudaz.[275] Thus that party seem to be favoured, and carried the other business in common council contrary to expectation.

[fo. 49v] The count of Egmont, whose progenitor was [be]headed by duke d'Alva, has been here 4 years and is now gone into France about agreeing with that crown. He is said to be a man of parts and not a rigid Catholic, [and] has had always able men about him; he's the only prince of Flanders alive. There has been some months since at the court of France some to treat about the surrenders [sic] of Lille, which had ere this been done had there not been put into it 3,000 Spaniards and Italians. The king of France promises to all the [sic] come in the enjoyment of all their liberties and liberty of religion. There be very many in those parts that are well inclined though appear not. 'Tis said the French in Germany [are] to deliver the several places they take to the right owners if they judge them able to keep them, only they must do homage to that crown. They have restored many places to the elector of Trier, who has been long imprisoned by the emperor, being of the French faction, but now released against this diet at Münster.

It is the judgement of wise men that as the former king of France engaged his ministers to prosecute this war upon the reasons and rules laid down – which they gallantly do, and not without a miracle considering the great discontents that were; the unsettled humour of the nation and [fo. 50] the several factions that have always been, the duke of Orléans still making stir and Condé against him [inserted], the queen a Spaniard, the king an infant, Mazarin a stranger an Julian[276] – yet do they carry on their wars with more vigour than ever, the queen and duke d'Orléans striving who shall most oblige the Huguenots (for their own ends). The duke is employed at the head of an army; the Gastione,[277] whom he favours, much do the work and are resolved, as they have already done this summer, so to make the enemy quarter

---

[275] Bermuda, or Somers Islands, on 27 October 1645: *CJ*, iv. 325.
[276] A reference to his Italian birth.
[277] i.e. the Gascons.

and maintain their army. Besides, the dukes de Guise and Elbeuf there also this winter. Then Count Harcourt commands another, who is of the House of Guise. And duke d'Enghien[278] in Germany, who is against duke d'Orléans. Besides, Prince Thomas in Savoy. So that all the busy heads are sent abroad while they sit quietly at home providing them money and cutting them out work. And certainly during the minority of the king will not engage in any other war.

Not many months since came of Salamanca, an old councillor of Spain, from thence with full power to agree with the Hollanders; landed at Dover, came to London, and stayed some days. Was, by a States man, conveyed for Holland; is since gone for Münster.

'Tis said that this [sic] too late to treat now the country's lost, and it cannot be done without the French. [fo. 50v] Since that Rákóczi has made his agreement with the emperor, or rather the emperor with him, the emperor does recruit apace, and the Swedes the like.

The king of Denmark is at peace, but if he shall again attempt anything he must look to the 2nd time. No doubt but the commanders of his forces and others of his faction will be putting him upon some new design for revenge.

<28 [October]> News came that Prince Rupert and Maurice, who not long before went to the king at Newark, came away upon a discontent with [Sir Richard] Willis, the governor, [with] Gerard and many others to the number of 400. Sent to Colonel Rosseter for a pass to go over sea, which he told them could not do without order; then [a pass] for Worcester – that neither. The Prince Rupert told him he must needs connive that his brother might go thither because all their things were there and lest the king should send before them, so he went; the Prince Rupert engaging himself for them and the rest that they had deserted the service and would never take up arms against the parliament. 'Tis said the prince told the king that Digby and his father had been for above 30 years enemies to his family. He might have known that before. [fo. 51] And how miserable they were gulled to engage so desperately to the ruin of their only and best friends, [and] serving the designs of their worst enemies. The king sent to him to return, but [he] refused it.

<3rd November [1645]> Monday. News came that the marriage between the king of Poland and Princess Maria of Mantua was celebrate[d] by an extraordinary ambassador, who was most richly attended and extremely magnificent.

There is a tax now in Paris upon the poll to 80,000 [livres]. One goldsmith was assessed 24,000 livres; the people do very much grumble.

The kingdom of France as it extends itself so it is not without great

---

[278] Louis de Bourbon, duke of Enghien, son of the prince of Condé.

pain to the body, and however the state design is carried on and they applaud that manage it, yet the people were never more miserable. And may from hence, and the several risings at Paris, wherein they [i.e. the people] have had their wills, conclude that that state is in no settled nor certain condition, and if ever they have an opportunity will never be reduced again.

This seems to be clear (granting the prince to have n'other religion than they use to have): that their governments are generally so tyrannous and insupportable that, besides God's design, they do bespeak their own ruin.

[fo. 51v] Letters being read that were taken of Digby's, there was amongst them one from Jermyn wherein he tells him what the queen said when she heard the cabinet was taken at Naseby:[279] 'a pox take him for a fool; one may know what countryman he is by carrying his pack at his back'. There were also letters that discovered a treaty of March 9 with the prince of Orange's daughter and Prince Charles, agented by Doctor Goffe.[280] The conditions were: that the States should declare against the propositions of the parliament at Uxbridge; 2. that they should take as good price and sell all the parliament ships they met with; 3. to assist him to their utmost.

Thus God seems to crush the prince of Orange in all his designs towards sovereignty. The good prince comes too late upon the stage to act that part, and by his attempts lays a groundwork for his own ruin in the hearts of that people, and teaches them the great danger and snare in giving so much power and so absolute into one hand; withal [inserted] that 'tis not safe to let the same man long in that charge, much less suffer it to be hereditary.

In the treaty of marriage with our daughter and his son [crossed out] What his brother could not effect he undertakes to carry on, and so from one to other lay down the design and means to be used.

[fo. 52] It argues a strange spirit in the [crossed out) What cannot be done this may be the next year, and if the States General or Provincial are not fit now, stay till they fall, and in the interim fit [crossed out] breed up and oblige others who may succeed.

And thus has the prince done that 'tis strange to see how they are departed from their interests,[281] else durst he not have entertained a treaty upon the forenamed grounds with the king. An example of this is plain: when the former treaty was for his son with a daughter of

---

[279] Much of Digby's correspondence seized after the battle at Sherburn was subsequently printed: *The Lord George Digby's cabinet*. Nowhere in any of his correspondence, printed or otherwise, does this quotation appear, and it seems likely that Juxon was reporting an embellished version of the letters read in the Commons.

[280] Dr Stephen Goffe, chief agent of Lord Jermyn.

[281] Lit. interesses.

ours, first the articles were drawn for the Princess Elizabeth, then by endeavours altered and drawn with a blank. Then Jermyn, Sir Henry Vane senior, madam nurse etc., being well greased, obtained it for the eldest Princess Mary, but the queen never intended it for good,[282] and that they should not come together till she were 12 years of age.

When the queen went over with her 'twas but only to oblige them to supply her, resolving never to have the marriage consummated but to leave her as a pawn. And left her with Madam Stanhope in charge [that] they should never come together, resolving rather to poison her than it should be. But the princess Orange, being as subtle as she, discovered it and so ordered it by corrupting the lady that appointed her son to go in to her [i.e. Princess Mary] one night, [fo. 52v] and the next morning told her she might now go to her father if she would. Our queen when she heard of it tore her hair and was extremely vexed.

The queen's court when at London was the greatest bawdy house in England. Madam nurses her 2 daughters, and all about her were whores. Jermyn came into favour after had got with child Mrs [Eleanor] Villiers and put into the Tower. The queen, upon his letters to her, examined the business to the bottom, and, finding him able, got his release and reserved him for herself [as a] Weckherlyn.[283]

For domestic news this week: the army in the west have taken up winter quarters at Chard. His majesty is come to Oxford with 400 horse; 'tis said no matter where so not at London. The king will do nothing without Digby, and it may be 'tis according the queen's little note and then must not. In the intercepted letters, though Digby confesses the king to be low yet will not come to the parliament. The remainder of the forces commanded by Digby and Langdale, who intended for Montrose, were met by one Brown, a Scots commander, and totally defeated; forced them 2 to take ship and whither is not yet known.[284]

We now being in part delivered, see in what in [sic] ill condition we were in last year – [fo. 53] the king having garrisons almost in every place; which paid [for] itself out of contributions and hindered us. Besides, could at any time in short warning have drawn forth a body

[282] i.e. she never intended that the match should stand.

[283] This is a reference to the scandalous affair between Henry Jermyn, one of Henrietta Maria's favourites, and Eleanor Villiers in the early 1630s which landed them both in the Tower. There was some tension between the queen's gaiety and sociability and Charles's gravity and strict morality, but the court was a model of moral propriety when compared with both its predecessor and successor: HMC, *Cowper*, ii. pp. 40–41; K. Sharpe, *The personal rule of Charles I* (Yale, 1992), pp. 170, 190, 212. George Weckherlyn was Charles's secretary.

[284] Sir John Brown, a colonel of horse in the Scottish army, defeated George Lord Digby and Sir Marmaduke Langdale at Annan Moor, near Carlisle, on 23 October 1645: PRO, SP41/2/125. Digby and his officers took ship for the Isle of Man on 24 October.

of veteran soldiers. This way he would have tired us out by being at no great charge but when in the field, and then, before taken, each of them would cost us dear.

We had also letters that there came a party of 1,600 horse and foot drawn from the several garrisons to relieve Chester, command[ed] by Colonel [Henry] Washington. Colonel [Michael] Jones drew out, fought and beat them totally and took most of them.

'Tis said from foreign [sic] that Hulst was taken by the prince [of] Orange 10 days since. That the forces raised by the king [of] Denmark are delivered over to the French, so that fear's over from us. The Turk's armado was defeated by the Venetians near Candia,[285] which 'tis said they'll surrender. Our English ships in the state's service got the day.

Sir Thomas Fairfax is said to be wax, which as often as melted receives impression. Sir Henry Vane junior is reserved and will not be taken notice of to do much [inserted] and has this faculty – to be irreconcilable where out. Mr Pym and he did never well agree, nor does he with Nathaniel Fiennes; it may be [he] loves no rival.[286] Lord Wharton and solicitor[287] are alike in this – they will sometimes be familiar and another time not own you. The last has not a pleasing deportment.[288]

[fo. 53v] The Scots press for an accommodation with the king. The reasons are thus rendered: they designed to have England melted into their church discipline, and by that means a national assembly of both joined might govern and have the management of all as it has in Scotland. They now see a party risen up in England of Independents, which (they thought not considerable yet) have the chief stroke in affairs and counsels, and will not be overborne. Besides, the parliament is fully resolved not to assent to Presbytery as jure divino, and thereby disappoint them as to that. They then consider their own country as like to be ruined, and suddenly, by Montrose, whom alone and without our help they can never subdue; no more than our nation them when had wars with them, and had beaten and driven them into the mountains [and] were forced to leave them and come back, and then would they recover themselves. We are not like to be (as yet) in a condition to help them, and in the interim the Irish may be poured

---

[285] i.e. Crete.

[286] According to V. Rowe, Pym and the younger Vane were friends and close political allies, although they could 'disagree on occasion'. Vane and Fiennes were also allies, if nothing more, during the mid-1640s: V. A. Rowe, *Sir Henry Vane the younger* (1970), pp. 10, 11, 19–20, 21, 23, 27, 63, 96, 99; Baillie, iii. 16.

[287] Oliver St John, solicitor-general.

[288] Juxon speaks as if he was personally acquainted with Vane, Wharton and St John. His observation on St John, that he lacked a 'pleasing deportment', certainly accords closely with that of Clarendon who described St John as having 'a great cloud in his face', and of a 'dark and clouded countenance': Clarendon, i. 183, 246.

into their country. That we are grown poor and not able to give them much money, and all the best plunder is gone; therefore an agreement is best for them.

Those here that are of the Scots' party are willing we should grow to some difference with them, which they will certainly lay upon the Independents to bring them into the odium of the people. [fo. 54] And if by that means can but get the managing of affairs and the armies into their hands (from them in whose they now are <u>in</u> [inserted]), 'tis enough. So that indeed the business is carried on rather by faction than for public advantage.

<17th Monday November> The greatest business of this week was the carrying on of the former petition, though in another way; for the ministers having under their hands delivered in their quce[289] to the ordinance, it was referred to a committee for for [sic] the drawing up a petition, but conformable to the covenant, which was resolved on this day and dispatched against Wednesday. At what [sic] time it was carried up by several aldermen and many of the common council in their gowns, delivered by Alderman Gibbs, but not at all resented. The answer was that they would not take any reports of their actions but from themselves, desiring they might be let alone to it.[290] **<19th [November]>** After the same day came another from the foresaid ministers to that purpose, but it was very ill resented and they sent home.[291] **<20 [November]>** Yet the next day the said aldermen and common council presented another of the same nature to the Lords, but this was extremely ill taken of the Commons; looking upon it as that which might make the 2 Houses clash, and that they would have their wills one way or other.[292]

[fo. 54v] This business thus carried, being stirred up and fomented by the ministers, puts the greater resolution in the House and are resolved never to give them any more power than they judge fit for them, nor ever to grant it (jure divino). There is a committee of Lords, Commons and ministers for the accommodating the difference between the Presbyterians and Independents so far as it may be,[293] who find it a hard matter to do that which shall please them that dissent and to acquit themselves with the reputation of wise men. For now the business comes to be not whether they shall connive at a toleration but whether they shall by a law allow them one. They confess in Holland 'tis connived at, and that only, but no act of that state made for the

---

[289] A contracted form of the Latin 'quaestiones', meaning questions, queries.

[290] CLRO, Jor. 40, fos. 150, 153; BL, Add. Ms. 31,116, fos. 243–4; ibid., 37,344, fos. 26–7; CJ, iv. 348.

[291] CJ, iv. 348.

[292] LJ, vii. 714–18; CLRO, Jor. 40, fo. 154v; BL, Add. Ms. 37,344, fo. 27.

[293] Set up on 14 November 1645: CJ, iv. 342; LJ, vii. 703.

allowance of a toleration. And indeed to do that were a thing as without a precedent, so opposite and destructive to any settlement of discipline.

<December 1st [1645]> This Monday Mr Solicitor [St John] made several very good motions, as to dismiss all causes depending before the parliament or any committee that might be determined by the law, and by this eased many that were tired out with waiting upon them.[294] Then, that whereas there were many committees for affairs of consequence and whose chairmen had been so for a long time [fo. 55], and that it proved that standing waters did gather filth, it was desired that henceforth the chairmen of such committee [sic] might be moveable. Further, that notice might be given by putting up papers in Westminster and [the] Exchange [that] if any of the parliament men had directly or indirectly received bribes they should make it known, and it to be accounted as a good service to the state, and what other oppression or grievance by any member. That all protections should be examined given by the members, and that though the persons of the members were to be free and privileged, yet that their estates to all ends and purposes to be liable to pay their debts. Towards the effecting of which a committee of the new and disengaged members to be chosen for it, of whom Sir John Danvers is chairman.[295]

Not long since, the prince of Wales, who is in the west, sent a letter to the general [i.e. Sir Thomas Fairfax] desiring a conduct for [Sir Ralph] Hopton and [Sir John] Culpepper to go towards the king to persuade him to accommodate with the parliament. The letter was sent up to the parliament, who returned no answer. Sir Thomas, with great civilities, offered, if he [i.e. the king] pleased to disband his army, himself would be his conductor to them. But in answer to that, by the Lord Capel's[296] letter to the general [inserted], seemed not to be contented with that, yet were resolved not to be over reached by them.

[fo. 55v] The king, by a trumpet, sent a letter to the Lords' House, or the speaker of it [rest of the page is blank].

[fo. 56] The French lost Mardyk, being surprised by a party of foot from Dunkirk.

Princes Robert, Maurice etc., who came out of Newark with a pretence to take ship, having demanded high terms from the parliament, were refused and they returned to Oxford again. Their first demands were granted, and more than was expected, for they were of the

---

[294] That St John was the instigator of these motions is confirmed by Walter Yonge and the author of *The Scottish dove*: BL, Add. Ms. 18,777, fos. 173v–74; *The Scottish dove* (3–10 December 1645), BL, E311/19, p. 883.

[295] This committee was appointed on 1 December 1645: *CJ*, iv. 362.

[296] Arthur, Lord Capel of Hadham.

uncapables,[297] and yet were with difficulty passed by. Having now refused this offer [they] are not like to meet with any more, but must stand to the adventure, for the Houses have nulled what was voted in favour to them. By playing their game ill [they] have lost first the king – in falling foul on Digby – and by slighting and abusing the parliament's offers, rendered themselves under their displeasure. And certainly this part was not acted without a finger of the Spanish side to lose them wholly to their best friends.

<**January primo [1646]**> The king intimates a desire to come to London, which is the 2nd part of Prince Rupert's offer, and only to attempt something upon London. He resolves to come alone. The parliament fear it, which is sad – that they should thus long manage the war, and upon such a point, that his coming in should make them more miserable. therefore [crossed out] So that if he must come, better if before; if not, change the name.[298]

[fo. 56v] Upon St Thomas day[299] there was a petition to the effect of the last put on foot in most wards, and put into the aldermen's hands to read and gain their consent and so prefer it generally to the parliament. To this end, there was a sermon in every ward; all of them drove one and the same way – not to choose men of erroneous opinions. The petition was principally against schism etc.,[300] and all wrote by the same hand. In several wards it was cried up, and in many not, so that nothing came of it. And certainly 'twas to let the parliament see the generality of the City were of the mind of the former. <[marginal note to the above paragraph] The ministers were the contrivers of it> But yet stayed they not here, but set up papers to incite the promoting of it, but all does no good.[301]

'Tis at last resolved the king shall not come before he have signed and disbanded, in which the two Houses agree. And themselves resolve upon a letter that tells him the truth. The Scots will not concur in it; say 'tis too sour.[302] Yet their assembly of Scotland not long since sent him a letter which charged him more fully.

---

[297] Those royalists excluded from pardon under the terms of the Uxbridge propositions.

[298] Juxon appears to be saying that if the king must come to London to reach an accommodation then it would be better if he did so before he has disbanded his forces. If he failed to do the latter, the name of the proceedings should be changed from an accommodation to a capitulation.

[299] 21 December, the customary election-day for common council. Yet because it fell on a Sunday in 1645 the election was postponed to the following day.

[300] *To the right worshipful, the aldermen, and common councilmen of the ward of Farringdon Within, at their wardmote, 22 December 1645* (22 December 1645), BL, 669 f. 10/41.

[301] There is some further evidence to support Juxon's contention that this Presbyterian initiative met with only limited success in the City: Lindley, pp. 361–2 & n. 31.

[302] *LJ*, viii. 81–2, 85, 91, 99–100; *CJ*, iv. 395–9, 405; Rushworth, vi. 219–20.

The Lord Goring is gone for France to be cured of the p[ox?]. In the west they amuse our army to hinder the drawing part of them eastward, which had been ere this but that some of the western gentlemen have their lands beyond Exeter and were restless till they moved that way. Wise men say they have been several time [sic] as much,[303] as in them lies the cause of the loss of the kingdom, being carried only by their own interests.[304]

[fo. 57] The petition presented in the wardmotes was at a common council acknowledged by the lord mayor and aldermen, and, in order to it, referred the consideration of it and a petition to be drawn up by the committee that did the former, adding to them the committee for fortifications.[305] At the same time came in a debate concerning the retaking of the covenant not only by the new elected members but by all th'other. And to imitate the parliament, appointed a fast for that court upon the same Wednesday the parliament and assembly had theirs.[306] Mr [Edmund] Calamy and Mr [Simeon] Ashe preached for them.

<14 [January]> The Scots commissioners divided themselves that day: part being with the parliament and th'other with the lord mayor; which was to countenance the business and to keep them in order. It was taken by the greatest part, but refused by many [crossed out] some [inserted]. <15th [January)> Next day presented their petition to the Commons by Alderman Gibbs; 'twas extremely well received and thanks given. The same next day from the Lords.[307]

There came a letter from the king at what time came the letters from Ireland of the agreement with the rebels, which was seasonable.[308] God by all his dealings seems to drive the business to greater extremities and especially towards the utter ruin of the king, who in all his overtures for peace (which are upon design) intends nothing less, but is restless from one thing to another; to ruin by deceit and pretences of agreement.

Sir Thomas Fairfax, considering Dartmouth, did resolve not to stand long about it, but having got a list of the well-affected in the town, to preserve them from plundering, [fo. 57v] resolved to storm it. And having appointed them to their several posts entered it in the several places when they were at supper in the town, and though all possible

---

[303] Juxon's meaning here is obscure.

[304] Lit. intrests.

[305] CLRO, Jor. 40, fo. 160. The City committee previously appointed to confer with ministers about the eldership was given the task of drafting the petition. There is no reference in the journals of common council to support Juxon's claim that members of the committee for fortifications were added.

[306] CLRO, Jor. 40, fo. 160.

[307] CLRO, Jor. 40, fos. 160v–61; CJ, iv. 407; LJ, viii. 104–5; Baillie, ii. 337.

[308] Glamorgan's treaties with the Irish Catholics, news of which reached Westminster on 16 January 1646: Rushworth, vi. 239–46; CJ, iv. 409.

resistance was made, by small and great shot, yet with the loss only of 2 men gained the town and in it great quantities of artillery and ammunition etc., it being their magazine.[309] This frightened them [i.e. the royalist forces] into Cornwall and actually set them of Plymouth at liberty, who had now for some years past been blocked up.

The king continues his seeming overtures for a treaty, which [he] desires may be personal, and many letters have been sent to that purpose; which at, has drawn forth a resolution in the parliament that 7 propositions should first be signed and the rest referred to a treaty: 1. Religion. [2.] The militia. [3.] Payment of the kingdom's debts. [4.] Delinquents punished. [5.] Prosecution of the war in Ireland left to them. [6.] No honours to be bestowed but on persons that have appeared for the parliament. [7.] The charter of London confirmed.[310]

But these must be first sent to have the concurrence of the parliament of Scotland, which will in all take up 5 or 6 months [inserted], so the the [sic] summer's business will be in a good forwardness ere that. And in the interim, may possibly be masters of the greatest part not yet ours, and also shall one way or other find what assistance the king will have from abroad, and what hopes, and how real his offers are, which if Q[311] will certainly be attended with suitable actions.

[fo. 58] The Scots seem to be very sensible that they are not so much interested[312] in these as in the propositions at Uxbridge, and say if there be any alteration farewell the peace of the 2 kingdoms. Their design certainly is to incorporate with this kingdom and to share equally in honours and employments, but 'twill not stand with the safety and honour of England to permit it.

<**February [1646]**> News came to us that a ship from France came into Dartmouth not knowing it was in our hands, we hanging out the king's colours. The master had order if they were in any danger to fling the packet overboard, which, when he perceived it was ours, did and upon examination confessed it. We ordered several boats to go out to see if they could find it. Providence so ordered it that they were cast ashore and taken up by us.[313] That which was legible and not in characters was about the prince's transportation. It seems 'twas thought fit he should go for Denmark and, upon reasons, that 'twas fatal to go to France; that the Protestants there would be jealous of it. But the queen overruled it for France as that which was best suiting the cabinet resolutions. There was also th'end and expectation of the king's coming to a personal treaty – which was to engage the City and

---

[309] On 19 January 1646.
[310] Juxon is referring here to what became known as the Newcastle propositions.
[311] This is a small capital 'Q' in superscript. Its meaning is not known.
[312] Lit. intressd.
[313] *CJ*, iv. 428–9.

his friends, upon our refusal or not agreeing with him, to rise and over-persuade the parliament to consent; but there's little hope of that.

<[marginal note to the above paragraph] The other[s] were given to decipher and will certainly hinder the treaty or make the zealous more moderate in it>

[fo. 58v] There came news likewise of the surrender of Chester upon terms very reasonable for the governor and persons of condition, who marched out **Tuesday the 3rd February**. The native Irish were left prisoners and shall b'executed. There came also the news of the surrender of Belvoir Castle to us,[314] which was upon the honourablest conditions yet granted – colours flying, drums beating, match lighted, bullet in mouth, bag and baggage.

Some 14 days since, there came letters from France to the solicitor [i.e. St John] with information that the Scots were tampering with the king and crown of France. They were presented to the committee of both kingdoms by Mr Pierrepont.[315] The Scots commissioners were highly vexed and put in a paper wherein the [sic] peremptorily desired reparation. The House had the hearing of it and did vote the gentleman to have thanks for his care in the information and so let the business die.[316]

Monday 9th February. There came over in the last passage from Calais one Sir David Cunningham and [William] Murray, of the bedchamber to the king, as servant to Sir David, who being suspected at Rochester were stayed, and the packet of letters to the French ambassador taken from the post. Sent up to and directed to [the] earl [of] Northumberland, Sir Philip Stapilton etc.,[317] they were first brought to Sir Philip. He [fo. 59] sent them to the earl [of] Northumberland, and, being night, though the committee sat at Derby House, kept them, intending the next morning to acquaint the House with them, [and] laid them with his gloves etc. in his withdrawing room. The next morning came the French agent to speak with my lord about the packet; was conducted into the lodgings and went to the withdrawing room, where, staying for my lord, espied in the next room upon the table the packet, which the courier that brought it assured him was the same. Upon this, he stepped in and took it into his pocket. My lord

---

[314] The Commons were informed on 2 February 1646: *CJ*, iv. 427.

[315] William Pierrepont, MP, a member of the committee of both kingdoms and a moderate Independent.

[316] This alludes to the 'unknown knight' controversy. The 'gentleman' who received the thanks of the House – the eponymous 'unknown knight' – was later revealed as the Yorkshire MP, Sir Henry Cholmley: *CJ*, iv. 412, 436–8, 466, 479, 486; *LJ*, viii. 123–4; Rushworth, vi. 235–7; Meikle (ed.), *Correspondence of the Scots commissioners*, p. 164.

[317] Northumberland and Stapilton were leading members of the committee of both kingdoms.

coming out he desired reason for the stay of the packet; in fine, told him he had it and would keep it, and after some dispute went away with it.

Upon **Wednesday [11 February]** there was a common council and the Scots commissioners came down to bring them a letter from the parliament of Scotland, which was read and contained matter of thanks for th'expressions of love to them; 2. for their zeal and endeavours towards the settling the government of the Church according to their covenant; 3. to tell them that though there were many jealousies whispered abroad of them, yet not to give them credit; but to assure them they always should be firm to their covenant, [fo. 59v] and to live and die with them in the full prosecution of that etc.[318]

They withdrawing, debate was what answer to give: some to have a letter presently drawn in way of thanks – but that was to run upon a rock and to undertake transactions with another nation without consulting the parliament – others to desire their armies might be active. But the result was to give them a verbal and complemental thanks, which, when the lord mayor had done in good language, they desired and did reply something, <[marginal note] That though the kingdom and parliament, army and commissioners of Scotland, and themselves were aspersed by malignants and incendiaries, yet they should see they would remain faithful, and especially to the City> with great expressions of content, to which the court gave a general hum, and the lord mayor told them they might by that understand the sense of the court. The letter was recorded in the court. The next [crossed out] same [inserted] day Mr Allen,[319] a member of the court and one of the parliament, was commanded to give them account of the whole carriage, and did it wisely.[320] The House ordered the lord mayor should bring the letter to them.

There is assurance given that last Friday the king, at a meeting of his great council at Oxford, told them they well knew how he had, by many messages, invited the parliament to a treaty and had received nothing in answer from them but scorns; [fo. 60] that he was resolved not to part with anything of his prerogative, the Church, nor his friends, and therefore desired them, as the former year so now, they would provide for his assistance, for he resolved to hazard with them the last drop of his blood in this cause.

'Tis also certain the Prince Charles, upon the approach of our army

---

[318] CLRO, Jor. 40, fos. 170–70v. The letter was dated 27 January 1646.

[319] Francis Allen or Alleyn, recruiter MP for Cockermouth 1645–53 and common councillor 1645–46. Allen was a factional ally of the Independent peer, the earl of Northumberland: Adamson, 'Of armies and architecture', pp. 52–3.

[320] The account was entered in the Commons' journals but later expunged by order of the House: *CJ*, iv. 437, 449.

towards him, Hopton (who is general in Grenville's place, and he committed for not fighting Sir Thomas Fairfax) came and told him they must be gone into Cornwall. The prince demanded, 'why, what will you do with me?' He answered that the rebels were coming and would take him prisoner if he stayed. The prince told him, he know [sic] not whither were his worst enemies, and said further, he did not believe they would do him any harm.

There came news that the parliament of Scotland was rejourned and had made the earl [of] Callander,[321] who has ever been suspected, general for Scotland; and that they had executed several of their delinquents and had given larger commission to their commissioners here.

There was upon **Wednesday [11 February]** great muttering of some intelligence in reference to the Scots, but the next day there passed a vote in both Houses to assure them all jealousies were laid aside and new resolutions for new amity [crossed out] Thus they play the children and change with the wind; lose their reputation to ground jealousies today against the nation [i.e. Scotland] and tomorrow vindicate them again. [fo. 60v] This is the unhappiness of a popularity, where things are transacted by multitudes, who are men taken out of them [sic] lump.

The common council appoint a committee[322] to call before them those that would not retake the covenant, who told them they had once taken it and did believe it was enough and said no more. The court begin to take upon them. They are earnest to have the choice of the militia in themselves, and then we know of what sort they shall be; therefore the parliament refused and will have it in themselves with their approbation.

<16th [February])> Monday. The House of Lords assent to the desires of the common council to have the choice of the militia in themselves, and send a letter with thanks to them, and in particular to Alderman Fowke, who was their mouth in the business; and this to ingratiate with the City.

<14 [February]> The desires of the House [of Commons] to have a relation of what passed the common [council], with a desire also to have the letter sent [to] the House, was considered in the common council. There did the lord mayor, and in fine the court, deny that the Scots commissioners named the word 'incendiaries', though 'tis most true 'twas spoken by the lord;[323] yet here by the way may see how

---

[321] James Livingstone, first earl of Callander.

[322] On 9 February 1646: CLRO, Jor. 40, fo. 166v.

[323] John Maitland, Lord Lauderdale, spokesman for the Scots commissioners before common council on 11 February 1646. He was said to have denounced the 'malignants' or 'incendiaries' who were trying to disturb the unity between Scotland and England. Baillie acknowledged that Lauderdale used the word 'malignants' (Baillie, ii. 352), while Juxon claimed that it was 'incendiaries'.

desperately they're engaged to the denying of the truth. [fo. 61] There were some of them very violent against [Francis] Allen, and that they would have him called to account for not only breaking his oath in revealing the votes of common council but giving a false report. They beginning to grow high against the parliament, as if they took too much upon them in questioning what they did in the common council. To them join the malignants, if it were possible to disunite or to put the City and them upon some bad understanding. The excisemen and customers are most of them very active for the Scots' interest.[324] The ministers do very much press the common council forwards and make them active.

Now the Scots are cried up more then ever and the covenant pressed. The godly party in the House[325] represented as men of no justice, as men that would have no peace, no government, nor no kingly power, and as men that would disunite the 2 kingdoms. So that every man's tongue is against them, though none drive less particular interests[326] than they nor have served them everywhere more faithfully. And it so comes to pass that not only bad and interested[327] men are against them, but good and conscientious – being over credulous – and think they drive on some design against the public peace. The House vote that they take nothing in ill part against the City of London for this or any other thing.[328]

[fo. 61v] <18 [February])> Wednesday. There was another common council, in which there was the committee formerly appointed to treat with the ministers[329] to consider of an answer to the parliament and what further to desire of them. Yet the leading men, who have the favour of the lord mayor and are permitted to speak as often as they please to one thing, when the committee was to be nominated and that Colonel Player[330] and Mr [Stephen] Estwicke were nominated, they cried them down saying they were Independents, though far from it and only honest and ingenious men. They now resolve (though formerly Alderman [John] Fowke and Alderman [William] Gibbs and the wisest were contra) to have a letter sent to the Scots in answer if the parliament would permit, but it seems they were better informed now.

<20 [February]> This was carried up on Friday to the Commons[331]

[324] Lit. intrest.
[325] i.e. the political Independents in the Commons.
[326] Lit. intresses.
[327] Lit. intressd.
[328] CJ, iv. 439.
[329] The committee appointed on 20 October 1645 to confer with London ministers about elders: CLRO, Jor. 40, fos. 148–48v.
[330] Thomas Player, senior, colonel of the City's white regiment.
[331] CJ, iv. 448.

and being considered of – presented by Alderman Fowke who was very
bold with them and told them they were resolved to stand to their
covenant (in the Scots sense) – there was debate upon it. Sir Henry
Vane junior desired it might be deferred, and said he desired to take
the fear of God before his eyes in a business of this consequence. One
made answer,[332] he wondered that gentleman should now desire it, and
now when the new model was brought in, which came in overnight
and was passed at the lump the next day.[333] But the gentleman [i.e.
Vane] said the meaning was [that] the party was not now ready and
prepared to the business. [fo. 62] Nat Fiennes told them the City was
their wife, and they could not but [inserted] take it ill another should
come to draw away her affection from them. 'Twas replied, if the
addresses to their wife had been in secret then might because of
jealousy, but to do it openly and in their sight there was no danger.
The business was referred to next day and nothing passed of moment
but skirmishing. In conclusion, resolved that Allen had done nothing
but his duty in reporting to the House upon their command, and, in
regard the clerk had not entered the report true, 'twas to be defaced.[334]
In the meantime, Allen is unhappy in this: that 5 days have been spent
upon him in this, and Long's business since in the House.[335]

There was one that said,[336] they had drawn the Lords, the Scots, the
assembly and now the City about their ears and had only got Oliver
Cromwell to their friend [inserted]. The honest party in the House
begins now (though never before) to fail them [i.e. the godly party] and
to be jealous. The Scots, the assembly, City, Lords, Stapilton's party,[337]
and malignants, their interests[338] all meet in one upon several considerations against the godly party and are resolved to get the mastery
and to try how they can steer the commonwealth. And these men [of
the godly party] are the most contented and resolved to let God or
man do their pleasure, only to hold out their witness and give their
testimony. [fo. 62v] All the other lesser parties fall in against them [the
godly party]; so strangely are men desirous of change. Yet one thing is
observable: that during this war not one man of godly and ingenious
principles has deserted the parliament or betrayed their trust, and yet
men of all other principles have; that though none have served them

---

[332] It has proved impossible to discover the identity of this speaker.
[333] The speaker is saying that he wondered that Vane should now call for more time
to debate the matter, when he had taken the opposite view concerning the legislation for
the New Model Army, which had passed through the Commons very rapidly.
[334] *CJ*, iv. 449.
[335] This is a reference to parliament's investigation of an incident in which Walter
Long attacked Allen: *CJ*, iv. 395, 397, 400, 407–8, 412, 420.
[336] The identity of this speaker cannot be ascertained.
[337] Sir Philip Stapilton's political following in the Commons.
[338] Lit. intrests.

with such activity and diligence, yet before safe in the port would cast them off most imprudently and ingratefully.

Sir Thomas Fairfax falls upon Hopton[339] (who was quartered at Torrington and had slightly fortified the town) at 9 at night, and though several times repulsed yet beat them out, dispersed the foot (who were 300, most their veteran Cornish foot). That besides, 600 taken; not more went into Cornwall. Thus in th'extremity of winter acts [Rowland] Laugharne: defeats the high shreve of Cardigan, who, being put in commission by the parliament, raises forces for the king, besieges and takes in Cardigan. 'Twas now retaken.[340]

<20 [February]> The same day came into the House of Commons a letter from the parliament of Scotland, signed by earl [of] Callander (as president),[341] in which he said he was commanded by them to demand, and did demand, of the parliament that they should speedily (according to the covenant) settle the government of the Church [fo. 63] without tolerating of any heresy or schism, and that they should confirm by their civil sanction what the assembly had presented to them to that purpose. For the other, he did desire in the name of the parliament that seeing by their covenant they were to support and preserve the king (whose good they desired as their own) they would dispatch their propositions to him. That they would give them satisfaction for the loss sustained for want of those ships, which by agreement should have been upon their coasts. That whereas we desired the restitution of the garrisons[342] by the first of March, they had sent their commissioners to give them grounds why that could not be done. That they desire to have the arrears paid by the first of May,[343] which were due to their army upon account – and to the Irish[344] – which should come along with their commissioners.

And these things were [sic] being performed by us, they should, in reference to our desires of their return, be ready to leave the kingdom; having come in to our relief, suffered with us, but rather brought a fire into their own country for us.

Certainly these letters must lie dormant, they do always come in so patly to second others here.

---

[339] On 17 February 1646.

[340] Juxon has confused Cardigan with Cardiff, which was retaken on 18 February 1646: R. Hutton, *The royalist war effort 1642–46* (1982), pp. 195–6; *CJ*, iv. 457–8.

[341] There were two letters from the Scottish parliament dated 3 February 1646 directed to both Houses of the English parliament and signed by John Lindsay, earl of Crawford and Lindsay (and not the earl of Callander) as president of parliament: *CJ*, iv. 448; *LJ*, viii. 177–9; Rushworth, vi. 233–5.

[342] Carlisle and the other northern garrisons in the Scots' hands.

[343] Should read 3 May.

[344] i.e. the Scots Ulster army under Monro.

[fo. 63v] The House of Commons were much startled at these concurrences, and especially that they should demand of them to establish what the assembly had proposed, when they [had been] called only to advise with. The parliament are resolved never to suffer the [crossed out] a general assembly here, as in Scotland, to prescribe to them. And indeed such a demand were in effect to dissolve the parliament and lose their privileges quite.

<23 [February]> Monday. Sir Thomas [Fairfax] sent word he was gone for Cornwall, desiring them to take care of his rear from France. That at an assembly of the popish clergy at Paris, our queen prevailed with them to give her £60,000 sterling; which the council of France having notice of, sent to them for £200,000 sterling, telling them seeing they could lend so much to a stranger they might do more for their own king, especially having not yet been taxed. In fine, they were fain to condescend, but desired the £60,000 might be part of the £200,000 – but 'twas refused. This is a good ground of confidence that we're not to fear much from them. Besides, General Goring came into Gastione's[345] army in Picardy to entertain some of the officers for the queen. Gastione, having notice of it, does commit him; calls a council of war where it's resolved he must either acknowledge his error publicly before the army or be banished the kingdom.

[fo. 64] <26 [February]> The House of Commons this day concluded to set to the business of [church] government and resolved to follow it de die in diem[346] till 'twere perfected.[347] Upon this they begin to cry up the Scots, the City of London and the Lords for having been the occasioners of this, and thus things are carried by faction. For in London 'twas not the City nor the common council, but a few engaged men there that are triers; for it happens many times when a thing is put to the vote in that court there will be 30 or 40 hands for the affirmative and not five for the negative, and the rest, who are the major part, are silent, as either not willing or not daring to appear; so a party carry on things there. And for the House of Lords, all the world knows they affect not the Presbyterial government, at least in reference to their own practise, and certainly when 'tis established will have a dispensation. They lay heavy burthens which themselves will not touch. Their compliance herein is to gain the City and so the people (who will never trust them) and the clergy, the better to serve themselves and friends when there's occasion.

The court of wards was by both Houses voted down and resolved

---

[345] Gaston, duke d'Orléans.
[346] Every day.
[347] CJ, iv. 455.

to put it in for an 8th proposition to be now sent to the king.[348]

[fo. 64v] Sir Thomas, resolving for Cornwall, did dismiss those that he took at Torrington (that would not take up arms) to go home, giving to each two shillings to bear his charges; which has infinitely taken with them insomuch that their fears of our revenge is off and the trained bands appear for us. Since, Sir Thomas has given strict command that none do presume to take away any cattle or goods etc. upon pain of death.

<2nd March [1646]> Monday. A letter came this week from Scotland to know who were the authors of Mr Solicitor's letter wherein they were accused to have treated with the crown of France to receive of them the arrears due from the parliament,[349] and then to recover it of us.

This morning did a party of 2,000 horse and foot from Oxford fall upon Abingdon, [and] having surprised their horse guard and the foot guard, were come into the town before the alarm; and that being given, a dozen horse commanded by Colonel [Heriot] Washbourne and <u>Major</u> [inserted] Blundell checked them. The foot came in their shirts, and after some hours dispute beat them out [of the town], which was in great danger to have been lost, and this without the loss of 20 men on both sides.

[fo. 65] Ashby-de-la-Zouch was surrendered to the parliament, as the pardon of Hastings and his father[350] etc.

There came another letter from Scotland to desire an account of the unknown knight.

[The middle section of this page is blank]

The lord chancellor and Lord Wariston[351] came now to London, passed by, but did not so much as call at, their army nor gave any instructions to them publicly; nor have [they] any commissioners there and so David Leslie will not be governed by ours but by both upon the place.

The parliament passed the ordinance for church government appointing commissioners, who are to consider of supernumary scandals,[352] and not to leave all in the power of the clergy, which they would fain have.

---

[348] On 24 February 1646: *CJ*, iv. 452–3; *LJ*, viii. 183–4.

[349] This is again a reference to the 'unknown knight' controversy: above, p. 100 n. 316.

[350] Henry Hastings, Lord Loughborough, son of the earl of Huntingdon. Ashby-de-la-Zouch surrendered on 3 or 4 March 1646: *The true informer* (2–7 March 1646), BL, E327/10, p. 358.

[351] Lord Loudoun, chancellor of Scotland, and Sir Archibald Johnston of Wariston.

[352] The ordinance was passed on 14 March 1646. Its fourteenth clause provided for the appointment of parliamentary commissioners in each province who would have the final say on appeals against suspensions from communion for non-listed (or 'supernumary') offences: *CJ*, iv. 463–5, 475.

[fo. 65v] **<9th [March]>** Monday. There was a common council to which was presented a petition signed by some 100 persons[353] to desire the court to consider of their covenant, and that they would petition to the House that they might have nothing put upon them but what had footing in the Word. The ministers (upon the voting and passing the business of commissioners,[354] which had been 10 several times been debated in the House of Commons) sent to their several agents in the City to bring in their reasons against it, so that they occasioned it. There was some disputing the business; in fine, 'twas committed to the committee for the Scots letter.[355] **<11 [March]>** Upon Wednesday following there was a court in the morning where it was read, and though urged that the proceeding would prove a breach of parliament, yet 'twas voted. At the same time did they call upon the refusers to retake the covenant and demanded their reasons. In fine, would have had them [inserted] withdrawn while they debated it, but they refused unless the court would vote it, which they did, and they withdrew. The result was to desire power of the parliament either to take it [crossed out] make them take it or expel them the court.[356]

The same day they went with their petition in great pomp first to the House of Peers [fo. 66], which they did for 2 reasons: the one because the Commons had already passed the ordinance up to the Lords, and the other because they judged the peers to be their best friends in it, and the rather because they had courted each other several times. But it had not an acceptance to desire, for after some hours debate they voted it a high breach of parliament, there being 13 contra [inserted] and 10 pro the petition.[357] Amongst the 10 were earls [of] Essex, Warwick, Manchester etc., who entered their dissents.

<13 [March]> This put the business to a slur, yet did not discourage the parties, but Friday they came to the Commons with the same they had presented to the Lords. The recorder[358] came out to them, and, after some discourse and finding it the same with the other, did persuade them not to deliver it in regard the Lords had sent the other down to them and they also had voted it a great breach of privilege. They [i.e.

---

[353] The petition was signed by 24 citizens: CLRO, Jor. 40, fos. 173v, 174v.

[354] i.e. the parliamentary commissioners to hear appeals against suspensions from communion.

[355] CLRO, Jor. 40, fo. 173v.

[356] CLRO, Jor. 40, fos. 174–74v.

[357] The vote and proceedings on the City petition on 11 March were subsequently erased from the Lords' journals: *LJ*, viii. 207–8 truncated entry; *CJ*, iv. 479. The ten peers who entered their dissents were probably identical with those who protested against the vote on 13 March approving parliamentary commissioners to hear communion appeals: *LJ*, viii. 208.

[358] John Glynne.

the City petitioners] considering of it went away without offering to deliver it. Yet 'twas given out they [i.e. the Commons] refused their petition and great murmerings.[359] They [the petitioners] came to so great a heat in the business that some said they [the Commons] taxed them with breach of privilege but they would let them know it 'twas they that had broken their privileges. To this [they] were much encouraged by the ministers and others.

[fo. 66v] The House hereupon resolve to apply themselves to some expedient for the preventing with [sic] might follow from discontents. At first, thought of applying themselves to a common hall, which was altered fearing some disorder, and concluded for a common council. This begot great expectation on all sides, and the common councilmen so prepared that nothing was expected but a sad breach.

<16 [March]> Monday.[360] There came down a committee of both Houses, where was a very full appearance of the court. Each man that spake did so dexterously apply their discourses with all sweetness and love that they found themselves overcome by them. Mr [Samuel] Browne of the House had the greatest part and gave a full account what had passed in the business of the Church with the assembly.[361] The assembly were called to advise and not to command. When they gave in their model 'twas as a prudential thing, nor would they come to argue it as jure divino in the assembly, yet 'twas preached by some of them of London to be; at which the House resolved to consider and state some questions to them that might determine the business, which the assembly and their friends in the House by all means labour to hinder and persuade it etc. [fo. 67] Told them the House did not except against the matter but the season of the petition, which was that after the ordinance had passed the Commons to go to the Lords, they to come and engage the Lords against the Commons was the breach of privilege. But yet told them they did not believe they had any evil design in the petition and that it was ignorance in them; therefore demanded of them the petition[362] that was presented to them which occasioned theirs.

---

[359] BL, Add. Ms. 31,116, fo. 259; Baillie, ii. 361.

[360] Other sources give Tuesday, 17 March: T. Edwards, *Gangraena* (1646), ii. BL, E338/12, p. 8; T. Hawes, *A Christian relation of a Christian affliction* (31 March 1646), BL, E506/24. There is no record of the meeting in the journals, the City having apparently carried out the Commons' instructions to expunge proceedings on the petitions from their records: *CJ*, iv. 475.

[361] Juxon appears to be the only source for the content of Browne's speech to common council. For parliament's instructions to the delegation which addressed the City fathers on 16 March, see HLRO, main papers, 11 Mar 1646; Bodleian Library, Ms. Tanner 60, fo. 554.

[362] The citizens' petition of 9 March 1646.

Being withdrawn, there was much debate and then the party[363] found themselves at a loss, there being so full a court, which is not usual and so things are carried with more ease. But now their judgements being fully informed in matter of fact, and of what danger and ill consequence their opposing the House might be, did therefore return them this answer: that they were sensible 'twas a great breach but not intend[ed] by them, and therefore desired them all the votes concerning that petition, and it, might be razed out of their books,[364] and assured them that as they had covenanted so were resolved to maintain with their lives etc. the privileges of parliament. And so both sides [crossed out] remained well satisfied, especially such as were not wholly given up to the clergy interest,[365] and withal gave the petition with the names that signed it.

[fo. 67v] But now their friends without, and the engaged party within the court, reproach them and complain of their lâcheté;[366] that they had betrayed their friends, [and] had asked pardon when they should have justified the action etc. Nevertheless, the discreeter sort did acquiesce. This did clearly discover the firm affection and inclination of the common council to the parliament, and that 'twas labour lost to attempt them.

News came of the total surrender of the Lord Hopton's army[367] (who were driven beyond the Mount [i.e. St Michael's Mount] in Cornwall, consisting of 4,000 horse etc.). The prince of Wales shipped for (Scilly). A bark from Ireland put in with some of the native Irish, who by the inhabitants were destroyed except 2, and letters of the whole business found.[368] Thus Sir Thomas and his army conquered not only by the sword [but also by] love, especially that county [i.e. Cornwall] who were thought irreconcilable.

Sir Jacob Astley coming towards Oxford with 3,000 horse and foot to join with the king and then to return all for Wales, to entertain the Irish that were presently to land, viz. 6,000 instantly and 4,000 [on] 1 May, was set upon by [Colonel Thomas] Morgan, governor of Glouces- ter, and [Sir William] Brereton, totally defeated, 1,500 prisoners, the Lord Astley with many more.[369] This was a most seasonable and happy defeat, and that which not only puts an end to the king's field forces

---

[363] i.e. the high Presbyterian faction in common council, or the leaders of the 'covenant-engaged citizens' as they preferred to style themselves.

[364] Both Houses agreed to expunge all the offending items connected with the petition from their journals and urged common council to do likewise: *CJ*, iv. 475, 477, 479; BL, Add. Ms. 31,116, fo. 260; above p. 109 n. 360.

[365] Lit. interest.

[366] Cowardice.

[367] On 14 March 1646.

[368] i.e. Glamorgan's negotiations to gain Irish assistance for the king in England.

[369] The action took place at Stow-on-the-Wold on 21 March 1646.

[fo. 68] but utterly disables him from gaining another army; insomuch that Sir Jacob, being take [sic], told them: 'now you may put up your pipes and go to play for there's nothing more to be done, unless God be so just as to let your divisions ruin you'.[370]

<234 [crossed out]> Monday[371]

Tuesday there was a common council, at which court the party did importunately put on the petition again upon this ground: that the parliament excepted not against the matter but the time of the [crossed out] it, and that now the ordinance was passed they had liberty to petition. But [crossed out] The dissenting party did not appear against them, but let it alone to the moderate party, who strongly opposed it as also the lord mayor upon this ground: that government was either divine or human; if human, enough had been said to it, if divine, it remained with the assembly to prove. And further said, that seeing the business of the former petition was razed out and not to be more thought of, did also desire the same in that court. And then told them, that they had entrusted the parliament with their lives, liberties etc., that they had sworn to be faithful to them in the same and therefore to leave it wholly to them. And being advertised that there was a resolution in the Houses to keep a day of thanksgiving [fo. 68v] in London, 'twas resolved to invite them etc. to a dinner.[372] Thus by degrees recover themselves.

In the interim [crossed out]

<27 [March]> There came down a committee of both Houses to the common council[373] to give them an account to their desires in reference to their petition and votes; was accordingly done.

[The middle section of the page is left blank]

The assembly the day before had put in a petition to the Commons to show that commissioners were not of divine authority etc.[374]

[fo. 69] This week came forth the letters taken in Lord Digby's coach, which give a clear light to all their foreign designs.[375] And upon the communicating of them to the States of Holland, they immediately

[370] According to John Vicars, Astley said 'Gentlemen, ye may sit down and play, for you have done all your work, if you fall not out among yourselves': J. Vicars, *The burning bush not consumed. Or, the fourth and last part of the parliamentary-chronicle* (1646), BL, E348, p. 399.

[371] The rest of this line is left blank.

[372] The City invited parliament to dine with them at Grocers' Hall after the day of thanksgiving in Christ Church on 2 April: *CJ*, iv. 492.

[373] On 26 March 1646: *CJ*, iv. 492; CLRO, Jor. 40, fo. 175v.

[374] A. F. Mitchell and J. Struthers (eds.), *Minutes of the sessions of the Westminster assembly of divines* (Edinburgh, 1874), pp. 209–11. The petition was presented to both Houses on 23 March 1646: *CJ*, iv. 485, 492; *LJ*, viii. 232–3.

[375] *The Lord George Digby's cabinet and Dr Goff's negotiations*, BL, E329/15, printed on 26 March 1646.

discharged both the fleet and men that were to be provided for the queen of England, under the command of [Jonkheer Philips van] Dorp, but pretended for the French, so that now all their hopes fail them, especially since the Irish cannot land neither.

The States of Holland are very inclinable to a peace with the Spaniard, mistrusting some underhand dealing between the Spanish and French. They have been offered by the Spanish ambassador a carta blanca. The crown of France sending to them to be early in the field, the States at a meeting said they had no money; but the prince, taking his time when one of his friends was president (according to course) of the States, together with [Cornelis] Musch, his secretary, sent a dispatch to tell the crown of France they were ready to comply with their desires, but wanted money, which [they] desired to supply them. The States having notice hereof presently met in great discontent, but the prince quickly charmed them with his good tongue, so that there seemed to be a consent; but one of them stood up and told the prince, 'Que Oldenbarnevelt n'a jamais fait tant'[376] (and yet lost his head). [fo. 69v] Thus discontents do daily grow and arise, which are as so many waves that beat off and retard the design of the prince.

<30 [March]> Monday. There came intelligence of the king's coming to London, which [he] was resolved to do and not stay the propositions; which was taken into a debate considering the danger of it, which could not be but in order to some design. And to speak truth 'tis his best and only way, for hereby might encourage a middle party to importune the parliament to conclude in favour to the king and raise great discontents. Besides, being here in our garrison and under custody, whatsoever should sign were by our laws invalid, for he might urge it was done p[er] minus,[377] and so in conclusion nothing would be done. The rigid Presbyterians are very much for his coming and so are the Scots, who will not suffer anything to be said that reflects on the king, and all of them cry out against Independents as those [who] would have no king, and so by all ways bring them into hatred.

The parliament vote if he come, his person, i.e. the king's, [is] to be secured from danger in St James's, and none to come to him without the parliament's leave. Those that come with him, to be committed, and, in case of resistance herein, then to kill and slay. The committee of Lords and Commons for the army were joined to the [London] committee for the militia to manage together this business.[378]

[fo. 70] <April 3rd [1646]> Thursday.[379] The 2 houses of par-

[376] 'That Oldenbarnevelt never did as much'.
[377] Under duress.
[378] *CJ*, iv. 495–6; *LJ*, viii. 248; Rushworth, vi. 249–50. The vote was taken on 31 March 1646.
[379] Should read April 2nd Thursday.

liament, Scots commissioners, th'assembly, <u>lord mayor etc. and</u> [inserted] common council, the Lord Inchiquin[380] and Major-General Massey <and Prince Elector> were at Christ Church to keep the day of thanksgiving for [the] defeat of Hopton and Astley, and were afterwards magnificently feasted in Grocers' Hall by the City, the red regiment of the trained band being a guard to them, and Cheapside th'wackt with people as at a lord mayor's day. There come daily very many from the king's quarters, which speaks him following.

<7th [April]> Monday.[381] There came this night at 11 o'clock the committee for the army to the committee for the militia[382] to acquaint them with some intelligence, newly come from Oxford and other of the king's quarters, intimating the assurance the king had to be in few days in London and in a very good condition; and this from the great numbers of malignants, prisoners and those lately come in, in all 40,000, in which the lord mayor [Thomas Adams] was to act a chief part. It was debated whether or no to acquaint the lord mayor with it or if then. Both were concluded affirmative, and so did at 12 o'clock. It startled him, but with much cheerfulness assured them how unlikely he was for such an engagement and, in fine, gave them good satisfaction. [fo. 70v] But withal told them he wondered how they should find him in such a business, and could not believe it any other than a design, which might be therefore done because he has lately showed himself forward, according to the covenant, for settlement of discipline.[383] The letters were attested to be from persons of credit (that daily give us intelligence from Oxford) by Major-General [Richard] Browne, who has received many from him and very true. The lord mayor, though [he] seemed satisfied, yet since is extremely nettled at it, at [which] all that party cry it up for a design to take him off.

Saturday [11 April] there came forth in print some of the Scots papers which they had presented at their conference, and joined with it a narrative or stating the question between the parliament and the Scots. This was known several days before it came forth and expected by their party.[384]

This day the parliament or House of Commons, after a very long debate, did vote the manner of the petition[385] to be a breach of privilege,

---

[380] Murrough O'Brien, Lord Inchiquin, president of Munster.

[381] Monday was 6 April.

[382] i.e. the parliamentary army committee to the London militia committee.

[383] A vindication of Mayor Adams was to be called for in the City's remonstrance of 26 May 1646.

[384] *Some papers of the commissioners of Scotland given in lately to the Houses of Parliament concerning the propositions of peace* (11 April 1646), BL, E333/1; *CJ*, iv. 507; *LJ*, viii. 271–2; Rushworth, vi. 253–57.

[385] The petition of the assembly of divines of 23 March 1646: *CJ*, iv. 485, 506.

because they being only called to advise did undertake to prescribe them what they ought to do. This puts their party out of all patience, and say though the votes were against them yet the reason was for them.

[fo. 71] <13 [April)> Monday. The Scots papers being read in the House of Commons, sent to know if the commissioners did order the printing, they renounce it. The House orders it to be burnt by the common hangman, and *Truth's manifest*, which was [David] Buchanan's, who was voted an incendiary, sent for, but gone the [sic] their army.[386]

The party in the City, having their instructions from Sir Philip Stapilton by Colonel [Lionel] Copley and Colonel [Edmund] Harvey,[387] put them to a desperate resolution to petition no more, but put forth a remonstrance and pay no taxes or excise, yet cry for the king and wish him with them, [and] condemn the House of Commons or the godly party for men of no conscience or honesty, no king, no church government.

<16th [April]> Tuesday. There [was] a common council intended for to act their designs there.[388] The lord mayor [i.e. Adams] must be vindicated and this were encouraged too from their party in the House, telling them it was only a party and design. Instructions given them to manage their business. The lord mayor was desired to give an account of the business – though seemed to refuse it – and by degrees did it. Then concluded on a petition to the House and a remonstrance[389] which should invert their own votes and ordinances upon them, and this was carried on very unanimously.

[fo. 71v] The news of the surrender of Exeter[390] came and of the remaining garrisons in the west. A letter from the parliament has lately been sent to the prince, who remains in Scilly, to desire him to come into the kingdom, promising to conduct him whither he pleased. Provisions sent him of all sorts by Sir Thomas Fairfax. The king remains in Oxford; has attempted to break out several times but was repulsed.

<18 [April]> Saturday. Came forth a declaration from the parliament, and ordered to be read in all churches, partly to disabuse the people in reference to the Scots papers and to antidote the remonstrance

---

[386] *CJ*, iv. 507–8. David Buchanan was the Covenanters' leading apologist during the mid-1640s and his tract, *Truth its manifest* (12 November 1645), BL, E1179/5, his most controversial work: Kishlansky, *New Model Army*, pp. 96–7.

[387] All three were leading figures in Essex's party.

[388] The common council meeting was on Tuesday, 14 April 1646: CLRO, Jor. 40, fo. 176.

[389] Which became the City remonstrance of 26 May 1646.

[390] On 13 April 1646.

that was in fieri[391] by the common council to them.[392] The same day was Mr [Stephen] Marshall, Mr [Richard] Vines, Mr Thomas Goodwin and Mr [Philip] Nye at the committee of common council, being desired thereunto by them, having sent them several q[uestions?] to give them their advice upon in order to their remonstrance. Being come, Mr Goodwin delivered in to them a paper where did tell them that they were, and always should be, willing to give an account of their faith or judgement whensoever desired, and were willing to dispute it [fo. 72]. But as to the things in which they desired their advice, viz. if the ordinances of parliament touching the government of the Church were not against their covenant etc., desired to be excused in, especially in order to their present act (though had in th'assembly declared their opinions), and that the parliament was the sole judge of the covenant, at least of their own act. But if they would dispute the lawfulness of what they [i.e. the common council] then were about would do it, professing that what was in hand by them was not lawful. Yet Mr Marshall etc. would not say so, and certainly this was to ensnare them by engaging them to contribute towards the declaration.

20 [April] Monday. The preface to the Scots papers and the stating of the question in them were burnt by the hangman,[393] which did not a little grieve their friends, who gave out many great words in their favour, saying they would suddenly reprint the papers with alone [sic] and justify them, but not done yet. The Scots deliver in many papers to the parliament, which contain their whole complaints and desires; and amongst the rest, that ruling elders have no right to be members of classical, provincial or national meetings, and in this concur our rigid divines, [fo. 72v] though they dare not openly hold it forth for fear of disobliging the people, who will by no means be shut out. This point has been disputed at Sion College by our London ministers, where they have been divided: Doctor [William] Gouge for the negative and many with him; Doctor [Cornelius] Burgess for the affirmative and many with him.

<27 [April]> Monday. Sir Thomas Fairfax, having mastered the whole west rather by love than force – though that has a kind of omnipotency in it – speeds his march towards Oxford, as to that part where is most work.

'Tis by the Northern Association desired there may be 1,000 horse and foot raised for their defence; partly in case Montrose should break through, and also to see fair play in the return of the Scots, that there

---

[391] In preparation.
[392] The declaration of 17 April 1646: *CJ*, iv. 512–14; *LJ*, viii. 277.
[393] On 21 April 1646: *CJ*, iv. 516–17.

may be not plundering etc.[394] And to be under Sir Thomas's command because his countrymen; and the rather he, and Cromwell to attend Oxford etc., because the Scots do not at all relish him [i.e. Cromwell]. In the interim, the Scots loiter before Newark and their horse quarter 30 miles from the leaguer, plundering and devouring the country.

Colonel [Charles] Fleetwood being about Oxford, Sir William <u>Fleetwood, his brother and</u> [inserted] cupbearer to the king [fo. 73], comes to him and tells him his majesty will put himself into his hands, he assuring him security <u>for his person</u> [added in the left margin]. The colonel having no power for such things informs the parliament by letter, who command him not to meddle.

In the meantime, all the Scots' party do make a great noise for his coming to London before the propositions signed, and say all would then be agreed, counting them Independents that are not of their minds. And indeed many wise and good men are of this opinion: to wish the king here that thereby men might be taken off from pursuing their several interests[395] and from seeking to devour each other, and to mind the common good and their own preservation, knowing the king would be using all means to be revenged, and to work about his ends, and thereby unite them more closely. And certainly here lies a great part of the delay; everyone almost has sought himself and driven particular interest,[396] which was not so sensible, things being at some distance from accommodation. But now that all must be gathered up into one head (viz. salus populi) 'tis hard, nay impossible, that each particular should preserve his pretensions, but relinquish for the public good; and men being corrupt, here lies the difficulty.

[fo. 73v] Each faction labours to engage the king to themself and to be the means of <u>his</u> [inserted] reconciliation (and here's the emulation), that they may not only establish themselves and have the principal part in governing, but certainly to the ruin of the other. They both are courted and privately treated with by the king; the Scots on this hope – to separate them from the parliament, and then an assurance of foreign assistance against the parliament, besides their party amongst us. But the rock the king by this runs upon is that they will have what they will, and though they will make <u>case</u> [crossed out] <u>good</u> [inserted] terms for him <u>and themselves</u> [added in left-hand margin] in reference to England, yet for their own kingdom will have all their demands. And, which is worst of all, will have the presbytery established and so

---

[394] Juxon has either written '1,000' for '10,000' or is mistaken in his figures. The Northern Association committee at Westminster proposed that parliament's northern army consist of 10,000 horse and foot – a proposal which the Commons accepted on 6 April 1646: *CJ*, iv. 501; Meikle (ed.), *Correspondence of the Scots commissioners*, p. 172.

[395] Lit. intrests.

[396] Lit. intrest.

all hopes of episcopacy buried; and that irrecoverably in regard they will have both kingdoms capable of one national assembly, where the ministers shall be well instructed to preach for and maintain their own interest[397] and authority, and by this be enabled to keep a good correspondency between the twa[398] kingdoms, which the king must endeavour to prevent in hopes of a more favourable season for himself.

The Independents, though the king knows their principles do incline them against the civil power etc., are rigid in their way and not to be taken off; yet in regard they are not to expect their desires of a liberty from the Presbyterians, nor much fair quarter,<he [the king] believes and is assured they will ruin him and his family>[fo. 74] and being at present the most active and brave men, if he can but take them off cares not for the other. Besides, these will admit of a moderate episcopacy provided they may have their liberty. This the king does infinitely desire rather than the other, believing that if he have the bishops again he shall in time work out the rest, and them too. That which makes him firm to the bishops is that he believes no bishop, no king. <'Tis a prophecy, says De La March,[399] and both are to cease together> And for the Scots and their party, he'll assure them from having a great part, first of his own, then of those that are for a moderate episcopacy, and the Independents. And for foreign supplies [he] may easily secure them, and if the Scots remain obstinate, chastise them, by which means may have an opportunity to be revenged on them. In the interim, they suspect each other mutually, the king them, they him, and each other, and all intends to overreach th'other.

The Scots pretend to stand for the king's prerogative (and thereby think to draw their party) and for discipline, and cry down th'other for the contrary. But this will not do; the king will not trust them nor will venture to come unless [he] may have assurance to ruin the other party and get good conditions for his friends. They cry out, 'the Independents will have no king', and yet say they treat him privately; the others say the latter of them.

In the interim, he's enclosed in Oxford and they say the Independents will keep him there till the propositions be sent (then they intend to continue him still). So that there's now nothing but jealousy lest the one should have and engage him and not the other; [fo. 74v] both labouring to supplant.

The City of London are courted for their favour, but not out of any

---

[397] Lit. interest.
[398] Juxon is being facetious here, using the Scottish pronunciation of 'twa' for 'two'.
[399] *A complaint of the false prophets mariners upon the drying up of their hierarchical Euphrates. As it was preached in the Island of Guernsey by John De La March*, [September 1641], BL, E169/4.

affection to them from the king or any party, which they shall find unless wise timely.

The king sends <u>Lord</u> [inserted] Southampton and Secretary Nicholas[400] to treat about the surrender of Woodstock, which is besieged by <u>Colonel</u> [inserted] [Henry] Ireton[401] and Colonel [Thomas] Rainborowe; and coming to agreement, Southampton tells them he could make a proposition should [sic] not only give them all the places in the king's hands but put an end to this unnatural war. In fine, tells them the parliament had lately put forth a declaration, which if they would stand to, the king should, with only five or 6, deliver himself into their hands.[402] <25th [April]> This was in a letter sent up some days past to Cromwell, who acquainted the House with it, showing an extreme dislike (that they should meddle to treat without any order), which the other party say was but feigned. Upon this the House order that now [sic] should presume to treat without their commands.[403]

These things in agitation, they're advised from Oxford the king intends to escape (and 'tis believed into the Scots army, which they desire), [and] double their guards; and yet on Monday morning by 2 of the clock, [John] Ashburnham, having a pass for himself and servants to come to London and make his composition, the king puts himself in disguise with a white periwig and as servant to Ashburnham, and another for guide in a minister's habit, who was Secretary Nicholas,[404] [fo. 75] and thus without difficulty pass the guards. On Tuesday comes out duke [of] Richmond, earl [of] Lindsey[405] etc., desiring to come up and make their peace, and then assured them the king was gone, withal that he lay that night in his chamber; asked him whither he went, told him 'twas not convenient for him to know, but assured him he went both to his, and the parliament's, friends.[406] The parliament being informed of this commands the foresaid lords to Warwick Castle.[407]

[400] Thomas Wriothesley, fourth earl of Southampton, and Sir Edward Nicholas, secretary of state to the king.

[401] The siege of Woodstock was conducted by Colonel Charles Fleetwood and Rainborowe. Ireton and his regiment were involved in the siege of Oxford: *CJ*, iv. 523–4; C. H. Firth and G. Davies, *Regimental history of Cromwell's army* (Oxford, 1940), pp. 92, 117. Juxon has conflated the king's overtures to Ireton at Oxford and to Rainborowe at Woodstock: Gardiner, iii. 95–6.

[402] Gardiner, iii. 96; *CJ*, iv. 523–4.

[403] *CJ*, iv. 523.

[404] The guide was not Sir Edward Nicholas but Dr Michael Hudson, a royal chaplain, as Juxon later acknowledges: below, p. 120; Gardiner, iii. 97–9.

[405] James Stuart, first duke of Richmond and fourth duke of Lennox, and Montagu Bertie, second earl of Lindsey.

[406] The identity of the 'him' in this sentence is unclear, although in the context Juxon implies that it is the king.

[407] On 30 April 1646, the Commons resolved that Richmond and Lindsey be imprisoned in Warwick Castle. However, on 2 May the Lords ordered that the two peers be held in

<29th [April]> This news came to the House on Wednesday morning and puts all parties from their old work to some new thoughts; is the only discourse, the other being laid aside, and expect where he will next appear. During these things the parliament's late declaration[408] satisfies and settles many; and besides, the House of Commons, having proposed some queries to the assembly [of divines] in reference to [church] government,[409] stays the minds of many for their answers to them.

<[marginal note to the above paragraph] The Scots papers, being also under consideration and hopes of agreeing men's minds, do, in fine, seem to take some rest; and it cannot be otherwise, for our citizens, being active beyond themselves and their understandings, could not long continue, having a principle of self love in them and a desire rather to get money than to tell news.>

And for the City remonstrance, it finds great cause of debate. Sir John Wollaston, Alderman Fowke, Gibbs and Foot[410] being against the body of it (all considerate and considerable men, this seemed to be the sum of their desires); that party[411] are calm and expects the issue of it. So that all are held in a kind of suspense (and the rather fortifying themselves with the hopes of the king's coming and their rewards for appearing, as they think, for him). He, like a fox, gets out of all their hands and puts them upon new counsels.

[fo. 75v] While some hope for, others feared, his coming, all were unsatisfied and wise men at a stand, not being able to see what might be the issue or how God would satisfy Himself for all his actions, many expecting an end rather than continuance of that sort of persons; he secretly absents, seems to vanish or presages an end.

<Monday 4 May [1646]> The parliament not knowing which way he may be gone, and having intelligence he may be about London, do mutually vote that whosoever shall, without discovering, entertain the king's person shall be accounted a traitor and die without mercy, and this to be proclaimed in England and Ireland.[412]

By last week's letters from Paris, Monsieur Augier, our agent, writes the king was to escape out of Oxford (the Friday before he did) in a miller's habit, and that the Lord Jermyn was gone to Guernsey[413] to

custody at Windsor Castle. The Commons objected, but the Lords appear to have prevailed: *CJ*, iv. 527, 541–2; *LJ*, viii. 291, 305, 313, 315.

[408] Their declaration of 17 April 1646: *CJ*, iv. 512–14. See above pp. 114–15.

[409] *CJ*, iv. 519–20.

[410] Sir John Wollaston was a senior alderman who had been lord mayor in 1643–44. The other three aldermen were John Fowke, William Gibbs and Thomas Foot.

[411] i.e. the 'covenant-engaged' faction.

[412] *CJ*, iv. 531–2; *LJ*, viii. 297.

[413] Juxon consistently confuses Guernsey with Jersey, which was the Channel Island in question.

fetch our prince into France. So that though the king seemed to make many overtures of coming, and now lately so plausible a one by [the] earl [of] Southampton, yet never intended it unless upon such terms and probabilities as might content and advantage him very much, nor ever intended to trust himself in their hands, though they thought him sure theirs. But while he amuses them with coming, gets out, and this upon counsel laid with the queen and Lord Digby, who is gone from Dublin. As a proof of it the prince was sent to and desired by the parliament to come back from Scilly. He took time to know his father's mind (and, 'tis like, his mother's too), [fo. 76] who commands him to the contrary, which certainly would not have done had he intended to have come to London as pretended and settled things; what then should the prince do in France?

<[marginal note to the above paragraph] Some say if the prince had come the Independents would have took and adhered to him, and the other [party] to the king.>

The prince did last week send word to the parliament he was gone by order from his father to Guernsey,[414] so that all things concur to make up the story; (i.e.) the king and himself, true to his principles and party and perfectly skilled in kingcraft.

'Tis certainly said his going out was in this manner: upon Sabbath day, called his lords and in short told them: 'My lords, I call you not for your advice but to acquaint you with my resolution. I intend to go out of Oxford this night and to go to London. There, ask me no questions, nor use any arguments to dissuade me, for I am resolved, though all the world were against it, I will do it, and if [sic] will only choose Ashburnham and a guide to go with me'. Having thus amazed them left them.[415]

And about eleven of the clock [and several other words which are illegible] [crossed out] But first sent for Ashburnham to come to him and told him what he had resolved upon. Ashburnham did, upon his knees, beseech his majesty to excuse him in a business of such hazard, for if anything should fall out otherwise than well with his person 'twould be his ruin. The king would take no denial but commanded him upon his allegiance and the duty he owed him to do it. [fo. 76v] About eleven o'clock at night, rises and calls to Ashburnham, bids him send for a barber, who cut off his locks and shaved him, and so taking one Hudson,[416] a jovial priest, along for a guide, went away. Took [the] London road and 'tis said came within ten miles of London, thinking to have come hither, but was assured if he came they would imprison

---

[414] i.e. Jersey.

[415] The source of this purported speech of Charles's has not been found.

[416] Dr Michael Hudson, one of the royal chaplains.

him as long as he lived. Resolved therefore for the Scots army and was there in a disguise some days up and down, labouring to disaffect them toward the parliament. In fine, came into the French agent's chamber and then discovered himself to them.

<[marginal note to above paragraph] If the general training day had [been] held as intended (**5th [May]**) present, the king had certainly come into the park and have put it to a venture, therefore was wisely put off.[417] Colonel[418] had notice, a letter sent to him to his quarters at Woodstock, of the king's going out, but being absent it was kept by the corporal and so he lost the opportunity of taking him, which God, as now appears, had not designed, who has ordered all things in favour to His>

Earl [of] Leven[419] sends word of it to our commissioners there and they send it to the parliament. This news seemed strangely to affect according to the several opinions and interests[420] of men; and, which is strange, the active men of the parliament did never consult what to do in case he should be gone into Ireland, Scotland or their army, so that the news surprised them, as appears by the sequel, which seems to intimate that God would manage the whole business without them.

[fo. 77] Upon this the Commons vote he should be desired of the Scots to dispose him as they should think fit, then to be secured in Warwick Castle, and that Sir Thomas Fairfax should be sent with 6,000 horse to demand him.[421] This startled when it came to the Lords; they voted point blank against the 2 latter, though but 13 to 10. The 10 entered their dissents peremptorily, but is [sic] was carried non obstante.[422] However, t'observe the humour of the people, they questioned not this, yet when [crossed out] there was but a few of the affirmative that the City petition was a breach of privilege, the slighted being carried by a few.[423]

---

[417] A general training of the City forces in Hyde Park had been planned for 5 May but was put off by order of parliament: Rushworth, vi. 267; *CJ*, iv. 531.

[418] Either Thomas Rainborowe or Charles Fleetwood: *CJ*, iv. 526; *LJ*, viii. 291; Gardiner, iii. 96.

[419] Alexander Leslie, first earl of Leven, the commander of the Scottish army in England.

[420] Lit. intresses.

[421] On 6 May 1646: *CJ*, iv. 537–8; *LJ*, viii. 308; Rushworth, vi. 268; Bodleian Library, Ms. Tanner 59, fo. 161.

[422] Eleven peers entered their dissents to the vote in the Lords against demanding custody of the king, not ten as Juxon states: *LJ*, viii. 309.

[423] Juxon is referring here to an earlier Lords' vote, that of 11 March 1646, condemning the City's recent petition as a gross breach of parliamentary privilege by the same margin of 13 votes to 10, with the latter similarly entering their dissents: above, p. 108. The last phrase should probably be rendered 'the slighting [i.e. the slighting of the petition] being carried by a few [votes]'. The point he appears to be making is that London citizens raised no objections to the close vote in the Lords on this occasion, but they had previously not accepted a vote by the same margin that ran counter to their wishes.

Mr [Alexander] Henderson departed for the [Scottish] army and to wait on the king as his chaplain.

Newark was surrendered upon honourable terms,[424] though the king would not have it slighted but delivered to the Scots, thinking to make it an apple of strife. But nor the one nor the other could be obtained. General Leven told him he preferred his honour and the peace of the 2 kingdoms before 10 kings.

News came that Lord Digby was arrived in France; from thence comes the design of the king's going to the Scots [fo. 77v] and therefore all the heads meet there. Though certainly (Digby) is neither beloved by the French or the king's party in Scotland.

The Lord Essex's party grow very active and labour exceedingly a remonstrance from the common council, which the [sic] give instructions for and must serve their ends to advance themselves and ruin the solicitor's party.[425] St John unhappily moves to have the king sent to dismantle his garrisons and, it taking, did consider that such an act of the king's would would [sic] make the world believe him much changed, when the truth is one month will bring them in, and therefore not to be beholding to him.[426] However, this was construed by their enemies to be an assurance these [crossed out] that [that] party were not for peace but for lengthening the war, and so laboured everywhere to make them odious, and telling that many of their party were now fallen from them, that they were quite undone, and do hope to make delinquents of them and to have them impeached. Thus strangely are we changed and turned.

[fo. 78] <May 4th [crossed out] 11> Monday

Wednesday, the so much expected remonstrance was brought into common council and read, but sent back with [crossed out] for some amendments.[427]

<19 [May]>[428] And was again on Tuesday brought again and, to the end it might not be retarded, there was a vote passed that none should speak above 3 times to any point. It happened that Mr [Stephen] Estwicke, going to speak and having begun, said, 'My lord, this court deals unjustly with the parliament', and before he could go on was

---

[424] Newark surrendered to commissioners appointed by the committee of both kingdoms on 6 May 1646.

[425] i.e. Oliver St John, a leading figure in the political Independents.

[426] Juxon seems to be referring here to a debate and series of divisions in the Commons on 11 May 1646 concerning the disposal of the king and the delivery of the garrisons still in royalist hands. Juxon appears to be the only source to identify Oliver St John as the author of the 'unhappy motion' concerning the king's garrisons, which was opposed by St John's allies among the political Independents: *CJ*, iv. 542.

[427] There is no record of such a meeting in the journals of common council.

[428] The following common council debate was held on Wednesday, 20 May: CLRO, Jor. 40, fos. 178v–80v.

interrupted, and though he desired to be permitted to go on yet was not suffered, but cried to have him [brought] to the bar. At last he went, it having been first argued if it were the custom of that court to do so and there was a case cited. He demanded to have delivered to him in writing the crime he had committed. In fine, told them he intended not to say anything to the prejudice of the court etc., and so the thing was passed over.

[fo. 78v] But when they were ready to vote the whole body of it, Lieutenant-Colonel [Robert] Tichborne desired to have the freedom to speak, and then did solemnly and gravely make his protestation against every particular and the whole; after him, Alderman Fowke and Alderman Andrews, and to the number of 11, all persons considerable, and desired it might be entered. This was not done without many bitter words given them. There was desired, to one particular of it [i.e. the remonstance] proof to be made, but the court would not and left it wholly to the committee that drew it, though some of the committee declared he [sic] never saw any, and though he demanded, yet was there none brought but the court require any [inserted].

The king told them he was divided in pieces: England had his revenue, the Scots his body, but God his conscience.

<22nd [May]> Friday. The common council met again about the remonstrance,[429] where was passed one to the House of Peers; at which time was brought in from some hundred of Independents a petition,[430] which the lord mayor [Thomas Adams] hearing of was willing to break up the court, but, being persuaded, took it in, and having first read it to himself [fo. 79] told them there was no danger in it. And so 'twas publicly read and contained only thanks to them for their pains and care for the City's preservation etc., and desired them to intimate, in their petition to the parliament, thankfulness for theirs[431] with a resolution to adhere to them and that nothing might be put in theirs[432] that might grieve the parliament. 'Twas in general answered that their desires were already granted (without any thanks). The same day, Captain [John] Jones and [John] Bellamy[433] etc. went to the Lords' House and spake with my lord general,[434] to know what day it should be delivered, who ordered it to be on Tuesday following.

[429] CLRO, Jor. 40, fos. 181–2v.

[430] *A petition of citizens of London presented to the common council for their concurrence ... for submission to parliament* (22 May 1646), BL, 669 f. 10/57. George Thomason claimed that it was signed by only 93 petitioners: Fortescue, i. 440.

[431] i.e. parliament's pains and care etc.

[432] i.e. the City's petition.

[433] John Jones was a friend of the high Presbyterian minister, James Cranford and a signatory of the City petition of 12 November 1645. John Bellamy was a Presbyterian bookseller and a leading apologist for the City's remonstrance of 26 May 1646.

[434] The earl of Essex, leader of the political Presbyterians.

<25 [May]> Monday. This day came a letter from the king to the parliament wherein seems to assure them of a good compliance etc.[435] At the same time come[s] a letter to the City from the [committee of] estates of Scotland, and another from the king to the lord mayor, court of aldermen and common council, which seemed extreme luckily to favour the remonstrance.[436] And though he be debarred from his servants etc., yet is well informed in all things and how to favour the Scots' interest;[437] certainly he cannot desire the settlement of Presbytery out of love to it.

[fo. 79v] <26 [May]> Tuesday. Many of the aldermen, with most of the common council, went to deliver their remonstrance first to the Lords, who accepted it most kindly and gave them an answer in writing.[438] For the Commons they were fain to wait a little from this occasion: the lord mayor was advised by Alderman Penington to send the king's letter to the City to the parliament, and not to open it, in regard it came from an enemy, but my lord would not be persuaded. Penington reporting this to the House, Colonel [George] Thomson said, 'If such a thing had been done by the lord mayor a year backwards he would have given his vote to have had him sent for to the House, and then to the Tower, and last to Tyburn'. At which some cried him to the bar but others 2nd what he said, and it was judged only a piece of zeal as a true Englishman.[439]

When the remonstrance came 'twas delivered by the 2 sheriffs. The House having read it were long in debate whether to call them in or not, or only to call them in and tell them they would consider of it, it [sic] or whether they should have thanks given them. But it was concluded for the 2nd: to call them in and tell them they would consider of it, which amounts to nothing, and this was carried by 40 voices.[440] This made them look something blank upon the business, [fo. 80] expecting a greater number for them and another like answer. They had printed it the day before, and dispersed it by 3 o'clock in

[435] *CJ*, iv. 554–5; *LJ*, viii. 328–9.

[436] *CJ*, iv. 555; *LJ*, viii. 334; CLRO, Jor. 40. fo. 183; Rushworth, vi. 271–2, 274–5.

[437] Lit. intrest.

[438] But the Lords' resolution that the text should be published led nine peers to enter their dissent: *LJ*, viii. 331–4.

[439] *CJ*, iv. 555; BL, Add. Ms. 31,116, fo. 271v. Juxon appears to be the only source for Thomson's speech.

[440] The whole day was said to have been taken up in debate on the remonstrance. Many 'sober men' were reported to have been displeased at what they saw as 'wholly a design of the Presbyterian party'. The eventual Commons vote on their answer to the City, that it would be considered when the time was convenient, was carried 151 to 108. The tellers for the yeas were Sir Philip Stapilton and Sir John Clotworthy; for the noes, Sir Arthur Hesilrige and Sir John Evelyn: BL, Add. Ms. 31,116, fo. 271; ibid., 37,344, fos. 52–3; *CJ*, iv. 555–6.

the afternoon, though they had not their answer till 7.

\<June 2nd [1646]\> There was a petition presented to the House of Commons from a party of the Independents,[441] and though the contrary party did not expect it should have been received, yet was and had several hours debate. 'Twas well liked, it being indeed only a long compliment, and debated to have thanks, which some were unwilling to have been at that time and especially in regard the remonstrance had none, but, in fine, 'twas carried affirmative and had it.[442]

The day before there was a common council wherein the said petition was considered[443] and by the violent party there adjudged to be scandalous (not in the matter but as to the manner of getting hands) and also seditious. And, in regard some of that court had a hand in it, would have had some brand of ignominy set upon them because they acted against the sense of that court. 'Twas told them that the court had no cognizance of it, being a petition of many as well without as within the City, and that it belonged to the parliament, to whom it was to be presented, to judge wholly of it [fo. 80v] and not for them to undertake to condemn it. Nothing would serve but voted it in the manner to be scandalous and seditious. Yet had it a contrary reception of the parliament, which made some of the common council to say, 'Could none of them take notice what we voted the day before?', which expressed the end of that censure, viz. to point out what they would have <u>had</u> [inserted].

A letter was sent from Ireland printed by marquess [of] Ormond, sent him by the king dated in Oxford and signed (Nicholas),[444] where <u>testifies assures him</u> [crossed out] <u>tells him</u> [inserted] <u>and all others</u> [crossed out] <u>and commands to publish it</u> [inserted] that the Scots were resolved, if he came to them, to protect his person etc. and all his friends under that consideration and had hopes to engage them further.[445]

The Scots commissioners disavow the thing and say 'tis scandalous.[446] But there is a true story which is: when the Scots army was at Hereford, in their way took one Allen and Barr, that had served the king and were retired to their homes, yet carried them away and set upon Barr's head a fine of £50. But observing him an ingenious and able man, did

---

[441] *The humble acknowledgement and petition of divers inhabitants in and about the City of London* (2 June 1646), BL, E339/12. This petition came to be commonly referred to as the 'anti-petition' opposing the remonstrance.

[442] The resolution to thank the petitioners was carried by 112 votes to 108, with Sir John Evelyn and Sir Arthur Hesilrige acting as tellers for the yeas, and Denzil Holles and Sir Philip Stapilton for the noes: *CJ*, iv. 561.

[443] CLRO, Jor. 40, fo. 183v.

[444] Sir Edward Nicholas, the king's secretary.

[445] Rushworth, vi. 266–7.

[446] On 8 June 1646: Rushworth, vi. 272–4.

not only discharge him of his fine but gave him money, viz. the Lord [Hugh] Montgomery, Lord St Leger[447] etc. [fo. 81], and not long after sends him with a letter to the governor of Raglan Castle where the king then was. 'Twas not long ere the king came to him, and in discourse he understood the contents of the letter, brought back an answer, carried again; upon it [i.e. the letter] were several meetings, one of them at the house of Barr. When 'twas concluded, if the king would come into the Scots army, he and his friends should have protection, and of this the several men before named have deposed upon oath.

Not long after, the Scots army being in Yorkshire, a countryman came with a letter from the king to the Lord Montgomery, but was directed to Colonel Montgomery's[448] quarters, a man very affectionate to the parliament. The countryman, seeing him in good equipage and hearing them call him my lord etc. as a colonel, imagined him the Lord Montgomery; hereupon privately tells him he had a letter to him from the king, which the colonel took, read and copied out and returned it again, telling him 'twas a mistake and directed him to the Lord Montgomery. The colonel quickly acquaints the General Leven with it, who resented it highly, and said they were all traitors and would have them hanged, and that there were so many of [them] they over voted him and could not do what he desires. [fo. 81v] That the army would never come to good till reformed, which they labour against as some did against ours.

Upon this a council of war was determined to hear it, but the Lord Callander being president of the council and their friend kept his chamber some days to defer it. At last it was referred to the state of Scotland, and the 3 lords that were accessory were sent thither. It fell out suddenly after that that state had need of an experienced man to command their army there, and at last were necessitated to send to offer the command to Callander. He refuses several times, but it being intimated to him that if he accepted of it 'twould engage the state to him and might procure the discharge of his friends; upon which was willing, got his friends quitted and presently quitted this charge. These lords are since come to the king at Newcastle, and Callander is the man that governs all in their army there. These lords were they who gave private encouragement to the king to come to the army and assured him of a general concurrence.

[447] Juxon has misheard or mistranscribed 'Lord St Leger' for John, ninth Lord Sinclair, who was closely involved in the Scots' secret negotiations with the king during the siege of Hereford. There was no 'Lord St Leger' among the Scottish contingent in England: Gardiner, ii. 285.

[448] Colonel Robert Montgomery, an officer in the earl of Leven's army.

About this time, Ned Hyde[449] writes from Guernsey[450] to Jay,[451] who was in Pendennis. The letter was intercepted by the parliament.[452]

[a written page of MS torn out here]

[fo. 82] The parliament, after the former relations made to them of some in the Scots army, do vote and declare that the Scots nation had performed and kept their covenant with them and resolved to send them a declaration.

In a letter intercepted from Hyde to Jay, one[?] Jay in Pendennis tells him ere that could come to hand would hear that the Scots army had declared for the king and then says he you may [section crossed out]. About this time the Scots army in Ireland under Monro received a great defeat from the rebels.[453]

The ministers of London [inserted] at last resolve to set upon the work of government, and yet in a printed paper declare upon what terms they do it.[454]

<12 June> The propositions[455] are now finished, to the reproach of those that say they[456] never did intend it, nor to have any king; and this is the very language of the malignants.

<15 [June]> The king writes to the parliament, if they please he'll come to London etc. and sign such bills they shall desire him and send for the prince to come to London.

There was taken going to the prince in Guernsey[457] a letter from the king in his own hand, and dated the 2nd of June, the same with that to the parliament [fo. 82v] to the purpose: Charles etc. [inserted] 'I command you to obey your mother's commands in all things except in the matter of religion, wherein I hope she will not importune you. If Ashburnham come to you let him wait on you as formerly. If you come to the queen, and she desire it, let him wait on her. I have sent my mind to her per Montreuil'.[458]

[449] Sir Edward Hyde, the future earl of Clarendon.

[450] i.e. Jersey.

[451] Probably James, first duke of Hamilton, whom Charles had had imprisoned in Pendennis Castle in 1643.

[452] *CJ*, iv. 575.

[453] The battle of Benburb (county Tyrone) on 5 June 1646.

[454] *Certain considerations and cautions agreed upon by the ministers of London according to which they resolve to put the Presbyterial government in execution upon the ordinances of parliament* (19 June 1646), BL, E341/11.

[455] The Newcastle propositions, which were despatched to the king on 13 July 1646.

[456] It is unclear whether by 'they' Juxon means parliament or the political Independents, who were thought by some contemporaries, notably the Scots, to be the main authors of the Newcastle propositions. See D. Scott, 'The "northern gentlemen", the parliamentary Independents, and Anglo-Scottish relations in the Long Parliament', *Historical Journal*, 42 (1999), 347–75.

[457] i.e. Jersey.

[458] Charles's original letter, as recorded in the Lords' journals on 17 June (*LJ*, viii. 379–

'Tis endeavoured to give Leslie[459] a writ of ease and put [the earl of] Callander[460] in the place. The old man is too honest for their designs. Lord of Argyle[461] comes to London and in the Painted Chamber speaks a very honest speech and moderate.[462] Duke [of] Hamilton takes the covenant.

<23 [June]> There were several Lords, Commoners, aldermen, citizens and others dined at Thomas Browne's,[463] wherein the design is mutually carried on; the ass is fearfully rid.

<24 [June]> Wednesday. Oxford surrendered; there marched out near 5,000. The articles were too favourable; the reason – because they desired to despatch to be ready for the Scots, against whom 'twas wished some odd man or other would begin the business, their fingers itching at it, under the hopes of obtain[ing] a liberty of conscience and continuing things in such a way as they might always rule. But God in His providence has prevented the one and suffered authority to set up Presbytery.

[fo. 83] **<26 [June]>** The Lords sent an order down to the lord mayor wherein [they] do take notice of the articles and surrender of Oxford not communicated to them, and, out of their care to prevent the concurrence of disaffected persons to London, desire the lord mayor to have a care of the City for the well government of it and the militia to be assistant to him.[464] The ground of this was 'twas fancied the army would now come up to London to affront it, or rather [the Lords sought] to usher in a power in my lord mayor over the militia, and the Lords over all, trying hereby if their orders would be obeyed and to ingratiate themselves to the City, as if their care were very great.

<30 June> 'Twas moved by Alderman [James] Bunce in common council to have a petition go from that court to accompany the [Newcastle] propositions, and to desire the king's concurrence in them and return thanks for his letter to them.[465] The marquess of Argyle dined at the lord mayor's.

<2nd July [1646]> The common council voted the letter to the king, but first to communicate it to the parliament and to have

---

80), contained no reference to Jean de Montreuil (alt. Montereul), the French ambassador in Scotland.

[459] Alexander Leslie, first earl of Leven.

[460] James Livingstone, first earl of Callander.

[461] Archibald Campbell, first marquess of Argyle.

[462] Argyle addressed a grand committee of both Houses appointed to receive him on 25 June: *LJ*, viii. 392–3. His speech is in Rushworth, vi. 298–99.

[463] Browne was a leading parishioner of St Peter Westcheap and a signatory of the London Presbyterian petition of 12 November 1645.

[464] On 25 June 1646: *LJ*, viii. 390–91.

[465] CLRO, Jor. 40, fo. 186v.

their leave.[466] Chose their commissioners to go with it: Alderman [James] Bunce, Alderman [Samuel] Avery, Mr [Richard] Venner, Mr [Thomas] Vyner, Colonel [Edward] Hooker and Deputy [Alexander] Jones.

<[marginal note to the above paragraph] The Lords returned thanks for it.>[467]

'Twas presented the next day to the parliament, who answered they were then busy and would consider of it;[468] and while 'twas under debate there was presented the copy of a petition from the general and Scots officers to the king of the same purpose.[469]

<[marginal note to the above paragraph] The concurrence is strange and things run in a line, notably>

[fo. 83v] **<5 [July]>** Monday.[470] News came by this post of the prince of Wales his being in France, and that he lay 2nd present [July] at St Germains, which clearly shows the king's intentions, for had he any real intent towards us would not have suffered the prince to have gone, especially having promised the Scots he would send to him to come into England. But the game is there playing now, for thither are gone all the gamesters, and this certainly, she [i.e. the queen] that laid the plot of it. The comfort is 'tis a Catholic plot and certainly to serve their interests.[471] The truth is, the business is a juggle.

The king of Poland arms strongly to make a diversion upon the Turk, and together with his confederates brings in a huge army to the field. 'Tis considerable that being so puissant he should stand neuter all this while to the war in Germany, <Especially having so many Jesuits and favouring them so much> but the truth is he ever favoured the Protestant party and was ever suspected by the Catholic.

The Venetian does notably defend himself against the Turk, and gives him great interruption. The French, having a mind to Italy, hug the discontented Barbarino and in their favour send a great fleet under their admiral, marquis de Brezé,[472] neveu to Richelieu, [fo. 84] and in it 10,000 men under the command of Prince Thoms [sic] of Savoy. The Fleet passed quietly, landed their men near Orbetello. The Spanish fleet followed unexpected, found them secure, not believing they durst attack them; but finding them in earnest the French refused to fight but betook themselves to flight, yet not without some blows, in which

---

[466] It was on 3 July that common council approved their answer to the king's letter to the City of the previous 19 May: CLRO, Jor. 40, fos. 187–87v.

[467] On 4 July: *LJ*, viii. 411.

[468] This was the response of the Commons: *CJ*, iv. 602.

[469] *CJ*, iv. 602; *LJ*, viii. 411, 413; Rushworth, vi. 304–5.

[470] Monday was 6 July.

[471] Lit. intresses.

[472] Jean-Armand de Maillé, duc de Brezé, admiral of France.

rencounter [sic] the admiral marquis de Brezé was slain with a cannon shot, the whole fleet routed etc.

<9th [crossed out]> There arrived here an extraordinary [ambassador] from France. Monsieur Bellièvre[473] was lodged at Goring House. The Lord Digby came from Paris to Guernsey[474] to the prince, and from thence went to Ireland.

<9th [July]> There came a letter from the assembly of Scotland to the lord mayor, aldermen and common council;[475] the main [sic] was to take notice of their remonstrance, with most high expressions of contentment etc.

The empress dead, and buried in great solemnity. Casamir, brother to the king of Poland, made a cardinal in acknowledgement of the king's preparation contra the Turk.

[fo. 84v] <16th [July]> The French ambassador presents himself to the parliament,[476] tells them he came at the same time to have audience and to take his leave. His business to them was to speed the [Newcastle] propositions, which, find[ing] gone, his work was done. Then desired to go into Scotland to the assembly of estates, and by the way to kiss the king's hand. The Lords presently condescended; the Commons considered of it.

<13 [July]> Tuesday.[477] The propositions went. The messengers.

<14 [July]> The report of the House of Commons about their desired [sic] of sending a petition and messengers with the propositions etc. was reported in common council by the knights of London.[478] They pressed strongly to have them at the instant expelled that would not retake the covenant, and that they would not suffer any man to sit there that was not of their minds, nor have any enemies amongst them. They were persuaded not to attempt what they had no power to command, as not in this. Would have all the commanders and officers retake it or be discharged. Their violent heat was such my lord mayor was fain to break up.[479]

<21 [July]> The French [ambassador] extraordinary went post to the king the same day the marquess [of] Argyle etc., all to be present to bait the lion. [fo. 85] The Spanish ambassador went also to the king to see how the cards are shuffled. So that a very great expectation was

---

[473] Pompone de Bellièvre, French ambassador to England.

[474] i.e. Jersey.

[475] Rushworth, vi. 307–8. The letter had been despatched from Edinburgh on 18 June 1646.

[476] On 17 July: *CJ*, iv. 620–21; *LJ*, viii. 436.

[477] Should read 13 July, Monday.

[478] Sir Thomas Soames and Samuel Vassall (two of the City's MPs) appeared before common council on 15 July to explain why the Commons could not approve of the City sending their proposed petition to the king: *CJ*, iv. 615–6; CLRO, Jor. 40, fo. 189.

[479] There is no record of this in the journals of common council for 15 July 1646.

raised by the concurrence of so many persons of condition. When our commissioners came they were civilly used by the Scots, and the king seemed to be pleased. Having delivered the proportions [sic], asked them if they had any power to treat, or to give longer time, who answered, no. Then he told them the parliament might have sent a trumpeter with them. He took time allotted, viz. 10 days and said would in that time give them a positive answer.[480]

<31st [July]> There was a motion for sending of some regiments of the army into Ireland, and had a long debate. In th'end carried for the negative but by one voice. The design was to weaken or rather dissolve the army. 'Twas Stapilton's motion, who never loved them.[481] 'Tis observed [that] at the first settling of the Model 'twas carried but by one voice.

Letters are intercepted going from the queen to Ormond, and in them one from the king, wherein does command him, notwithstanding any letters or order to the contrary, to pursue the business in Ireland [fo. 85v] to his best advantage. And in order to this, Ormond has concluded since the last arrival of Digby a peace with the rebels and proclaimed it.[482] And in Scotland there remains Antrim, Crawford[483] etc. in arms for him, so that he drives on his former design and builds upon these and his allies.

France has lately discovered, in letters intercepted by the Swedes going to the emperor, a private agreement to drive out the Swedes forth of Germany. And in pursuance of it did neglect to join their army under Colonel Turenne[484] with them, when they thereby might have hindered the conjunction of the emperor and Bavarians, and tho[ught?] at least ruined one of them.

The French are forced to leave their Italian expedition and return home with loss. They begin to be discontented at court, for the Prince Condé pretends to have the admiralty as of right, though born 13 months post morte patre.[485] The cardinal would also have it, but the queen regent keeps it in her hands undisposed. The crown of Swede has sent an ambassador to France to expostulate the late business.

The Hollander go on in that treaty with the Spaniard, though the French ambassador[s] at Münster and the Hague have there made

---

[480] On 24 July 1646: *CJ*, iv. 642.

[481] The motion was lost by 91 votes to 90, with Hesilrige and Sir John Evelyn tellers for the noes and Stapilton and Holles tellers for the yeas: *CJ*, iv. 631–2.

[482] On 30 July, the first Ormond peace: Rushworth, vi. 401–2.

[483] Randal MacDonnell, second earl of Antrim, and Ludovic Lindsay, sixteenth earl of Crawford.

[484] Henri de la Tour d'Auvergne, viscount of Turenne.

[485] After his father's death, i.e. he is a bastard.

[inserted] their protestations a l'encontre.[486] [fo. 86] The articles of agreement were shown to the French ambassador at the Hague by one of the States, who boasted of them to be very advantageous. But the ambassador replied, that the Spaniard offered his master all the 17 provinces in marriage, but refused to treat without them [i.e. the Dutch]. But herein they had not requited them, yet were free to do what they pleased.

The French, after some attempts upon Mardyk wherein they lost many men – and 300 of Colonel [Henry] Tillier's regiment who came out of Oxford, besides many persons of condition – did at last by a general assault take it in, and in it above 2,000 prisoners. The French sent 6,000 men under the command of Maréchal Grammont to join with the Hollanders. But they agree so ill that they pillage the convoys of each other. And certainly th'antipathy of the Hollanders against them is very great and such as may end in blows.

The prince of Wales – though visited by the queen regent, yet invited only by the Cardinal Mazarin – with Prince Rupert and the rest of the nobility [dined?] all at the same table, and not in the English fashion.

[fo. 86v] The king of Poland, having lately drawn many forces together upon pretence of making a diversion upon the Turks in favour of Venice – into which parts had sent his brother, Casamir, who is lately made a cardinal – but having in the said design wholly declined the estates of Poland in whom the power resides (he being but elective); they hereupon, having met and considered the business, did clearly apprehend the king to intend the surprisal of Danzig, or some other town of consequence, did issue out their commands prohibiting all persons to come to the rendezvous upon pain of death, in regard they should have been, but were never, consulted with in the business. And then went to the king to complain of his proceeding. He seemed innocent, but wisely put it up and told them if they did not approve of it, would not meddle with it, and so dismissed them. So that this king as well as ours and the king of Denmark (whom his own subjects compelled to agree with the Swede, though to disadvantage) have lately attempted to make themselves masters of their subjects. The other 2 have been wise in making their agreement, but our king stands it out most obstinately.

[fo. 87] When the king got away from Oxford and went to the Scots, 'twas with full expectation to set us by the ears with them, having first cajoled the Independents and exasperated the Presbyterians against them or mutually. Then had confidence of a concurrence in the Scots army, and certainly there was n'other discourse for many weeks but we must fall out, and order was given to begin it, but [Sydenham]

[486] In opposition.

Poyntz was wiser.[487] At which time all the royalists, though [they] abhorred them, yet took the Scots' part; the City also and most of the parliament. The [English] forces were under Independents. The king loses no time – courts them [i.e. the Scots and their allies] at Newcastle, lets his friends know his hopes were great.

The forces in Scotland continue in arms, and the peace with the Irish rebels concluded by Ormond and Digby, who came from France. Digby tells Ormond must not take notice what the king does at this time write or command but to prosecute his advantage.

Monsieur Bellièvre pretends the affairs as concerning England and Scotland were represented as irreconcilable and ready to give the stroke, but did see if far otherwise, intending certainly, if it had been so, to have struck in with them against us. [fo. 87v] Montreuil writes to France that 'twas not possible to break the accord between the 2 kingdoms, so that now the king was utterly cheated, and he obstinately refuses the propositions.[488]

By this time all their designs are come to light, and the issue is that the Scots declare themselves gallantly, and both fall to a quick accord. Thus the king is still driven from one to another desperate course and always the loser; and in this unhappy: that though no prince ever used more dissimulation yet never thrived and his designs were always discovered.

Pendennis and Raglan surrendered,[489] being the last garrisons in England etc. All done in 14 months and the kingdom cleared.

<22 [August 1646]> The House of Commons vote down all allowances formerly to their members in regard the kingdom's free.[490]

<August 24> Monday. The emperor had lately caused his son to be crowned king of Bohemia and so in election to succeed his father.

Our commissioners returned from the king re infecta;[491] that he could not pass them [i.e. the propositions], they were ridiculous and

[487] Colonel Sydenham Poyntz commanded the force of cavalry that shadowed the Scottish army as it moved northwards with the king: Baillie, ii. 375. In contrast to Juxon, Viscount Saye and Sele believed that Poyntz was ready and willing to fight with the Scots, and would have done so had he received orders from parliament: [Saye], *Vindiciae veritatis*, p. 101.

[488] Juxon is probably referring here to the French diplomatic correspondence seized by a parliamentary vessel in the Channel in July 1646 and subsequently examined by a Commons committee: *CJ*, iv. 641; J. G. Fotheringham (ed.), *The diplomatic correspondence of Jean de Montereul* (Scottish Hist. Soc. n.s. xxix, 2 vols., 1898), i. 245–6; S. R. Gardiner (ed.), *The Hamilton papers* (Camden Soc. n.s. xxvii, 1880), pp. 107–8.

[489] On 17 and 19 August 1646 respectively.

[490] The Commons took this action on 20 August: *CJ*, iv. 649.

[491] 'With matters unaccomplished'.

unreasonable; but the Scots commissioners came a day before them and with them Lord Dunfermline.[492]

[fo. 88] There is now a resolution of sending away the Scots.[493] Their demands were brought in and amount to £1,900,000. We, to balance, say they have received in money, clothes etc. and taxes (besides plunder) £2,200,000. The Scots demand more to cut scores and clear all, £500,000. We offer 2, they come to 4, we offer 3; in th'end we agree to £400,000. At first desired but £100,000 presently, the rest at 3, 3, and 3 months. But having, as they pretend, received new instructions from above, demand £200,000 present, and without which cannot march; and upon that condition to depart and surrender up all their garrisons. 'Tis, in fine, agreed to by the Commons, but then the difficulty is where to find it.[494]

They repair to the common council, offer the sale of bishops' lands and the security of excise, or what should be desired. The common council accept of it provided what is lent (by such as shall underwrite) upon the public faith may be secured with interest, and then the sum [crossed out] so much more to be advanced de novo.[495] The Commons assent to their propositions, adding to their security delinquents' lands,[496] hoping by this means to persuade the Lords to the sale of them, who had hitherto refused, but with exceptions. [fo. 88v] This addition made by the Commons, though the common council have formerly desired the same, yet the interest[497] of the Lords was so great as to make them decline it and be content only with the former.

By the sale of these lands the bishops will be put out of all hope to be re-established; and certainly, had not this been done, they might have had some hopes. But herein God overrules and has unexpectedly ruined them so as never to rise again, and by the same way Henry 4[498] took to destroy monasteries – by selling them to persons of all sorts and so to interest[499] the whole kingdom in the business.

Mardyk was retake[n] by the French, but with great loss, especially of persons of quality, having been stoutly maintained by the Spaniard.

<7th September [1646]> Monday, my Lord General Essex died at his house in the Strand of an apoplex,[500] having been sick about a week, taking cold in hunting the stag, leaving Sir Walter Devereux to

[492] Charles Seton, second earl of Dunfermline.
[493] On 14 August 1646: *CJ*, iv. 644.
[494] *CJ*, iv. 647, 649, 654–6, 659; *LJ*, viii. 487.
[495] CLRO, Jor. 40, fos. 191–2; 'de novo' means 'anew'.
[496] On 10 September: *CJ*, iv. 665.
[497] Lit. intrest.
[498] Henry VIII is surely intended.
[499] Lit. intrest.
[500] Essex died on 14 September 1646.

succeed to the viscountcy of Hereford etc. His will was made before the battaigle at Kineton,[501] wherein earl [of] Northumberland, earl [of] Warwick, Mr Hampden, defunct, and the solicitor, St John, were made executors, and not without some astonishment. [fo. 89] It shows that noble lord then to have had a good opinion on the said persons, though now 2 of them are of a contrary faction,[502] and may teach thus much - that both parties should understand and love each other better and endeavour union.

However, this unexpected blow made a deep resentment in the party of which he was caput, and drove them to a very great stand whom to choose that might succeed.[503] 'Tis apprehend as an irrecoverable loss, and the malignants boldly say the king has lost a very good friend, that he would be the saddest man. He was the only popular person to attempt, if it could have been done, against the Independents, to whom he was made irreconcilable. The Houses upon the news adjourn to the next day to testify their sense of his loss.

The duke [of] Hamilton applies himself to the king and joins against Argyle's party, who are the only honest in the kingdom. Many tamperings are made with the army and others, and honours conferred on several of Hamilton's family. And 'tis believed the king has assurance that if such terms cannot be obtained for him as he desires, he shall be connived at to escape.

[fo. 89v] In the interim, a [Scottish] parliament is to assemble, and does in this month of September, where had been much labouring; yet the honest party was the most and so their votes were tending to peace.[504] The parliament, i.e. the House of Commons, vote that the king during [his] stay in England was to be disposed of by them exclusive, and that their sum of £200,000, being paid, there was nothing that could or should hinder the Scots' departure; that the commissioners here were to be acquainted with their resolutions but not consultative.[505] In these votes both parties concurred. The parliament in Scotland concur in the first as to their marching home and surrendering up of garrisons upon payment of the £200,000.

The general assembly in Scotland sent some of the ministers [as] commissioners to the king to persuade him [to] sign the propositions

[501] Edgehill.
[502] Northumberland and St John.
[503] Baillie, ii. 401.
[504] The Scottish parliament assembled on 3 November 1646. It had a higher membership, especially of burgesses, than its recent predecessors and the majority of the gentry and burgesses continued to adhere to Argyle: J. R. Young, *The Scottish parliament 1639–1661: a political and constitutional analysis* (Edinburgh, 1996), pp. 163, 185, 331, 334–5.
[505] On 18 September 1646: *CJ*, iv. 672.

etc. To whom made reply: that he desired to see their commission if they had power to treat in a business so foreign to that kingdom of Scotland. And further said he believed that they had nothing to do with altering the laws of England, they being distinct from them, [fo. 90] and that the ecclesiasticy and civil government of England were so interwoven as not to be separated without the ruin of both. But he was ever in the mind that upon a general and free debate he would be content to take away what was justly offensive and also to make provision for tender consciences.

The queen of Poland has been crowned in the greatest pomp imaginable. The emperor has caused his son to be crowned at Prague, but could not obtain so much in Hungaria. He has lately married his eldest daughter to the Infant [sic] of Spain. These two Houses are faithful friends and support each other in their declining condition.

About this time it fell out that the peace being concluded with the rebels in Ireland, marquess [of] Ormond with about 1,400 foot and 300 horse marches towards the rebels thinking to join with them; and in his march came the earl of Castlehaven[506] and assured him they had laid a plot to cut off himself and all his forces [fo. 90v], and therefore advises him not to advance but with all speed to return to Dublin. Having given him ground for this fear, the marquess with a few horse makes home in post and after him his forces. Upon this news the parliament appoint Sir Robert King and Sir John Clotworthy to be commissioners to the marquess, promising him all fair terms and an entertainment of £4,000 per annum in regard his whole estate is in the hands of the rebels.[507]

<October primo [1646]> Dunkirk is besieged by the French under the command of duke d'Enghien, who leaning upon one of his page's shoulders, the page had his head carried away with a great shot from the town. Though [Ottavio] Piccolomini was not far off, yet durst not adventure upon the French, so that this week it was taken in upon composition; that fisher town which has been for many years the scourge to all her neighbours – English, French, Dutch.[508]

The French have again sent an army of 10,000, under the command of maréchal de Milray, who are landed near Orbetello to recover the loss and dishonour this last summer. L'Italie est le cimetière au France.[509]

[fo. 91] There was <u>for</u> [inserted] this year chosen for lord mayor Sir

---

[506] James Tuchet, third earl of Castlehaven.

[507] Clotworthy and King had been appointed commissioners to treat with Ormond (for the surrender of Dublin) by 29 September 1646: *CSP Ireland, 1633–47*, p. 520.

[508] Dunkirk was surrendered to the French on 1 October 1646.

[509] 'Italy is the graveyard of France.'

John Gayre,[510] a man competently wise and of grave comportment, but not over well-affected to the parliament, having been distrained for his 20th part.[511] This happened contrary to all expectations, [Gayre] having been laid by for several years. The violent Presbyterians, having laid all their designs for Alderman [John] Langham – whom they persuaded should be elected, and he resolved not to suffer any private meetings[512] – to carry with the better, cried down Alderman John Warner[513] for an Independent (who was next in course) and one that was against the remonstrance. Then resolved to give their hands for Langham and Bunce that the other [i.e. Langham] might have it. The Independents and many others gave for Warner only. The honest party being thus divided into 3, the malignants all resolved and gave their hands for Sir John Gayre, who, next to Langham, had most hands. They 2 being presented, the elder was chosen,[514] but certainly not without a providence, for Warner, being disgusted by the Presbyterian party, they might have occasioned quarrelling and more envy against that party; [fo. 91v] and then Langham, being a most violent man (like an English mastiff, whatsoever you set him upon can hardly pull off), would have been furious against the Independents, and occasioned clashing with the parliament and common council. Now Gayre is like to mind them both alike, and silently to teach them love and amity. And the truth is, considering the temper of the people, 'tis best, for there will b'ever a jealous eye over him and we're better under jealousy than security.

<4th [October]> Monday.[515] The Scots desired there might be a conference about the disposing of the king's person, which was performed in the Painted Chamber very stoutly on both sides.[516] In fine,

[510] Sir John Gayre, a senior alderman who had been passed over for the mayoralty for several years because of his neo-royalism, was finally elected on 29 September 1646.

[511] Gayre had been imprisoned for refusing to pay his assessments.

[512] i.e. conventicles or gathered churches.

[513] John Warner was a leading political Independent who had been resolutely opposed to the City remonstrance of May 1646. He was to serve as lord mayor in 1647–48 as the army's nominee following their purge of the City.

[514] In the selection of a new lord mayor, the traditional practice was for common hall to forward two names, including the senior alderman under the chair, to the court of aldermen, which duly chose the latter. According to Juxon's account of the 1646 election, John Warner, the most senior eligible alderman, secured the vote of Independents and their supporters, while the Presbyterian vote went to John Langham and James Bunce with the hope of gaining their selection as the two nominees and the eventual endorsement of Langham. However, with the 'honest party' vote thus split three ways, Sir John Gayre emerged as runner-up to Langham on the combined 'malignant' vote; their two names went forward to the court of aldermen and Gayre, as the senior candidate, was duly chosen.

[515] Monday was 5 October.

[516] There were conferences on 1, 6 and 10 October 1646: Rushworth, vi. 329–36; *CJ*, iv. 729.

some of ours told them they should make a report of the whole to the Commons' House, for only their members disputed it; to which the Lord Lauderdale[517] said they should protest against any verbal report, being resolved not to give account for words – especially because there might many pass which were not fit for report – but told them that in few days they would deliver it themselves in writing, with which ours remained satisfied.

[fo. 92] The next week, instead of bringing in the papers promised, they send their speeches to the press with order to print 8,000, and this by Lord Loudoun's own <u>hand</u> [crossed out] warrant.[518] The Commons' House, upon notice, send aforesaid, [and] find his secretary correcting the said copies with a preamble to them, which was very popular. The House resent this very deeply – that they should in a clandestine and seditious way go about to court the people, especially considering what went before and that the House had not as yet received any report of it. The printer was committed to Newgate etc.;[519] all their friends dislike and disapprove of it.

<21st [October]> The [sic] send in their papers: to the Lords in six sheets, to the Commons in four.[520]

Sir Thomas [Fairfax] was voted a week since for 6 months longer and [Colonel Edward] Massey's [western] brigade paid and disbanded.[521]

<22 [October]> Thursday. The earl [of] Essex's funerals [sic] were solemnised in very great pomp, coming from his house and carried to Westminster Abbey. All the trained band and our regiment of horse attended, with 400 reformadoes trailing their pikes before the mourners etc. and led by Sir William Waller.[522]

<[marginal note to the above paragraph] Had he lived but a week longer, the Lords had voted him generalissimo and Sir Thomas laid aside for his good service. And then Massey's horse and [Colonel Thomas] Sheffield and others should have declared for him, and many malignants and the City, and forced the House of Commons to concur towards the king. But in the season God rather took him away than would permit so great mischief>

[fo. 92v] Upon a resolution to have no member a commissioner for the great seal, the Lords nominated (4) for commissioners and sent

[517] John Maitland, second earl of Lauderdale.
[518] John Campbell, first earl of Loudoun, chancellor of Scotland.
[519] *CJ*, iv. 692–6.
[520] The papers from the Scots commissioners were delivered into both Houses on 20 October: *LJ*, viii. 532–40; *CJ*, iv. 701.
[521] *CJ*, iv. 687, 692, 697.
[522] *The true manner and form of the proceeding to the funeral of Robert earl of Essex* (22 October 1646), BL, E360/1. Waller had been the most senior serving officer under Essex and had become a leading political Presbyterian.

them to the Commons. The Commons pass them by and vote other (3), [and] send them to the Lords. The Lords and Commons both resolve to adhere to their votes. In fine, the Lords would have all seven, the Commons rather than so the former,[523] but nothing resolved though the term be already begun. 'Twas at last pro tempore concluded that the speakers of both Houses should keep and officiate the seal; for the judicative part, that the judges alternatively should do it.

<November [1646]> The Scots, seeing they could not print their papers here, cause them, as they say, to be printed in Scotland and dispersed here, though the truth is they were here printed, for they were exposed to sale wet out of the press [MS torn] under the name of Tyler, the printer at Edinburgh.[524] The Scots declare that the money being paid (viz. £200,000), nothing should hinder their departure – no, not the disposing of the king. The assembly of estates in Scotland concur in it.

[fo. 93] But yet at this very time the commissioners here, operating on their party of ministers in London, press a 2nd remonstrance that the parliament might have some new work, which though it has been dashed quite twice, yet the covenant upon the army has been again put to vote, but carried for the negative.[525]

Towards the raising the money for them, there was an universal concurrence in the House because none durst seem to oppose it, but 'twas believed the money would not be raised, and then new things demanded.

The Independents would fain have a touch with the Scots, because they say 'tis only they that oppose their liberty, and would be willing to give good conditions to the king, who has promised all shall be in their hands, they preserving his regality and suffering him and his friends to enjoy their religion, which is far the safer way for the king.

But the Scots that are desperate, and the cavaliers on the other side, offer to assist, but the danger will be that not only the Scots will prove [fo. 93v] by that to be masters of England but 'twill draw in a foreign force, and then 'twill be difficult to drive them out. 'Twill happen with us as with Cleves and Jülich while the dispute was about it.[526] All arm

---

[523] i.e. the Commons would rather have had this compromise of all seven commissioners than the Lords' four nominees.

[524] *Some papers given in by the commissioners of the parliament of Scotland, to the parliament of England* (29 October 1646), BL, E360/12. Although purporting to have been printed by Evan Tyler, the actual printer was Robert Bostock according to Thomason: Fortescue, i. 472.

[525] The only parliamentary vote on the covenant at this time was on 18 November 1646, when the Independents won a division against giving a second reading to an ordinance requiring subscription to the covenant by everyone in the kingdom: *CJ*, iv. 725.

[526] The reference is to the disputed succession, producing rival Catholic and Protestant

in prudence to preserve from affronts, but in conclusion the Spaniard intended to dispossess the right owners, begin to seize upon places. Which seeing, the Dutch he was resolved to put in for a share, and so divided it with the Spaniard, under pretence of preserving it from them who were their enemies and might prove bad neighbours.

Mr Jeremiah Burroughs died, a man much lamented.[527]

The king of Tunis's eldest son came over to Sicily and was baptised and became Christian. From thence to Rome, where the Jesuits have engaged him, taking him into their tuition.

The king has made Sir Archibald Johnston his attorney general of Scotland, which was done expressly for the speeches he made in the Painted Chamber in the king's behalf. [fo. 94] He has also made Dunfermline one of his bedchamber. Thus they receive honours, though will not allow of those conferred upon Montrose etc. And though he [i.e. the king] be with them, yet is not therefore the nearer in heart, for resolves not to take the covenant nor sign the propositions.

<18th [November]> This day was the first for the subscription of the bishops' lands, and by Friday night the 17th[528] there was come in £220,000 and upwards, and within this time there was one Lord's Day and a fast day; so that it came in 8 days, to the great wonder of all and the high reputation of the parliament, who are able to raise such a sum upon confidence of their prosperity. And it may argue the bishops are not much re-desired; nor are the Scots much desired.

This year and about this time died the earl of Arundel at Padua in Italy, Sir Kenelm Digby, the flower of the English nation, at Rome, and Sir Francis Windebank, principal secretary to the king, at Paris. <[marginal note to the last named] Died a professed papist and had the extreme unction>

[fo. 94v] There has been for this whole month an almost continual rain, no day excepted, which has caused floods to a wonderment the like not known.

The French have not only taken in Piombino but Porto Longono, and now are complimented by the pope and the duke of Tuscany according to the ordinary course, [which is] to adore the rising sun and weary of their old guests.

Th'effigies of the noble earl of Essex was basely and unworthily defaced and mangled,[529] to the great scorn of the parliament.

---

alliances, to these substantially Protestant north-western German territories, beginning in 1609 and ending with their partition in 1614.

[527] Burroughs and his fellow Stepney preacher, William Greenhill, were two of the most influential Independent divines in London and vocal opponents of Presbyterian church government. He died on 13 November 1646.

[528] Should read 27 November.

[529] On 26 November 1646.

There was at this time a printed petition spread abroad in the City for hands, addressed to the common council and from them to the parliament, which contained many unreasonable and at this time dangerous things; which having been brought into the parliament and read, a committee was appointed to examine the authors and printers and admonish them.[530] Accordingly the committee ordered, but by the direction of some members of the committee the chairman, instead of a summons, signs a warrant, but ignorantly. There was upon [fo. 95] **<December [1646]>** it three well-affected citizens sent for by a messenger, which the citizens resented very ill; and therefore on **<5th [December]>** Saturday, when they were to appear at the committee, many came there also in their behalf and cried, 'one and all'.[531] The committee acknowledged it an error to have committed them, appointed them to return on Monday, but discharged them from restraint.

<6th [December]> Sunday. Many of them repaired to the lord mayor and desired him to call a common council about it, that some care might be taken to do them reason, it being a grand usurpation to commit without showing cause. The mayor promised them to do it.

<7th [December]> Monday. Many hundreds went to Westminster and there the committee declared to them they were sorry for that great mistake, which was the clerk's fault. The House ordered they should have their fees again and the clerk committed. The House disclaimed it and sent out 2 of their members to certify the same.[532]

<10th [December]> Thursday. There was a common council, before sitting of which were met in Guildhall some hundreds of people, amongst them many malignants. Drake's son in Cheapside,[533] upon the hustings, and the sheriffs' court read the petition with a long enlargement, desiring hands to the one and their concurrence to the other, both to be presently delivered to the common council, [fo. 95v] which was done with a total submission of it to them; at which time in open court the 3 persons committed related the history of the business. The court, for [the] present, returned them thanks for their good affections, expressions, and their submission etc., and after chose a committee to

[530] *The humble petition of many well-affected freemen and covenant-engaged citizens of the City of London* was read in the Commons on 2 December and was referred to the committee for complaints: *CJ*, iv. 735.

[531] See *The moderate intelligencer* (3–10 December 1646), BL, E365/16, p. 786; *A perfect diurnall* (30 Nov.–7 December 1646), BL, E513/27, p. 1406; *The humble petition of the lord mayor, aldermen and commons of the City of London* (1646), BL, E366/16, p. 9; M. Mahony, 'Presbyterianism in the City of London, 1645–1647', *Historical Journal*, 22 (1979), p. 109.

[532] Bulstrode Whitelocke records that a parliamentary committee was appointed to deal with the business of the petition and find some expedient to preserve the peace: BL, Add. Ms. 37,344, fos. 71–2. He does not reveal the committee's actions as noted by Juxon.

[533] William Drake, fourth son of Roger Drake, of St Peter Westcheap.

consider of it and to draw up what might be fit to be presented;[534] <[marginal note to the above] The common council were in that tune that they would have voted it in the lump: Adams, Sir George Clark,[535] Bunce, Langham, Avery, and Vyner – not a man noted for any religion> which was done on Friday last, where they sat from 10 in the morning to seven at night, and having passed it resolved to carry it up next morning.

The Scots, having in the interim received satisfaction about money (being to have £200,000, which was to be convoyed by Major-General [inserted] Skippon, who was to be governor of Newcastle), made new demands the next day after the petition was presented to the common council. Whereas before they urged for that sum to th'end they might pay their quarters, now demand an addition else they could not; (2) desired to have particular security for the other £200,000; and 3rdly to have forces from England sent to subdue the enemy there, and tax upon this kingdom till it were done.

We answer, to the first, that they concur with them and if they can find any that will be engaged they shall be glad, whether in their House or in the City, [fo. 96] for they could not give better security than the public faith. To the other, answered that they should be willing to assist their brethren when there should be need, but did hope that as when they came to our assistance 'twas at our charge, so did expect when we went to them it should be at theirs. And for forces to be sent thither did believe there was no present need, because when their House did vote the return of their army, instead thereof they brought in more forces. And besides, they did assure them the enemy was not above 3,000 strong, whom they had driven into the mountains, and had not only a competent force already in their own kingdom for the work, but when their army did return would certainly have force enough. Yet to show their willingness for compliance, agreed, and ordered them £50,000 out of Goldsmiths' Hall.[536]

<19th [December]> The petition was presented to the Lords and Commons upon Saturday, accompanied with many of the subscribers,[537] according to the desire of some of the common council; (though improper) seeing 'twas by them presented to our representative body and they only ought to have appeared. The House of Lords quickly returned an answer of thanks and ordered their petition should be

[534] CLRO, Jor. 40, fo. 199; BL, Add. Ms. 37,344, fo. 72.
[535] Sir George Clark was an alderman of eminent standing in the City.
[536] On 13 January 1647: CJ, v. 51–2; LJ, viii. 670–71.
[537] HLRO, main papers, 19 December 1646, petition of the lord mayor, aldermen and commons of the City of London and annexed 'representation'; BL, Add. Ms. 37,344, fo. 73.

printed.[538] It was certainly to carry on their own designs, for some of the sticklers could say the Lords must do their work for them. [fo. 96v] The Commons, after some debate, gave them also thanks for their good expressions and constant affections; promise suddenly to consider of it.[539] In this petition there was a great concurrence of the malignants, yet [it was] wondered [that] they wholly left out that part which concerned the king and the commands of one house of parliament, but desired there might be a concurrence of both Houses in all things that required their obedience, which was also left out.[540]

The king had hoped ere now to have brought us to blows, by making [the] Scots desire extraordinary things and believing the Independent party would not consent, and so to have drawn on a disagreement. Herein the Scots concurred to make great demands and to obtain them too, having the City to back them – for all their motions were mutual and upon design – and upon this point carried they all their work and obtained all their desires; for what was desired by the Scots, the City would solicit for them in remonstrances and petitions, and what the City desired, the Scots would not fail to second. But in the close of all, the king thought to have brought his business of Ireland into a good condition for help, or his friends in Scotland or abroad, or else to have shuffled them off without taking the covenant or signed the propositions.

[fo. 97] **<21st December, Monday>** But all failed him. The Scots must depart; they can bring him to nothing but must leave him (as they had promised him) to his freedom as well in going as in staying. The Lords vote his coming to Newmarket, and the Commons concur with a letter which came from the king this week (wherein he desires he may come to Holmby House <u>near</u> [inserted] <u>where Northampton</u> [crossed out] with honour and safety; and for assurance of it desires the faith of both Houses, the commissioners of Scotland, and the City of London, which was his old offer). They would have him come, and vote he shall be there with security according to the covenant.[541] By which both nations are interested[542]

---

[538] *LJ*, viii. 617–8.

[539] *CJ*, v. 20–21.

[540] It is not entirely clear what Juxon's meaning is here. He seems to be implying that the Lords had unilaterally made order for the disposal of the king ('the king and the commands of one house of parliament'), yet no such order had been made. He also seems to indicate that he has seen, or otherwise has knowledge of, an earlier draft of the City petition. However, he is wrong to state that reference to the 'concurrence of both Houses' was left out of the final draft – the City petition acknowledged that the 'bringing home' of the king should be left wholly to the wisdom of both Houses: *To the right honourable the Lords ... the humble petition of the lord mayor, aldermen, and commons of the City of London* (29 December 1646), BL, E366/14, pp. 5–6.

[541] *LJ*, viii. 621–22, 626–28; *CJ*, v. 28.

[542] Lit. intressed.

in his disposal because both concurred in that and make their interpretations of it.

And for all this, not 2 days before this letter came it was discovered that the king had sent a letter to the duke of York wishing him to escape either into France or to him, which[ever] he could best do. The duke did ingenuously confess it. Thus it falls out perpetually that when the king seems to make the fairest offers of returning he then has something working underhand to the contrary.

He has been most most [sic] extremely unhappy in his undertakings for Ireland. [fo. 97v] The peace concluded by Glamorgan[543] was what he seemed before to disrelish, and yet being done, Digby to colour it over. And it may be to get himself [i.e. the king] some little reputation, committed him and the opportunity was [let?] slip, which he thought to recover by his releasement and a ratification of the peace.[544] And now we are to expect him [i.e. Glamorgan] from thence at the head of an army, which certainly had been done if God had not so unexpectedly despatched things here. And yet to hinder it, the pope's nuncio[545] had debauched all the native Irish, or the most rigid of them, not only to renounce that peace as not being enough advantageous for them, but to pronounce excommunication against them that adhered to it and repute them as enemies, which was a mighty disservice to the king and prevented a conjunction.

As to France etc., he depends upon the issue of the diet at Münster, where if peace be once concluded, expects his friends will appear for him, or at least may procure forces from France or Holland etc.

At the choice of common councilmen this year there was a general design, which took effect, to the putting out all not only Independents but such as favoured them, and herein were so violent as took in several known malignants – nay, in the fury put out some of their own party.[546]

[fo. 98] <**1646 January**>[547] The Count Harcourt was some weeks since totally defeated by the Spaniard, having lain seven months before

---

[543] The second Glamorgan treaty concluded by Edward Somerset, first earl of Glamorgan, who succeeded to the marquessate of Worcester on 18 December 1646.

[544] Glamorgan had been imprisoned on 4 January 1646 and released on the following 21 January. The Irish peace was eventually proclaimed on 30 July 1646.

[545] Jean Baptist Rinuccini, archbishop of Fermo, papal agent in Ireland from 22 October 1645.

[546] The poor showing of the Independents in the common council elections of 21 December 1646 is confirmed by both royalist intelligence and the record of returns in wards like Coleman Street and Farringdon Without: Bodleian Library, Ms. Clarendon 26, fo. 161v; Guild., Ms. 4458/1, fo. 141; ibid., 4415/1, fo. 135; ibid., 3016/1, fos. 286–7; ibid., 3018, fo. 132. Furthermore, Thomas Juxon's uncle, Arthur Juxon, may have been a casualty of this and the previous year's election, for there is no evidence that he served on common council again after 1645 until 1648.

[547] i.e. January 1647.

Lerida in Catalonia, where the Spaniard set upon them at night in their trenches, relieved the town and beat the French, taking their cannon and baggage. 'Tis said Mazarin was not his friend and so lost him by neglecting to supply the army.

The elector of Brandenburg was in this month married to the prince of Orange's eldest daughter at the Hague. His mother was sister to the prince elector and a Calvinist, by whose means the elector and his court became of Lutheran Calvinist. By this post came the news of the death of the prince of Condé – an old covetous man, a might [sic] enemy to the Protestants, a Jesuited papist and one that was never content, nor could the cardinal know what to do with him. The duke d'Enghien, his son, is now prince of Condé – a most gallant prince, a true gentleman and one who has been extremely fortunate; inclines, and is very favourable to, the Protestant [sic].

At the parliament now holden in Scotland was was [sic] called upon hopes to have advantaged the king's business, Hamilton having made a party there for him and laboured to have engaged them to assist against us [fo. 98v] in case we would not receive him with honour, freedom and safety. Expected the Lord Wariston should have spoken in the king's behalf, but on the contrary showed himself a true patriot, and, in fine, 'twas concluded unanimously that, till the king did sign the propositions and take the covenant, he should not execute the duties of his place;[548] ordered his guard should be doubled that he might not escape, though a ship from Holland has many weeks lain there to serve him. And the parliament, having thus voted, sent to the assembly to desire their opinions in point of conscience to the former things. Who declared that they ought not only not to assist, but to oppose whatsoever should be done to that end, being thereunto obliged by covenant. Thus God, who has His overruling hand upon the hearts of all, has not only disappointed the hopes of enemies, but united us more firmly than ever, and droven [sic] the king still farther off and beating him from all those things he thought to have saved himself by, be [i.e. but?] in vain.

Montreuil is gone again into Scotland; but 'twill, no question, but the French hoped upon their agreement at Münster to have spared forces for this service and come to the king's assistance, but yet out of expectation to be masters of some good ports, which the king would certainly have given them.

---

[548] Juxon appears to be referring to the ratification by the Scottish parliament on 24 December 1646 of a vote in the committee for common burdens on 16 December that the king must consent to all the Newcastle propositions or else the government of Scotland would be settled without him. The vote in the committee was 'a close and bitter one': Young, *The Scottish parliament 1639–1661*, pp. 171–2; D. Stevenson, *Revolution and counter-revolution in Scotland 1644–1651* (1977), pp. 77–8.

[fo. 99] The king has endeavoured to make an escape[549] in the Holland ship, toward a reward for which there was £100 paid the master. He should have gone in the night by the conveyance of William Murray, but 'twas discovered and prevented. He intended for Scotland, and thither to have drawn all the fugitives, but General Leven, upon receipt of the parliament's votes, doubles the guard and sends them word their votes were to him as a law. The French ambassador[550] told Leven they had sold their king for £200,000, which would turn to the eternal infamy of their nation. He only replied that he was a servant and so obliged to follow his commands.

The truth is, the Scots have discovered a very great constancy to their principles and engagements, though they have not only been courted by the king and offered very large sums to desert us, but also by the crown of France; by which means have not only lost them both, but a great part of England, and filled their own kingdom with war and misery. And as an effect of this the French, though they have for 800 years past continued to them very great and large privileges, yet now do exact from them the same payments as from other strangers and have proceeded to imprison some for nonpayment; which argues them very much disappointed [fo. 99v] and must certainly draw from us a brotherly sense and assistance.

The king, while he courts us for a personal treaty, does at the same time endeavour to have the duke [of] York escape,[551] and to go away himself. And then by letters sent from Laugharne,[552] which were sent to him from the king and [Dr Michael] Hudson, his guide, does labour to withdraw him from his obedience, intimating the restoring of the Church and ruining of this rebellious parliament.

The Venetians are defeated in Candia by the Turk, who slew them 5,000 upon the place, and so are become masters of that island, while the pope and princes of Italy are deaf to the solicitations of that seigniory. The emperor recalls Archduke Leopold from the command of his army and appoints Gallas – one who has been unfortunate and long out of use.

The marquess of Brandenburg though married yet not pleased; for that which drew him to the match was the promises of the prince of Orange for assistance to regain Jülich and Cleves – but they are not easily drawn where there's no appearance of profit to them. Therefore is suddenly to be gone, and 'tis said will not suffer his lady to carry any of her ladies with her. [fo. 100] He was, without peradventure,

---

[549] On 24 December 1646.
[550] Pompone de Bellièvre.
[551] The plan was discovered on 21 December 1646: *LJ*, viii. 620.
[552] i.e. intercepted by Rowland Laugharne, parliamentary commander in Wales.

over-persuaded to this match by some of his counsellors, who were for it not without suspicion of being bribed to it, though he has a report to have a brave and wise council. 'Tis said that at this marriage neither the old princess nor the princess royal were; the mother because she should have given place to her daughter, now an electress, and the princess royal because a king's daughter – such a hindrance is greatness to human society.

When the condition of the Scots is impartially considered, they had reason to apply themselves to the people and to make their party as strong as they could, else might the king and Independents have joined against them and they but left to shift for themselves.

The Lord Lisle[553] is despatching for Ireland as lord deputy and general, and his brother, Colonel [Algernon] Sidney, lieutenant-general [of the horse], and Sir Hardress Waller, major-general [of the foot].[554] 'Tis a sad story that the Independents, to support their own party, do not only court and do favours to the Lord Northumberland's party – whom they know are not godly – but send upon that account such men for the conduct of the Irish business as they do pre-intend and know shall come to nothing, but consume men and money; and all this for support of the faction, and it may be to the intent Cromwell may hereafter go and have his own conditions.[555]

[fo. 100v] <**February [1647]**> The common council received many petitions from the wards giving them thanks for their great pains; and especially in the business of the petition to the parliament wherein desired that none might preach in private though ordained that therein [crossed out]. It was then determined that the common councilmen of 2 wards should go up to the parliament de die in diem to have answer of their petition, and that the business for rating houses to increase the ministers' maintenance might be despatched.[556]

The Scots having sent their commissioners from their parliament to Newcastle to meet ours from the parliament there, and to solicit the king to the signing the propositions and taking the covenant, but he being wholly obstinate, they then declared in a declaration to him the resolution of the Scots parliament. And though the king made many demurs and questions and showed his resolution to go for Scotland,

[553] Philip Sidney, Viscount Lisle, the eldest son of the earl of Leicester.

[554] Sidney and Waller clashed with Inchiquin, president of Munster, over who should control the army in Ireland.

[555] For Viscount Lisle's lieutenancy of Ireland, and the backing it received from 'the Lord Northumberland's party', see J. Adamson, 'Strafford's ghost: the British context of Viscount Lisle's lieutenancy of Ireland', in J. H. Ohlmeyer (ed.), *Ireland from independence to occupation 1641–1660* (Cambridge, 1995), pp. 128–59.

[556] CLRO, Jor. 40, fo. 204v.

yet it could not be, and so, in fine, was delivered up to the earl of Pembroke[557] and other our commissioners.

<[marginal note to the above paragraph] 'Twas carried but by one voice in their parliament for his not coming to them>[558]

The king being desired by some that waited on him to declare whither he would go, answered, he would go rather to them that bought him than to them that sold him. He said the Scots had deceived him in his hopes; he would now try whether we would deceive him in his fears. He being in the hands of our nation, refuses to hear Mr [Joseph] Caryl and Mr [Stephen] Marshall (who were sent down to him) to preach or pray, and says though he granted the Scots the settlement of their government ecclesiastical yet has not done it to us, and therefore though he heard their ministers yet will not ours. [fo. 101] He desired to have had a chaplain of his own and to have heard the common prayers, but 'twas denied him.

There be several desires of the parliament of Scotland in reference to themselves and us and the king. There is a committee of them to be about the king. There was a sweet concurrence between the Scots and our commissioners, and their forces and ours. And now have they made a particular exception to the general practice of auxiliary forces that come to assist another nation, who seldom leave what they have once possessed. England was conquered by the Saxons and Danes, in that manner required aid from them.[559] General Leven sent to the prince elector to offer him 8,000 of his men to serve him for Germany.

Coin and all sorts of provisions have been and still are very dear, and the month past, being continually wet and extreme warm, gave sad apprehensions. But this month relieves in that point, beginning with a hard frost.

The king is very forward and discontented, and especially with the Scots (as also the queen extremely) when he had read their declaration touching their resignment of him into our hands. Told them he was about publishing something wherein he would set them forth, and that they should see he was neither knave nor fool. He is resolved against the covenant and intends to put on the design of liberty, hoping thereby to avoid it and so to introduce bishops again; which those that are for liberty are content with, believing them as lawful as Presbytery, especially if regulated.

[557] Philip Herbert, fourth earl of Pembroke.

[558] Juxon seems to be referring to the vote in the Scottish parliament of 16 January 1647 on whether or not the king should be left at Newcastle (i.e. to the custody of the English parliament). He appears to be the only source to state that the vote was carried by one voice: Young, *The Scottish parliament 1639–1661*, p. 174.

[559] Juxon appears to be saying that the English, having previously sought aid from the Saxons and Danes, came to be conquered by them.

[fo. 101v] Notwithstanding the old Lord Goring were always before-time of the French faction, and now in their country – yet not without leave from our king and the concurrence of the queen, [even] though the French ambassador and agent were at Newcastle expressly to serve him (or rather themselves by him) – yet old Lord Goring[560] came to Brussels, and, having received instructions, makes several voyages to the prince of Orange – upon pretence of seeing his sons – and back, and brought the treaty to a great forwardness, directly contrary to the interest[561] of France and the Protestant princes. Which must assure us of the constancy of the king to the crown of Spain rather than any other; and the many things of this kind tell us plainly he is more firmly united to them than to any other.

The Hollander did all the last year show their great desire of a peace with the Spaniard, for before they would take the field desired [from the French] not only extraordinary sums, but six thousand foot, which was done; and the [sic] quartered in the land of Waese, where only the Boares are armed, and in short time destroyed 1,500 of them for their plundering and insolencies. After, put them on several things incon-siderable to spin out time and consume their men that they might not gain any new advantage. [fo.102] And, in fine, of the 6,000 men there returned but 2,[000], and they were not sent till Dunkirk was over.

The emperor of Russia, by the advice of a late ambassador of his here, who had great entertainment and respect, seize upon the English merchants' goods unless they would pay custom as strangers, pretending that his alliance was with the king of England and his subjects, but they were traitors to him, and that unless they would procure a letter from the king to testify their loyalty, they should pay the tax; and this not without instigation from the king's ministers.

<[marginal note to the above paragraph] This and the plot of Sir Sackville Crow at Constantinople was with the king's advice>[562]

The king being come to Holmby writes to the parliament that they would permit 2 of his chaplains to come to him, professing he never dissembled his conscience to them.[563]

There was a notable mutiny in Smithfield made by the butchers and the rascally crew in opposition to the paying of excise, wherein they proceeded to the burning the house of excise, the taking the money

---

[560] George, first Lord Goring, created first earl of Norwich by the king in 1644, who was Charles's ambassador in France. Juxon appears to be the only source to claim that Goring was attempting to arrange a 'treaty' between the king and the Spanish at Brussels.
[561] Lit. intrest.
[562] Crow, English ambassador to Turkey, seized some of the property and persons of Levant company merchants trading there: *Subtlety and cruelty: or a true relation of the abuses and oppressions of Sir Sackville Crow, his majesty's ambassador at Constantinople* (4 July 1646), BL, E358/5.
[563] The request was refused on 8 March 1647: *LJ*, ix. 68–9.

and other things away.[564] Upon which the parliament put forth a declaration to satisfy the kingdom in point of excise, and the principal actors in the mutiny were committed to Newgate and to be there tried according to law. [fo. 102v] **<March [1647]>** There is since a new excise house built in the field and intended to be made a dwelling house, and so if hereafter any shall break open or burn 'tis by the law felony and shall suffer.

The lieutenant of Ireland arrived at Cork.

The king being come to Holmby sends for some of his chaplains; remains in the old strain.

The French ambassador, Bellièvre, had his audience in both Houses.[565] His business was formal and only to colour over his stay here, which else could not so well be done. They are spies and lie for their masters.

Upon Shrove Tuesday[566] I was married to my dear wife by brother Byfield[567] at St Giles-in-the-Fields.

The prince of Orange died the 4th of this present **[March]** at the Hague, recommending to the States religion and unity and not to forget the House of Nassau. The next day they swore his son into his father's places, but intend to restrain his power.

There was about this time a petition presented to the common council from many well-affected Presbyters. The purpose of it was to desire them to present to the parliament their constant good affections to them, [fo. 103] and to desire that till the king had signed the propositions and taken the covenant he might not be admitted nearer London, and that malignants that had neither taken the covenant nor submitted to the government under the parliament might not be permitted to come near the king nor remain in the City. This petition was vexing to the malignants, who stormed, imagining they should

---

[564] On 15 February 1647: *CJ*, v. 89.

[565] On 27 February 1647: *CJ*, v. 100–101; *LJ*, ix. 41.

[566] On 2 March 1647: St Giles-in-the-Fields, register of marriages 1615–1713, fo. 30v.

[567] Juxon is referring here to his brother-in-law, Richard Byfield (1598?–1664) who conducted the wedding but was not the incumbent. This was Henry Cornish: Camden local studies and archives centre, Holborn Library, St Giles-in-the-Fields vestry minute book, P/GF/M/1, p. 46. Byfield was rector of Long Ditton, Surrey, and had been added to the assembly of divines in 1645. He was reportedly 'a great covenanter' and was one of the City's Presbyterian ministers questioned for their role in the July 1647 riots. He was to be ejected from his living after the Restoration. His will, made in August 1662, has an extraordinary preamble in which he reaffirms his belief in the doctrine of the Trinity and the infallibility of scripture, and expresses his utter detestation of popery, Arminianism, Socinianism and Anabaptism 'with all the dreams and furies of Enthusiasts, Quakers and Familists'. After his ejection, he retired to Mortlake and was buried in the parish church in December 1664: *DNB*, iii. 565; J. Foster, *Alumni Oxonienses, 1500–1714*, ser. 1, vol. 1, p. 226; *The army anatomized* (4 December 1647), BL, E419/6, p. 35; PRO, PROB 11/317/9 will of Richard Byfield.

have had better service from the City and that party. It was referred to the old committee for the remonstrance.[568] They, when met, enjoined secrecy that none should divulge what was there debated; which done, 'twas advised not to meddle with the person of the king nor with malignants. In fine, the drawing of it up was left to Alderman [Thomas] Adams and [Thomas] Skinner, the City's remembrancer; the first referred it to the last – both sound for the king.

'Twas brought into the common council very lame and poor, very much to the dislike of the honest party there and without, who had knowledge of the carriage of the whole and were extremely enraged against the committee. It was recommitted by the common council and at last brought in, yet very low and imperfect and which was scarce ever seen. They were now so prepared, i.e. the common councilmen, that they would have had it to the vote without so much as consideration of it, which at last with much ado was obtained.[569] [fo.103v] Yet suffered it no great alteration (only added into it the quartering of the army so near London, i.e. within 10 miles, [of] some few troops, and that contrary [to] the general's order, which was that none should be within 15 miles of London in regard of the provisions of the City).

They also took notice of a petition (of which they had a copy) abroad for hands, gathered by such as were for liberty of conscience.[570] It was directed to the supreme court of judicature, the Commons etc., pray[ing] a toleration, [and] that there may be no House of Lords, no payment of tithes nor any taxes, nor the army disbanded till all be done. (This was a day or 2 before delivered to the Commons by another).[571]

Th'expressions concerning the king[572] were that means might be used to persuade him to take the covenant and give satisfaction <u>to</u> [inserted] (not sign) the propositions. There were very many thanks returned them.

Not long after this, there was a petition presented to the Commons by Sir Thomas Essex and many reformado officers,[573] wherein to beget

---

[568] CLRO, Jor. 40, fos. 204v, 205v–206.

[569] On 16 March 1647 common council approved the texts of the City petitions, which were presented to both Houses the following day: CLRO, Jor. 40, fos. 207–8; *CJ*, v. 115; *LJ*, ix. 82–5.

[570] *The humble petition of many thousands, earnestly desiring the glory of God, the freedom of the commonwealth, and the peace of all men.* This was the Leveller 'large petition' addressed to the Commons. Common council ordered that copies of this petition should be annexed to the City's petitions to the Houses: D. M. Wolfe (ed.), *Leveller manifestoes of the Puritan Revolution* (repr. London and New York, 1967), pp. 131–41; CLRO, Jor. 40, fos. 207–10.

[571] On 15 March 1647: *CJ*, v. 112.

[572] Juxon has now returned to discussion of the City's petition.

[573] *The humble petition of colonels, lieutenant-colonels, majors, and other officers, that have faithfully served the great cause of the kingdom, under the authority of parliament* (22 March 1647), BL, E382/4, which was presented to the Commons on 22 March 1647: *CJ*, v. 120.

a good opinion, and so render themselves capable of employment in the New Model, do first of all take notice of the miseries of the kingdom and pray a settlement of the Church according to their covenant. 'Tis strange from those that practise so contrary.

[fo. 104] **<April [1647]>** The parliament sent several of their members to the army to persuade them for Ireland; where being, had notice of a petition on foot wherein prayed care for arrears, who should command them if for Ireland etc., and an act for indemnity with the royal assent. This was brought up to the House by them,[574] and being in debate upon it came in two letters:[575] one said from [Edward] Rosseter's regiment, the other from the headquarters, which speak of the carriage and progress of the business, and that several officers of condition in the army which [sic] abetting to it.

This was so ill resented that the contrary party drove on furiously to revenge: order the officers named to be sent for (and the Lords would needs have the general also), and in this heat presently a disbanding of the army, which was gain for them and the royalists; and further, a declaration of both Houses published to the dislike of the petition and carriage of the army in it.[576] In few days the officers came[577] and, being at the bar of the Commons, were asked several questions according to the information; to all answered negative, and not being able to prove anything, nor the informer known, were dismissed to their charges, yet not without some wonder having been so hot in it.[578]

[fo. 104v] The House of Commons, taking into consideration the affairs of Ireland, vote that the civil government shall be in the hands of 2 lord justices as formerly, and that the military shall be under one, he subject to commissioners upon the place.[579] In pursuance of which, vote Major-General Skippon to be field marshal and Massey general of the horse, with general consent.[580] And for carrying on this business and maintaining the forces in England, vote £60,000 per mensem. They come down to the common council and propound the loan of £200,000 for the advancing of the Irish affairs,[581] and offer such assurance as is within their power. 'Tis immediately embraced and a committee appointed to consider of security.

[574] On 27 March 1647: *CJ*, v. 127.
[575] On 29 March 1647: *CJ*, v. 128–9.
[576] Holles's 'declaration of dislike', assented to by the Commons on 29 March 1647 and by the Lords on the following day: *CJ*, v. 129–30; *LJ*, ix. 111–12, 115.
[577] Lieutenant-General Thomas Hammond, Colonel Robert Hammond, Colonel Robert Lilburne, Lieutenant-Colonel Thomas Pride and Lieutenant-Colonel Mark Grime on 1 April 1647: *CJ*, v. 132.
[578] *CJ*, v. 132; Rushworth, vi. 444–5.
[579] On 1 April 1647: *CJ*, v. 131.
[580] Voted on 2 April 1647: *CJ*, v. 133.
[581] On 6 April 1647: CLRO, Jor. 40, fos. 212–12v.

The bishops' lands are now begun to be sold; the manor of Fulham being the first exposed to sale.

The common council, or rather a party amongst them that have much laboured to get the militia into their hands, prevailed that the money should not be furnished till the militia were settled; which the parliament taking into serious consideration came to a vote, [fo. 105] and resolve for one year, and no longer, that the common council shall have the nomination of the militia, to be approved on [sic] by the houses of parliament, and that the members of it to be chosen out (not only of the City) but of all the places within the lines of communication,[582] which makes the party fall extremely short of what was intended by them.

The Archduke Leopoldus William is arrived in Flanders to command the country. During that, the Hollanders have maligned the crown of France, [and] carried on a treaty with the Spaniard. They [i.e. the French] have secretly done the same with the duke of Bavaria, together with the crown of Swede for seven years [inserted], excluding the emperor, king of Spain and all others; which does a little startle them at Münster, and particularly the emperor, who does exclaim against him [i.e. the duke of Bavaria] and says the prince elector [of the Palatinate] never did so much against him and yet the emperor did reward Bavaria with the inheritance of the other. By this means France and Sweden have weakened the emperor and made this fox their friend. And for his part, had the treaty at Münster concluded, he must have resigned all to the prince elector, which now shall not only possess but take off the French, if not the other, from pressing after it. [fo. 105v] Besides, he well foresaw the emperor, to have procured his own peace, would have done it at the other's cost and have engaged him to restore [the Palatinate] or else must have looked to have lost all and had his own country destroyed, which [he] now prevents. And knows how to purchase the emperor's favour at greater [crossed out] a [inserted] cheap rate than the other way, especially considering how much the emperor does stand in need of his aid. So that, without peradventure, he has done best for himself, and the other two shall with more ease master the Austrian family. The States of Holland are strangely divided in reference to this peace, some being for it and others against it, so that 'tis like to turn into factions amongst them.

<May [crossed out]> The condition of Ireland crying aloud for our relief, especially since the surrender of Dublin by the marquess [of]

---

[582] On 16 April 1647: *CJ*, v. 145. The jurisdiction of the new militia committee was to extend over the suburbs as well as the City itself, but Juxon is wrong about the ordinance requiring the committee's members to be drawn from the suburbs too.

Ormond,[583] and the state of England being at this time in a good condition, it was thought the most expedient way to help Ireland was by sending over part of the army here.

Having concluded what garrisons and field forces were necessary to be here continued – which in horse, foot and dragooners [fo. 106] were to amount to the number of ten thousand – hereupon voted the remainder of the army and the other forces of the kingdom to be disbanded, ordering only six weeks pay for the army.[584]

Next, considering who were to command the forces in Ireland, resolved that it should not be by one single person but that civil matters by 2 lords justices as formerly, and military by a field marshall and general of the horse, together with a committee upon the place. Upon which the [parliamentary] lord lieutenant [Viscount Lisle] was discharged; and so accordingly, having received the votes of the House and his commission at an end, returns and gives an account to the parliament of his expedition and after receives thanks from them etc.[585] In whose room Major-General Skippon was voted the field marshall and Massey general of the horse. Skippon, being at Newcastle at his charge, receives the votes [and] desires to b'excused, pleading age and infirmity; is sent for to come to London. Where come [sic], is over persuaded by his friends to accept of it, though, as he professed, he should die before he arrived to Dublin in regard there seemed so great a necessity to lie upon it.[586]

In the meantime – the army finding themselves disbanded by vote, or to go to Ireland, and but 6 weeks pay for them; [fo. 106v] as also that many of them were called to account, imprisoned, and suffered for several things done in order to the parliament's service, and no act of indemnity passed to secure them – the officers of the army draw up a petition to deliver to the general, desiring he would in their behalf represent it to the House; a copy whereof was by someone sent up privately to the parliament, who presently fall into debate, and being somewhat exasperated by the parliament [crossed out] Stapiltonian party, who laboured above all to have them disbanded, voted to send

---

[583] This is probably a reference to Ormond's offering to surrender the lord lieutenantship to parliament on 6 February 1647: *LJ*, ix. 29–30.

[584] On 27 April 1647: *CJ*, v. 155; *LJ*, ix. 152.

[585] On 7 May 1647: *CJ*, v. 166. See above, Adamson, 'Strafford's ghost: the British context of Viscount Lisle's lieutenancy of Ireland'.

[586] According to *A perfect diurnall* (26 April–3 May 1647), BL, E515/10, p. 1571, Skippon desired to be excused 'by reason of his age and disability ... but seeing he is ordered by both houses of parliament and called thereunto, he shall deny himself to serve the public, and obey the commands of both houses'. No corroborating evidence has been found for Juxon's statement that Skippon was 'over persuaded' by his friends to accept command in Ireland, or that he professed he should die before he arrived in Dublin.

up for several of the officers who they were informed did promote it.[587] And at 9 at night, Holles went out and drew up a declaration, brought it in, and [the Commons] voted if they did not desist in the petition should be reputed as enemies to the state.[588]

The next day[589] **[1 April 1647]** the officers, being come and called for into the House, were asked several questions according to several letters of information sent up by some who were to be concealed, but to all answered negative. The House, not being able to prove anything, dismissed them to go to their charges; which over hasty act of the Commons was much censured.

The next thing was that several persons of both Houses, together with Massey, were appointed to go to the army and endeavour to [fo. 107] give them satisfaction, and also to communicate the votes for Ireland and see what numbers would engage for that kingdom.[590] Which was done, the officers being several times assembled, but seemed generally resolved not to go till had satisfaction to their demands and that their officers might go along with them.

During the commissioners' abode in the army, were informed of an ensign in the general's regiment that did obstruct the service of Ireland.[591] They sent for him and, without acquainting the general with it – who was in the army – do commit him and bring him afterwards prisoner to London. This they [sic] army resented very ill.

The commissioners at their return – being upon a Saturday, before report could be made to the House[592] – had conference with some of their party in London and gave an account of their journey, together with the state of the army, but with all the aggravation that could be, and so after did to the parliament. Insomuch that upon the coming down of Lords and Commons to the common council about the advancement of £200,000 for Ireland, [the] earl of Pembroke did in course affirm he had seen the copy of a petition (to the king) from the army wherein they pray him to come to them, and they promise to r'establish him upon his throne and to strengthen it; told them 'twas no longer the New Model for there were 7,000 cavaliers in it,[593] and

[587] On 29 March: CJ, v. 129. Juxon is repeating himself.

[588] Holles's 'declaration of dislike' drawn up on 29 March: above, p. 152.

[589] The officers appeared before the House on 1 April: CJ, v. 132; above p. 152.

[590] The parliamentary commissioners arrived at army headquarter at Saffron Walden on 15 April: Rushworth, vi. 457.

[591] Ensign Francis Nicholls.

[592] The commissioners made their report to the House of Commons on Tuesday, 27 April, hence the previous Saturday was 24 April: CJ, v. 154-5.

[593] Other sources report that Pembroke quoted the figure of 4,000 cavaliers: Gentles, p. 482, n. 95. For Pembroke's speech and rumours that the army was holding secret negotiations with the king, see Rushworth, vi. 476; Clarke papers, i. 24, 26; Kishlansky, New Model Army, pp. 208-9; Woolrych, Soldiers and statesmen, pp. 69-71; Gentles, p. 153.

that theirs and the king's hopes were upon the army. [fo. 107v] This was believed by some and divulged by others on purpose to serve their turn against the army. There was also framed a formal answer to their petition from the king; all done on purpose to exasperate the army, and thereby to ruin them and, with them, all that favoured them.

The common council, having promised to advance the money desired, after, make these demurs: that in regard the army did seem to threaten them and that there were many in the City of their opinions, pressed that for the security of the City and their satisfaction they might have power to choose their militia annually and to march forth at pleasure.[594]

<4 May [1647]> 'Twas at last granted them to nominate 31 persons for their [militia] committee, to be approved of by the parliament, and to continue only for one year.[595]

At the common council [crossed out]

The common council, to carry on the business more solemnly, concluded upon a day when to make choice of their new militia, and to have a sermon, and all the members of the court to retake the covenant. Which being done, several were absent upon several occasions; amongst the rest Mr [Stephen] Estwicke, being taken very ill, was constrained to go out of church, and coming in the afternoon to the common council 'twas objected against him his non-taking [fo. 108] of the covenant, and that he was not fit to sit in that court. Upon which 'twas desired by some that he might withdraw while they debated the business. The lord mayor persuaded him others would have had it voted presently; he refused. In fine, upon my lord's entreaty he did voluntarily go out, and then hearing himself much reviled, came in again and told my lord and the court that he could no longer hear himself so abused, and therefore, as he freely went forth so came in again. At this they were very much offended and cried out to have him go forth; he would not. In fine, my lord mayor commands some of the officers to pull him forth, and they violently did; afterwards passed a vote to warrant the action.[596]

Having made choice of their men for militia, 'twas quickly ratified by the parliament.[597] Then for their security for the £200,000, the Commons add to the former for the Scots, the papists' estates in arms

[594] The City asked for a new militia committee in March 1647 and the ordinance passed the Lords; it passed both Houses on 16 April 1647: *LJ*, ix. 82, 143. Juxon is repeating himself: above, p. 153.

[595] *CJ*, v. 160–61; *LJ*, ix. 143, 174–6.

[596] On 27 April 1647: CLRO, Jor. 40, fo. 215v; Rushworth, vi. 472–3. John Brett was a fellow recalcitrant common councillor.

[597] *CJ*, v. 160–61; *LJ*, ix. 175–6.

and delinquents'. The Lords leave out the latter and put in Goldsmiths' Hall.[598] The common council, being instructed, are unsatisfied without it, alleging it was promised them by their member what security they would. Which was true, but not to engross all that the parliament were able to give; by that means should leave them unable upon any emergency to raise any sums, having pawned all their security already. [fo. 108v] In fine, their party in the House of Commons do carry it for 1/2 of Goldsmiths' Hall.[599]

In the meantime, the army continues their resolution not to disband till satisfaction be given in their desires; join all together, officers and soldiers, send to Poyntz's horse to join with them, secure themselves in their quarters against any offence from the country, resolve to demand several of the members of parliament, and many things foreign to their cognizance.[600] This being put into them by some ill men, fills the kingdom with sad apprehensions, [and] enraged their enemies in the Houses, who resolve rather to put all to a hazard than to have terms put upon them by the army; that they would immediately conclude with Ireland, having offers from the rebels, then agree with the king, and all together [i.e. Presbyterians, Irish and the king] join against the army and destroy them.

And Cromwell and their friends in the House do publicly profess if they shall not content themselves with what's proper to them as soldiers, but go about to confound and disorder the whole business, they would certainly desert them, and so also did many of the principal officers resolve. Concluding that then there were many miscarriages in the parliament, must bear rather than seek to destroy them, and though the people were rationally the supreme power, yet the parliament legally was and therefore were bound to submit unto them. [fo. 109]

---

[598] *CJ*, v. 153, 159; *LJ*, ix. 163, 165; Rushworth, vi. 478. In other words, the Lords designated composition fines ('Goldsmiths' Hall') rather than the sale of delinquents' estates as security for the £200,000.

[599] On 5 May 1647: *CJ*, v. 163. The tellers on the question that the House shall insist on their former resolutions about security for the loan were Sir John Evelyn of Wiltshire and John Boys for the yeas (91); Walter Long and Richard Knightley for the noes (104). The victorious 'party' would appear to be that of the political Presbyterians.

[600] The agitators in the New Model Army resolved early in May to 'hold correspondence' with their fellow soldiers and the 'well affected' elsewhere in the kingdom, although Juxon appears to be the only source to state that they requested Poyntz's horse to join with them at this time. Certainly by June Poyntz was complaining that agitators from the 'southern army' were causing disturbances among his northern regiments: *Clarke papers*, i. 23, 142–6; H. Cary (ed.), *Memorials of the Great Civil War in England from 1646 to 1652* (2 vols., 1842), i. 233, 282. Juxon has apparently mistaken the calls from certain regiments for justice against the authors of the 'declaration of dislike' for the desire of the army in general. In fact, most senior officers were still anxious to confine the army's demands to purely military matters: Gentles, pp. 163–5.

Nay, though they should do things that tended apparently to the prejudice of the common good, rather to suffer and wait for a better time than resist. The common people never were fit for government.[601]

During these things a petition was presented to the Commons from the hands of many Independents, expressing many grievances by particular men, especially by Mr Holles etc. The petition was read and ordered to be burnt by the common hangman, and so was.[602]

Cromwell, having been with others at the army and returning, gave the House an account of his proceedings therein and had thanks returned him.[603]

There was another petition from the Independents in London, showing their great dislike of the changing the militia and turning out of many honest commanders, but had no answer.[604]

New commissioners are appointed, Lords and Commons, to go to the army and see them disbanded by several regiments,[605] with instructions thereto and 2 months pay upon the place. The general's regiment, being at Chelmsford in Essex, were to be the first; **<June>** the day, Tuesday the primo June. But the night before they sent a letter [fo. 109v] to the committee of both kingdoms, desiring they would save their labour in sending, for they were gone to a rendezvous, at [sic] so it appear the next day. They were all drawn towards [Saffron] Walden and resolve not to disband till their desires were granted.

<3rd [June]> Thursday, they [i.e. the Commons] fall into debate about them and vote them all their arrears – id est the common soldier; to the officers, a piece of money for present – to retract their declaration wherein they were accounted enemies;[606] [and] vote an act of oblivion

---

[601] Juxon goes further than most commentators in stressing the abhorrence felt by Cromwell, the New Model's friends at Westminster, and many senior officers at the prospect of the army challenging the authority of parliament. For Cromwell's position on this issue in the spring of 1647, see *Clarke papers*, i. pp. xvii–xx; Abbott, *Writings and speeches*, i. 435–7; Clarendon, iv. 223.

[602] 'The humble petition of divers well-affected people, in and about the City of London', which the Commons on 20 May ordered to be burnt along with the Leveller 'large petition': *CJ*, v. 179–80; BL, Add. Ms. 31,116, fo. 310; ibid., 37,344, fos. 87–8; above, p.151.

[603] On 21 May: *CJ*, v. 181.

[604] 'The humble petition of many thousands of well-affected people', read in the Commons on 2 June, but the motion to return an answer was defeated by 128 votes to 112: *CJ*, v. 195. The tellers for the yeas were Sir John Evelyn and Sir Michael Livesey and for the noes, Denzil Holles and Sir William Lewes.

[605] On 28 May: *CJ*, v. 192; *LJ*, ix. 216.

[606] The 'declaration of dislike' was voted to be expunged from the Commons' journals on the night of 3–4 June and the Lords were asked to do the same: *CJ*, v. 196–7; Rushworth, vi. 502; BL, Add. Ms. 31,116, fo. 311v. The declaration was subsequently repealed by ordinance on 8 June: *CJ*, v. 202; *LJ*, ix. 242, 247–8; Rushworth, vi. 547–8. In seeking to correct Juxon's chronology, Gentles confuses the two processes: Gentles, pp. 173, 489 n. 259.

to them for all things done in order to the good of the parliament. Sat till 2 of the clock next morning. The next morning were met many of my Lord Essex's officers, and fell upon several of the members. Told them they had always obeyed them, and when were commanded did disband, yet were not their arrears voted. Pressed them very uncivilly; went to the door, told them they should not stir till they had voted them money.[607] Within 2 days after, petitioned the House that in regard their privileges, together with their own liberties, were in danger by the army, did offer their service.[608]

[fo. 110] The army march up to St Albans, and a letter sent to the lord mayor and common council wherein they express a charge against (11) of the House [of] Commons, and advise them to concur with them for justice and not to be afraid at their approach, nor to raise any forces, and then might be confident of no hurt.[609] This being read, was sent a copy to the House, upon which they vote 'twas fit to consider of their own preservation and safety; thereupon nominate a committee of the Lords and Commons, of their own mind, to be a committee of safety for one month to come, and with a large power; order them to come and join with the [City] committee of the militia.[610] They presently come, and, against their coming, there were many reformadoes come down to Guildhall to be entertained, and animated the citizens not to take the affront.

<Friday [11 June 1647]> Being come about (7) at night, when the more part of the committee were absent, the [sic] passed many votes: as to have the guns carried to the forts; [fo. 110v] to have the blockhouses secured; to send to the adjacent counties to be up in arms; to send to their several forces, as Poyntz, Laugharne and those intended for Ireland, to keep them in a good understanding with the parliament – but there were privately letters sent to the aforesaid to march up to a certain rendezvous. Then to secure all the horses about London, and that none might pass without the lines, and lastly a general alarm in the City presently.

Then were the reformadoes called in – as Dalbier, Sir Thomas [inserted] Essex, Colonel [Edwin] Sandys etc. – to take the names and list the next day those that would offer their service, and a general expectation that the common council would the next day give concurrence in the whole. This being thus done, Colonel [John] Bellamy,

---

[607] CJ, v. 197; BL, Add. Ms. 31,116, fos. 311–12; M. F. Stieg (ed.), The diary of John Harington, MP, 1646–53 (Somerset Record Soc. 74, 1977), p. 55.

[608] On 7 June when MPs were again intimidated: CJ, v. 201–2; BL, Add. Ms. 31,116, fo. 312; Stieg (ed.), The diary of John Harington, p. 55.

[609] The army's letter was brought to the City on 11 June: CLRO, Jor. 40, fos. 219–20; CJ, v. 208. The eleven members were not charged until 16 June.

[610] On 11 June: CJ, v. 207; LJ, ix. 255.

the bookseller, made a motion that all ways might be taken to avoid the shedding of more blood [fo. 111] and to prevent the ruin of the City, which would follow if the reformadoes were entertained; and therefore desired they would permit the common council to send their commissioners to the army to know their desires and see if it might not be reconciled. 'Twas opposed, though seconded by himself and others, and nothing expected or intended but a vigorous opposition of the army.

The next morning, the common council considered of what had the night before been done at the militia and resolved to send commissioners, which accordingly did; [John] Warner, [John] Fowke, [William] Gibbs, aldermen, [Christopher] Pack, [Thomas] Noell, [Thomas] Chamberlaine, [Thomas] Player,[611] who were well entertained, it being that which they [i.e. the army] wished for – to hold the City in suspense and engage them in their desires. They send letters to the common council of nothing but fair intentions and that, if they would not raise or colour any levies against them, not a hair of their heads should be hurt by them, nor would they suffer anybody else to do it. This did in general seem to content and quiet the multitude, who desired nothing more than rest after so long a tempest.

[fo. 111v] The army send their particular [crossed out] charge to the House of Commons and demand they (11)[612] might be suspended till the business were tried. The House voted the contrary until a particular charge were brought in.[613]

In the meantime, there was a vote made and an ordinance for the payment of all that had served the parliament, a month's pay;[614] which was seemingly grounded upon a petition of some of the reformadoes for their arrears, but was indeed to oblige them and to have them ready in London when occasion should offer. By which means there came from all parts of the kingdom, and here were secretly entertained and listed, insomuch that here were not so few as 20,000 £ [crossed out] in and about London. And though, at the desire of the army and the order of the parliament, they were to b'excluded the lines of communication and that referred to the militia [committee] of the City, yet they were so well principled in their work that none were expulsed, and the £200,000 paid into Weavers' Hall was above 1/2 paid out to them, when indeed many of them had nothing due nor were any of their account[s] audited, but came in a tumultuous manner to the

---

[611] Alderman Thomas Vyner, William Hiccocks, Robert Lowther, Richard Waring and Walter Pell were also commissioners: Rushworth, vi. 558; CLRO, Jor. 40, fos. 220v–221.

[612] i.e. the 'eleven members'.

[613] Rushworth, vi. 585–92; *CJ*, v. 223. The vote was taken on 25 June 1647.

[614] On 16 June: *CJ*, v. 214; *LJ*, ix. 271.

treasurers in London and would not be disputed with, but all that came, had.

[fo. 112] The parliament voted that all the [sic] would come away from the army should have their arrears paid them, thinking thereby to have broken it to pieces, but that brought off not above 4 troops and 400 foot.[615]

The common council desire of the parliament not to raise any forces and that the reformadoes might b'expelled the line; and hereupon the (11) members, apprehending the City would <u>not</u> [crossed out] desert them, desired leave to go beyond sea – 'twas granted them.[616]

Then the House of Commons vote the army their army, and Sir Thomas Fairfax their general, and take them under their protection, and the army to be paid up – those that came off and they to be disbanded being then entertained,[617] and this done upon the desire of the army. The parliament, not finding the City to favour the proceeding, begin to incline to give them satisfaction.

The impeached members absent from the House but come into the City and hold private meetings with all sort of persons for to countermine the army; and in short do procure <u>an engagement</u> [crossed out] a petition to the common council, [fo. 112v] joined with an engagement to bring the king to London upon his granting what he did offer the 12 of May[618] – and this in the name of covenanters, citizens, apprentices, seamen and others – and with their utmost to oppose whoever should act contrary to this their engagement.[619] Copies hereof were dispersed in all the wards, and many of the trained band officers and others were engaged in it. The parliament, having notice hereof, do vote it traitorous, and, in case they do not desist, to be proceeded against.[620] The conspiracy was so strong that as 'twas cried in the streets, they in disdain tore it[621] and go on amain in getting hands.

[615] The Commons resolved on 3 and 11 June 1647 that any of the officers and common soldiers who agreed to disband or to serve in Ireland should have their full arrears of pay: *CJ*, v. 197, 207; *LJ*, ix. 241, 252; Gentles, p. 167.

[616] Common council petition of 2 July 1647: Rushworth, v. 597–600; *CJ*, v. 231; CLRO, Jor. 40, fos. 231v–32v. The Commons granted leave to the eleven members to go overseas on 20 July: *CJ*, v. 251–2.

[617] On 17 July: *CJ*, v. 248–9.

[618] The king sent a letter to parliament from Holmby House, dated 12 May 1647, in which he agreed, if he was allowed to come to London to conclude a personal treaty, to the establishment of Presbyterianism for three years and to relinquish power over the militia for ten years: *LJ*, ix. 193–4.

[619] *The humble petition of the citizens, commanders, officers and soldiers of the trained bands and auxiliaries etc.* and the annexed *A solemn engagement* (21 July 1647), BL, 669 f. 11/47; *CJ*, v. 255.

[620] *CJ*, v. 257; *LJ*, ix. 351.

[621] i.e. the vote against the petition.

Sir Thomas desires the militia [committee] may be put into safe hands, alleging many things considerable against the present. 'Twas granted and the old [committeemen] put in again with an addition of others.[622] They meet at the accustomed place at Guildhall, but were quickly attended by a company of young men, who came boldly into them and wished them to begone and not to sit there, telling them if they caught them there again they would hang their guts about their ears; and never left them till they had compelled them to rise, and, as they went, followed them with ill language.

[fo. 113] Then went the aldermen, together with the common council [inserted], with a petition to the parliament, desiring the former militia might be restored and reinvested. The answer of both Houses was that they could not alter what they had done; upon which several of them told th'apprentices and others, who were there in great numbers, that they had done what they could and that now it rested in them to play their parts, who presently repaired to both Houses' doors. The Lords were threatened in case they did not vote the other in again, and so much that they condescended, and yet were fain to shift for themselves out at the backdoor. Then they come to the Commoners' House, force open the door, tell the speaker they would not nor should they stir till they had done it; cause them to put it to the vote, themselves standing at the bar, and proposed what they would have voted, and, though desired, would not withdraw to permit them liberty of voting. When the Commons voted the prentices voted with them, and when there appeared some difficulty in the negative and affirmative, desired them to withdraw that they might divide the House; but told them they would not, but they should do it where they were, [fo. 113v] and then they were not contented but would see it entered in their journal.[623] All this while there was in the Palace Yard Alderman [James] Bunce with some common councilmen and others as a committee for to give direction for the management of this business, to whom there came continually some from the Commons' door to give them account which [sic] was done and to receive directions what to do. This force upon the House remained till nine at night. In the meanwhile, the parliament sent to my lord mayor to send down some of the trained bands for their guard, but he refused, called a common council, and then, when they understood the House had done the thing, 'twas ordered that some of them that were gracious with the multitude should go to Westminster and quiet them;[624] where they no sooner came but they

[622] On 23 July: *CJ*, v. 254, 256–7; *LJ*, ix. 349.

[623] The force upon the Houses of 26 July: *LJ*, ix. 355–7; *CJ*, v. 258–9; Rushworth, vii. 747; BL, Add. Ms. 37,344, fo. 100.

[624] CLRO, Jor. 40, fo. 240v.

were quiet and departed everyone home, but with this general acclamation – to return the next day.

The next day **[27 July 1647]** the Houses met,[625] but neither of the speakers, viz. [the] earl [of] Manchester and Lenthall, came; sent to their houses, were not there but gone to the army, who, upon the news of these things, sent out orders for the army with all speed (who were dispersed upon [sic] and down the kingdom upon the granting of the old militia) [fo. 114] to march up to a general rendezvous at Hounslow.

In the meantime, the House of Commons resolved to <u>vote</u> [crossed out] choose a new speaker, which they did, it being one Mr Pelham,[626] reputed a moderate man; and the clerk, [Henry] Elsynge, was absent but returned within 2 hours; and the sergeant of their House was gone, chose a new one, and now they are pleased. The Lords choose Lord Willoughby[627] speaker and proceed roundly against th'army; vote the 11 members to return to the House, which they quickly did, being retired only into London.[628] They presently order the guns to be carried to the forts, and they to be manned, and then order given to list – being furnished beforehand with bodies upon the payment of the month's pay. In the interim, they send the commissioners to the army to cajole them, and tell them they would take care for the future for the guarding of the House, and disclaim that act of the apprentices; which gave some contentment to the general.[629]

<u>In the interim</u> [crossed out] But the common council go on to arm, and money was raised in the court by contribution for the work to the value of £10,000.[630] <u>They also appoint</u> [crossed out].

[fo. 114v] They debate about the choice of a major-general for the City. 'Twas replied in the common council that Major-General Skippon was already, and when he went to the army 'twas but lent and with condition to return when they should have occasion for him. Thereupon, the commissioners were ordered to treat with him in it, who, after much persuasion, consented, provided they would get him an order from the House of Commons to discharge him from being a commissioner in the army. For thither also did both Houses send their commissioners to have inspection upon all the carriage of th'army, together with ours [i.e. our commissioners] from London.[631]

---

[625] The Commons met on 27 July but immediately adjourned till the following Friday, 30 July: *CJ*, v. 259. The Lords had adjourned on 26 July until 30 July: *LJ*, ix. 358.

[626] Henry Pelham was chosen speaker on 30 July when the House reassembled: *CJ*, v. 259.

[627] Francis, fifth Baron Willoughby of Parham: *LJ*, ix. 358.

[628] On 30 July: *LJ*, ix. 361; *CJ*, v. 259–60.

[629] *CJ*, v. 260–61; CLRO, Jor. 40, fos. 242v–44; Rushworth, vi. 646.

[630] On 29 July 1647 it was resolved to borrow £20,000 for the defence of the City: CLRO, Jor. 40, fo. 243.

[631] *CJ*, v. 266; CLRO, Jor. 40, fo. 247.

During these things there was a motion made to the militia [com-mittee] for the choice of a major-general, but were put off till they might have Skippon's answers; though there was a part of the militia [committee] that openly maintained they had no power to choose a major-general (nor indeed had they). In fine, the lord mayor and that party pressed the choice of a major-general, and concluded if there were no answer from Skippon in such time [they] would conclude on the business. But the necessity of having one speedily, and not him, [fo. 115] made them resolve upon Massey for their major-general, and got him confirmed by both Houses,[632] and about 3 days after obtained an ordinance enabling them to the choice of a major-general. This done, they seized upon a [sic] horses within the City and appoint troopers to mount them, and all preparations for defence of the City against the army.

The House gave power to the militia [committee] to do all things in order to defence, and order also that whosoever should in word or action disparage or discourage this present action should be accounted as enemies.[633] Did intend to expell the army['s] friends out of the City, whither many of them were gone already, and did intend to put them on ship-board and also to disarm them; and when 'twas in the House of Commons moved that they also that had borne arms against the parliament might be disarmed, 'twas opposed, saying that they should then lose a great part of their friends.

Massey took upon him the disposing of the guards of the City, and great threatenings what to do. The common council were in this while drawing up a declaration against the army and for the justifying their defence. [fo.115v] This was referred to a committee; they it to [Alderman Thomas] Adams; he left it to [Thomas] Skinner, the remembrancer; and without reporting of it to the committee to be read and considered (the common council sitting) they brought it in, and being once read passed in the lump.[634]

The royal party depend much upon it and resolve to appear all for the king, expecting that it would be positive for him, without naming the covenant or Scots or anything, else they would not stir. But herein were disappointed, for 'twas too low for them and too high for the honest part that joined with them. The royalists were resolved to let all the prisoners everywhere loose and declare the duke of York their general, and force every man to contribute either in person or purse. The City declaration was by the lord mayor ordered to be read in

[632] On 31 July: *CJ*, v. 261; *LJ*, ix. 363; Rushworth, vi. 646; CLRO, Jor. 40, fos. 244, 246v.
[633] On 31 July: Firth and Rait, i. 992–4; *CJ*, v. 260–61; Rushworth, iv. 646.
[634] CLRO, Jor. 40, fos. 244v–46.

every church the Lord's Day, and the ministers to encourage the people to assist against the army. In the meantime, many of the commanders of the trained bands and auxiliaries lay down their commissions, and a strange unwillingness to engage against the army, especially the parliament not discharging the general of his commission, nor the army of their protection. But they durst not do it, yet resolved to wait an opportunity for it.

[fo. 116] The king sends Major-General [Richard] Browne to the City of London to stand upon their defence, and if they should declare for him, he would in due time acknowledge it; sends to the parliament to stand in the defence of their privileges; and sends privately to his friends not to engage on either sides, but let the rogues tug it out by th'ears.

The forces of the City had a general order to appear at their rendezvous upon the army's coming to Hounslow, but now, as formerly, there was an inconsiderable appearance.[635] The apprentices came not out as was promised. For the auxiliaries, could scarce any of them be got upon the guard. The seamen were promised by the Trinity House to 10,000, but came not above 300. There were none of the [Tower] hamlets would obey commands, all their officers having laid down.[636] And though there was all the means that could be possible used to make ready so many horse as might look the army's [horse] in the face (who were now come to Hammersmith) yet Massey [crossed out] – to the intent they might but engage and make a beginning, thinking that would run all into a desperate point – yet Massey declared in common council that he could not make 700 horse fit for to engage the night that the City concluded with th'army.[637]

[fo. 116v] The army well knew how things passed and therefore longed to have him peep out, intending to surprise the horse who were ordered to lie without the works.

And now that all possible endeavours were used to draw to an engagement, and so to a 2nd war, wherein the royalist would only [have] taken the spoils and the king reinstated without granting anything to the parliament; who indeed could never [have] been in a capacity to have demanded anything, for their new army were most reformadoes and for the king.

The king did all this while but tamper with the army and try if he

[635] Several newsbooks reported that there was 'great appearance' of reformadoes and militia officers at a rendezvous in St James's fields on 31 July: *A perfect diurnal of some passages in parliament* (26 July–2 August 1647), BL, E518/12, pp. 1682–3; *The kingdom's weekly intelligencer* (27 July–3 August 1647), BL, E400/39, p. 617.
[636] There had been a comprehensive purge of this suburban subcommittee for the militia: Worcester College, Oxford, Clarke Ms. 2/3, fos. 162v–163.
[637] The night of 2–3 August 1647.

could engage them for him; but finding contrary, slighted them, and the more as he understood any probability of opposing them. And his friends gave out that they and the king would never agree, there being a great labouring in the army to that purpose. Then 'twas expected the king should declare that he was restrained by the army to whet the City on, and he had to that purpose a declaration ready, only stayed till the armies were engaged. But finding things go contrary to expectation, courted the army and disliked the carriage at Westminster, and glad he did not declare. But 'twas known his intention; he knew the army knew it.

[fo.117] It is also to be considered that the apprentices, after the force upon the Houses, presented a petition to the common council wherein they tell them that they had obtained the votes the day before for them of both Houses, and desired them to put them in execution; to which the court called them in and returned them thanks, and accordingly prosecuted them [i.e. the votes].[638]

<2nd August 1647> Again, the Monday before the army and City agreed, the House of Commons voted the king to come presently to Whitehall without any satisfaction named,[639] on purpose to gratify the malignants and engage them, and to usher the king's declaration. The Scots commissioners were at the same time at the House of Commons door to promote them; and notice being given to them who dissented in the said vote, they sent for them out and used arguments to them to agree to it and, as 'twere, over-press them to it.[640]

There was one thing that happened not many days before all was given over: that many honest citizens went to Guildhall to persuade, by a petition, the lord mayor to avoid a new war; and, being there, there happened to be some of the reformadoes whom they jostled and broke his sword. Hereupon Poyntz and Massey and many more not being [fo. 117v] far off, but in the New Artillery Ground mounting their men, came suddenly thither and with their swords drawn fell upon the naked men, whom they slashed and cut barbarously, and some killed outright, and followed them up and down the streets cutting them; and at last the horsemen came into Cheapside with their swords drawn, crying out for King Charles.[641] This was a sad sight to all true-

[638] 'The petition of the young men and apprentices of the City of London' presented to common council on 27 July: CLRO, Jor. 40, fos. 240v–41.

[639] *CJ*, v. 264.

[640] Juxon appears to be the only source to claim that the Scots commissioners badgered those MPs who dissented to the motion that the king be invited to London to treat.

[641] The Guildhall incident of 2 August in which only two men may have been killed: *LJ*, ix. 401–2. Juxon appears to be the only source for the horsemen in Cheapside crying up the king, although an anonymous pamphleteer claimed that Massey's men came 'thick in companies to the Guildhall gate, shouting, hollowing, and crying for king, parliament and City': *The disconsolate reformado: or the sad look'd Presbyterian jack* (21 August

hearted citizens and told them what they were t'expect from such fellows.

Then the borough of Southwark refused to let in any of the City forces, but stood upon their guard at the bridge foot, and suffered none to come into the City but [inserted] whoever would to go out. So that there were many of all sorts that went to the army, besides many of the Lords and Commons, and many others, the 2 speakers being also there.[642]

The ministers of the assembly also made their request to the common council that they would avoid blood, and most did heartily desire a good accommodation, crying out that justice might be done upon them that had deserved it.[643]

In th'end, the common council sent their commissioners to the army to moderate the business, but they would not treat with them, only [fo. 118] sent them back with certain propositions, demanding their answer that night by (11) of the clock, viz. that they would the next day come with a party of horse and foot, and bring the speakers and members of both Houses to the parliament, and there be a guard to them; and that the fortifications from Crabtree fort southward to the Thames should be guarded by them, and all their guards to be after few days discharged; and that those that had assisted to the forcing of the Houses should be proceeded against. This was no sooner propounded but snapped at and accorded. And 'twas at such time when they were truly informed they were no ways able to defend themselves, not being so much as to relieve the guards one over; and were yet resolved, upon the refusal of the general to treat, to give the utmost resistance they were capable of. But were in a moment altered, and, being once agreed to, there was a general acclamation of joy, though not universal; for they did not only tremble at the thoughts of the success, but at their own men, whom if they should have prevailed had more cause to fear than the army.

[fo. 118v] The next day **[6 August 1647]**, they came all to the parliament again, and great multitudes, together with the common council, went in their gowns to Charing Cross to meet them.[644] 'Tis remarkable that it was never in the minds of the army to carry it on

---

1647), BL, E404/4, pp. 3–4. For other accounts of the Guildhall incident, see *The army anatomized* (4 December 1647), BL, E419/6, p. 24; *Two petitions from the City of London* (12 October 1647), BL, E401/20, pp. 4–5.

[642] For those members who fled to the army after the Presbyterian 'riots' of 26 July, see *Old parliamentary history*, xxvi. 241–4.

[643] The ministers delivered their message firstly to the Lords and Commons on 2 August and then to common council: *LJ*, ix. 368; *CJ*, v. 265; Mitchell and Struthers (eds.), *Minutes of the Westminster assembly*, pp. 407–8.

[644] CLRO, Jor. 40, fo. 251v.

so far, but were brought to it, one thing after another, and that by the design of their enemies, and were always confident of success.

Never was the king nearer the enjoyment of his desires to return to London upon a clear board; which, had it been done, we had been all ruined, and so great misery would have fallen upon all honest men – nay upon all that had adhered to the parliament – as is not to b'expressed, being to attend the revenge of so bitter enemies. And if in anything or at any time the compassions of God were strongly moving for this kingdom and City since this war began, 'twas at this time.

All the reformadoes and grand incendiaries were in a moment slunk away and not to be found; and, which was observable, not an ingenious man that was engaged in it yet was willing to own it, all looking back upon the danger escaped.

The parliament being again settled, the army had a great desire to give a testimony of their integrity. Whereas they were reported to be a plundering army, [fo. 119] it should appear to the contrary. And therefore did march in at <u>Tyburn</u> [crossed out] Hyde Park fort and through Cheapside over the bridge<with bag and baggage, and artillery etc.>in so great order and civility that 'twas not heard of so much as an apple took by any of them – to the great admiration of all that beheld them.[645] And, to speak the truth, they were able-bodied men, especially the horse, and most within 40 years of age. But it wrought 2 notable impressions in their enemies: one was that whereas they were reported to be 30 or 40,000, they marched not more through than 12,000 horse and foot (a great part of them were commanded out on other employment and were not there); and [that they were] very poorly armed – scarce a footman had a sword or good musket, or the horse any pistols etc.[646]

And then apprehended this to be done in way of triumph, as to conquered people, which was abhorred in the very thought of it. And every day began more and more to talk against the army and their proceedings; especially when the parliament began to question many citizens, the lord mayor and several aldermen (their own members being shipped for Calais), and talked of laying a great fine upon the City.

[fo. 119v] That which did very much occasion a repining against the army was that they took up their quarters roundabout London, and so made the citizens sensible of free quarter and brought them

---

[645] Other contemporary accounts of the army's conduct on 7 August are similarly favourable: CLRO, Jor. 40, fo. 252; BL, Add. Ms. 37,344, fo. 104; Gentles, pp. 193–4.

[646] It has been suggested that the soldiers had piled their weapons into carts so as to be less frightening to the citizens: Gentles, p. 495 n. 32.

more to be acquainted with their carriage and humours than ever; interrupted them at their country houses. Insomuch that now the [sic] was a general complaint, and the mouths of very many were opened; especially when, through this discontent, trading did very much abate.

Not many days after the army passed through London, Sir Thomas was made constable of the Tower and appointed Colonel [Robert] Tichborne the lieutenant;[647] was [sic] did very much startle the City. And then there was part of the army for the guard of the Tower until a regiment was raised for that purpose. This put the merchants into discontent and ordered their bullion for Holland.

The (11) [inserted] members, [having] most of them got out of the kingdom [and] shipped for Calais, were overtaken and stayed and then brought before [Sir William] Batten, who lay in the Downs; were dismissed, showing pass from the speaker (though it after cost Batten his place) when they came ashore. Sir Philip Stapilton [fell? – Ms. torn] sick and, being come to a lodging, in a few days died (as 'tis said) of the plague, which was very unfortunate for them, [fo. 120] for they forced them immediately to re-embark at a great charge and also to pay down so much money for having, as they pretended, brought the plague thither. Then made them pay an extraordinary fee to the physician that did visit him, besides to the host for bringing the sickness into his house and so prejudicing him. And for burial, carried him out upon a common bier and buried him in a common place. Thus died that brave and valiant wise Stapilton, to the great grief of all his friends and his enemies too.[648] The General Essex's and his deaths were the ruin of their party <[marginal note to the above lines] 'Tis observable that my Lord Essex hearse was strangely disfigured by an unknown man; pretended God commanded him to do it>

The rest went into Holland where they [met? – Ms. torn] with inhuman affronts from the fugitive [Ms. torn] letters which, in ordinary apprehension, was an omen upon them and spake them very unfortunate. The solicitor [crossed out] recorder remained and was committed to the Tower, as also Sir John Maynard and Colonel Copley. Anthony Nicoll was taken but did afterwards escape away. He confessed that he only intended the disbanding of the army, but no new war; but affirmed that the ministers were the men that did continually importune

---

[647] Fairfax was appointed on 6 August and Tichborne on 9 August 1647: *CJ*, v. 269; *LJ*, ix. 375, 379; Rushworth, vii. 760–61.

[648] *A perfect diurnall* (16–23 August 1647), BL, E518/21, p. 1708; *Perfect occurrences* (20–27 August 1647), BL, E518/23, p. 232; *A short and true narrative of the departure from England, sickness and death of Sir Philip Stapilton* (18 August 1647), BL, E409/3.

them to it by virtue of their covenant. [That? – Ms. torn] they were resolved to send the army into Ireland, but the ministers would not, lest they [i.e. the Independents] should possess that to themselves.[649]

[fo.120v–121v: blank]

---

[649] The first account of Nicoll's words to be published appears to have been in October 1647: Hugh Peter, *A word to the army. And two words to the kingdom* (11 October 1647), BL, E410/16, p. 6.

APPENDICES

1. THE WILL OF JOHN JUXON, SENIOR[650]

In the name of God amen, the seventeenth day of August anno domini 1626 and in the second year of the reign of our sovereign lord Charles by the grace of God of England, Scotland, France and Ireland king, defender of the faith, etc. I, John Juxon, citizen and merchant tailor of London, being in perfect health, mind and memory, for which I give Almighty God most hearty thanks, and remembering the great statute of heaven that all men must die, and considering the uncertainty of the time thereof, and how troublesome and uncomfortable it is to defer and put off the settling and disposing of such my worldly estate as it hath pleased God to bless me withal, and the declaration of my mind, will, purpose and desire concerning the ordering thereof until I be surprised by death or sickness, do make and ordain this my last will and testament in manner and form following, absolutely revoking hereby all other wills and testaments by me heretofore made whatsoever.

And first of all I commend and commit my soul into the hands of Almighty God, in full assurance and confidence to be made partaker of eternal happiness in the life to come by the only merits, mediation and intercession of my Lord and Saviour Jesus Christ. And my body to be decently buried in the daytime in the church of such parish wherein I shall happen to die. And further, I will and ordain that fifty poor men may have eleven shillings apiece to provide every of them respectively a good comely gown of black cloth to wear and go with my body to the grave. Item, I give and allow twenty pounds to be expended upon a dinner for such of the company of merchant taylors as be of the livery thereof, and shall go with my body to the church in the afternoon. And I desire that the company's almsmen that be in the house near the hall may there dine with the said company, and that the said dinner may be served in at one course. Item, I give five pounds to Christ's hospital to have fourscore of the boys there to go with my body to church, and my further will is that they also have bread as in such cases is used. Item, I will that thirty and five pounds shall be expended upon a dinner for my kindred and other my friends that shall be invited to go with my body to church in the afternoon and to have the dinner served in at one course.

[650] PRO, PROB 11/150/112.

Item, I give to my loving mother, Mrs Sara Sheppard, during her life twenty pounds per annum to be issuing and paid yearly out of the overplus of my rents of my messuage and tenements in Moore Lane in the parish of St Giles without Cripplegate, and to be paid unto her by equal portions at such times as the rents of the same houses or tenements are now payable and reserved unto me by the leases hereof made. And the first payment thereof to be made and begin at such of the said times as shall first and next happen to come or be after my decease.

Item, I give and bequeath to my Aunt Smallwood during her life also five pounds per annum to be issuing and paid yearly out of the said overplus of the said rents of the said messuage or tenements which are in Moore Lane aforesaid, and to be paid unto her by equal portions in such manner as the said twenty pounds per annum is set down and appointed to be paid to my said mother as aforesaid.

Item, I do give and bequeath unto my son John Juxon all the said overplus of the said rents of the said messuages or tenements which are in Moore Lane aforesaid for and during the first three whole years after my decease (my said mother, Sara Sheppard, and my said Aunt Smallwood being paid their said several and respective parts thereof as aforesaid).

Item, I do give and bequeath unto my daughter Elizabeth Juxon all the said overplus of the same rents of the said messuages or tenements from and after the end and expiration of the said last mentioned three years unto the full end of other three years then next following (my said mother, Sara Sheppard, and Aunt Smallwood being paid etc ... as aforesaid).

Item, I give and bequeath to my son Thomas Juxon all the said overplus of the same rents of the said messuages or tenements from and after the end and expiration of the said last mentioned three years until the full end of other three years then next ensuing (my said mother, Mrs Sara Sheppard, and Aunt Smallwood being paid etc ... as aforesaid).

Item, I do give and bequeath to my daughter Sara Juxon all the said overplus of the same rents of the said messuages or tenements from and after the end and expiration of the said last mentioned three years, until the full end of other three years then next ensuing (my said mother, Sara Sheppard, and Aunt Smallwood being paid etc ... as aforesaid).

Item, I do give and bequeath to my son Joseph Juxon all the said overplus of the same rents of the said messuages or tenements from and after the end and expiration of the said last mentioned three years, until the full end of five years then next ensuing (my said mother, Sara Sheppard, and Aunt Smallwood being paid etc ... as aforesaid).

Item, I do give and bequeath unto such child that my now wife shall have by me, and if she shall have none such, then to my son Joseph, his executors and assigns, all the said overplus of the same rents of the said messuages or tenements, from and after the end and expiration of the said last mentioned five years, until the full end and term of all the years which shall be then to come in the lease which I now have of the same messuages or tenements. But if my said wife shall not bring forth a child living that she now goeth withal, then all the said overplus of the same rents of the said messuages or tenements from and after the end and expiration of the said last mentioned five years given unto my said son Joseph Juxon shall be divided amongst those of my said children as shall be then living.

Item, I do give to my sister Mrs Mary Whitehead twenty pounds in money and the overplus of the rent of a house which I hold by lease in Walbrook, in London, wherein one Edward Hewlen, shoemaker, now dwelleth, being now eight pounds per annum over and above the rent reserved and payable out of the same to the parson and church-wardens of the parish of St Stephen's in Walbrook, London, or to the lessors thereof for and during so much of the term mentioned in the said lease as shall be to come at the time of my decease (if she shall so long live); she, during the time as she shall hold the same, performing the covenants in the said lease specified on the lessee's part to be performed, the payment of the rent thereby reserved to be paid to the lessors only excepted. But if she shall happen to die before the expiration of the said lease, then I give and bequeath the said overplus of the said rent to my brother Raph Juxon for and during so much of the term as shall be to come in the said lease at the time of the death of the said Mary Whitehead (if he shall be then living and shall live so long), he performing the covenants in the said lease as aforesaid (except before excepted). But if he shall not be living at the time of the death of my said sister or shall die before the expiration of the said lease, then I give and bequeath the overplus of the said rent to my brother Rowland Juxon for and during so much of the term as shall be to come in the said lease at the time of the death of the said Raph Juxon or Mary Whitehead, which of them shall last happen (if the said Rowland Juxon shall be then living and shall live so long), he performing the covenants in the said lease as aforesaid (except before excepted). But if the said Mary Whitehead, Raph Juxon and Rowland Juxon shall happen to die before the expiration of the said lease, then I give and bequeath the said lease and the residue of the term which shall be to come therein at the time of the last dying of them unto and amongst my own five children and the survivors of them, equally to be divided amongst them.

Item, I will that the sum of twenty pounds shall be employed, and the benefit thereof to and for the use and behoof of my brother Raph Juxon, in such sort as my loving friend Mr Stephen Denison (if he shall live; if not, then as my brother Arthur Juxon) shall think fit. Also I give to my said brother Rowland Juxon the sum of twenty pounds more to be given to himself.

Item, I give and bequeath to my sister Mrs Anne Bigge the sum of twenty pounds to be by her given and paid unto her daughter Anne Bigge the day of her marriage.

Item, I give and bequeath unto my brother Arthur Juxon the sum of thirty pounds.

Item, I give and bequeath unto my brother Matthew Sheppard ten pounds.

Item, I give and bequeath unto Richard Juxon, the son of my said brother Rowland Juxon, the sum of ten pounds towards placing him an apprentice with some honest, religious tradesman at the discretion of my said brother Arthur Juxon.

Item, I give and bequeath to mine especial friend Mr Stephen Denison[651] the overplus of the rent of an house which I hold by lease in the parish of St Margaret Moses in Friday Street, London, over and above the rent reserved and payable out of the same to the lessors thereof for and during so much of the term mentioned in the said lease as shall be to come at the time of my decease (if he shall so long live); he during the time as he shall hold the same performing the covenants in the said lease specified on the lessee's part to be performed, the payment of the rent thereby reserved to be paid to the lessors only excepted. But if he shall happen to die before the expiration of the said lease, then I give and bequeath the overplus of the said rent to my son Joseph Juxon for and during so much of the term as shall be to come in the said lease at the time of the death of the said Stephen Denison (if he shall be then living and shall live so long), he performing the covenants in the said lease as aforesaid (except before excepted). But if he shall not be living at the time of the death of the said Stephen Denison, or shall die before the expiration of the said lease, then I give and bequeath the said lease and the residue of the term which shall be to come therein at the time of the last dying of them unto my executor hereunder named. But if the said Stephen Denison shall live until the expiration of the said lease, then I give unto him ten pounds per annum to be paid him out of the rents, issues and profits of the lands and tenements which I bought off Anthony Calcott alias Calcocke, lying and being in the parish of Mortlake in the county of Surrey, yearly at two feasts or terms in the year, (that is to say) All Saints and St Philip

---

[651] Denison was curate of St Katherine Cree at the time and had lived in the Juxon household for twelve years or more: above, p. 6 n. 32.

and Jacob, by equal portions so long as the said Stephen Denison shall live.

Item, I give to so many of the godly ministers hereunder named as shall be living at the time of my decease the several sums of four pounds apiece hereafter mentioned to wear mourning gowns and to go with my body to the church at the time of burial: that is to say, to the said Stephen Denison four pounds, to Mr Richard Sibbes[652] four pounds, to Mr John Spendlove four pounds, to Mr [blank] Holbrooke four pounds, to Mr [Nathaniel] Culverwell[653] four pounds, to Mr [blank] Richardson four pounds, to Mr [blank] Watson four pounds, to my brother Rowland Juxon four pounds, to Mr [Elias] Crabtree[654] four pounds, to Mr [blank] Merriall four pounds, and to Mr George Landford[655] four pounds.

Item, I give and bequeath to Mr Alderman Rainton and his wife, Mr William Haynes, my father and mother Sheppard, my father and mother Kirrell, to each of these seven persons four pounds apiece to buy mourning cloth and to go with my body to the church at the time of my burial.

Item, I give and bequeath to my brother Bigge and his wife, my brother and sister Whitehead, my brother Raph Juxon and his wife, my brother Arthur Juxon and his wife, my brother Matthew Sheppard and his wife, and my Aunt Smallwood, to these eleven persons last mentioned to each of them three pounds to buy mourning cloth and to go with my body to church at the time of my burial. Also my will is that all our children and servants have mourning cloth. And as for any other money for mourning or mourning cloth to be given to any other person or persons, I leave to be disposed and given as my executor and overseers shall think fit. And my express will and meaning is that if any of the parties above named to whom I have given any legacy (not otherwise hereby specially by me disposed of) shall not be living at the time of my decease, then I will and bequeath his, her, or their legacies to be equally divided and paid to and amongst my own five children and the survivors of them which shall be then living.

Item, I give and bequeath to my servant Thomas Warren, if he be dwelling with me at the time of my decease, ten pounds.

---

[652] Richard Sibbes, as preacher at Gray's Inn and elsewhere, was one of the most popular and influential puritan divines of his generation: Greaves and Zaller, iii. 169–71.

[653] Nathaniel Culverwell was a popular London preacher: P. Collinson, *The religion of Protestants: the church in English society 1559–1625* (Oxford, 1982), p. 244.

[654] Elias Crabtree was curate of St Lawrence Pountney and was to be articled against in high commission and cited before Laud in January 1632 to be warned to conform: A. G. Matthews, *Calamy revised* (Oxford, 1934), p. 140.

[655] George Landford was vicar of Mortlake, Surrey, in 1617–30: Venn and Venn, *Alumni Cantabrigienses*, pt. 1, ii. 43.

Item, I give and bequeath to the churchwardens of the parish church of Mortlake in the county of Surrey which shall be at the time of my decease and to their successors for ever one annuity or yearly rent of five pounds and four shillings to be issuing out of all my lands and tenements which I purchased off the said Anthony Calcott alias Calcocke, lying and being in the parish of Mortlake, to be paid at the said two feasts or terms in the year, that is to say, All Saints and St Philip and Jacob, by even and equal portions; and for not payment thereof accordingly to distrain for the same and the arrearage thereof (if any shall be) and such distress to keep and detain until thereof they be satisfied. I will that the said churchwardens and their successors for the time being for ever shall, upon the sabbath day in every week in the forenoon after morning prayer or the sermon in the said church ended, pay out thereof to four poor widows six pence apiece which are or shall be placed to be in four houses or rooms in the said parish of Mortlake now or hereafter to be appointed by me; and if it shall happen any of the poor widows which shall be so placed in any of the said four houses or rooms at the time of my decease, or any other that shall succeed them, or any of them, to die or be for just cause removed or put out, then I will that the said Mr Stephen Denison, if he shall be living, if not, that then my heirs and assigns for the time being, shall have the nomination or appointing of some other widow or widows (always having two of the said four widows to be inhabitants in the said parish of Mortlake, and the other two to be taken out of London – preferring my own kindred if any of them be capable and desire it) in the place or stead of her or them that so shall die or be removed or put out.

Item, I give and bequeath to the said churchwardens of the said parish church of Mortlake, and their successors for ever, one other annuity or yearly rent of three pounds eighteen shillings per annum to be issuing and paid out of the said lands and tenements last above mentioned at the two feasts or terms aforesaid by the portions aforesaid and to distrain and the distress to keep and detain as aforesaid; which being to them paid or satisfied as aforesaid I will that the churchwardens and their successors for the time being for ever shall therewith buy, provide and deliver to and for the said four poor widows these things following in manner and form as hereafter is specified: (that is to say) for every one of them at the end of three years after my decease, and so at the end of every three years then next and consequently following, one gown of broadcloth with these letters J J embroidered with silver thereon, that is to say, on each side of the breast one of the said letters, every of the said gowns with the embroidering to be worth or to cost thirty shillings; and also to buy, provide and deliver to and for every one of the said widows every year yearly at the end of one year next after my decease, and so at the end of every year then next and consequently following for ever, one pair of cloth stockings worth two shillings, one pair of shoes worth two shillings, and one smock worth three shillings.

Item, I give and my will and mind is that the several sums of money hereafter mentioned shall be yearly for ever at the feast of St Thomas the Apostle well and truly out of the issues or profits of the said lands and tenements by me purchased off the said Anthony Calcott alias Calcocke paid as hereafter is mentioned: that is to say, twenty shillings towards the releasing of one person yearly out of Ludgate prison in London, and twenty shillings more to the two hospitals, the one at Hammersmith the other at Knightsbridge, in the county of Middlesex. And further I give, and my will and mind is, that the several sums of money hereafter also mentioned shall be yearly for ever after my decease at two feasts or terms in the year, (that is to say) the Annunciation of the blessed virgin Mary and St Michael the Archangel, by even and equal portions out of the said lands and tenements by me purchased off the said Anthony Calcott alias Calcocke paid for the better maintaining of the lectures following, so long as they shall continue: (that is to say) to him that is or shall be appointed to preach the lecture about six or seven of the clock on every Sunday morning at Allhallows in Lombard Street, London, forty shillings (if it shall be performed and continued the whole year), if not then but twenty shillings; to him that is or shall be appointed to preach the lecture about five of the clock in the afternoon on every Monday at St Margaret's at New Fish Street Hill, London, forty shillings (if it shall be performed and continued the whole year), if not then but twenty shillings; to him that is or shall be appointed to preach the lecture about five a clock in the afternoon on every Tuesday at Allhallows the Great in Thames Street, London, forty shillings (if it shall be performed and continued the whole year), if not then but twenty shillings; to him that is or shall be appointed to preach the lecture about five of the clock in the afternoon on every Wednesday at St Mildred's in Bread Street, London, forty shillings (if it shall be performed and continued the whole year), if not then but twenty shillings; to him that is or shall be appointed to preach the lecture about five of the clock in the afternoon on every Thursday at the church in Little Eastcheap in London forty shillings (if it shall be performed and continued the whole year), if not then but twenty shillings; to him that is or shall be appointed to preach the lecture about five of the clock in the afternoon on every Friday at Rood church, near the west end of Tower Street, forty shillings (if it shall be performed and continued the whole year), if not then but twenty shillings; to Mr [John] Spendlove being now one of the lecturers at St Antholin's in London on Saturday at six of the clock in the morning (so long as he shall live) forty shillings; and after his decease I will that the like sum of forty shillings shall be every year yearly for ever at the feasts or terms above mentioned by even and equal portions paid equally and amongst those ministers that shall perform the morning lectures (I mean the appointed lecturers) at St Antholin's aforesaid on the week days so long as the said lectures shall continue. And my will and meaning is that if the said lectures shall not continue as aforesaid, that then so much of the said money as is aforesaid appointed to be paid for so many of the said lectures as shall not be so continued (in case they had been continued) shall be every year yearly given and paid by mine heirs and assigns at the feast of All Saints unto the master and wardens of the company of merchant taylors in London, and their successors for the time being for ever, and by the said master and wardens and their successors paid according as they shall think fit at or before the feast of St Thomas the Apostle to some poor scholars, the one year in Oxford and the other year in Cambridge, for ever.

Item, I give the sum of five pounds (which I lent towards a stock for corn for the company of merchant taylors) to be given to and amongst the poor widows placed in the company's almshouses near Tower Hill.

Item, I give and bequeath to the company of merchant taylors in London one gilt pot with a cover with three several plates of gold enamelled set on the same to add to the plate belonging to the hall (which pot is amongst my plate).

Item, I give to my loving wife Judith Juxon nine hundred pounds in money, which (if she will) shall be continued in trade in the sugarhouse in Walbrook, London, or elsewhere in co-partnership with my brother Arthur Juxon for four years (if she so long remain a widow); and also that she shall then have her dwelling in the said sugarhouse for four years, the rent to be paid out of the stock; and also that she shall have the house which I now dwell in at East Sheen in the said county of Surrey, and the orchards and gardens and outhousing therewith now used by me, and four several small closes lying near to the same, containing by estimation eleven acres, be they more or less, for the said four years to dwell in and use, but not to let or anyway to dispose of otherwise, and so as she remain a widow the said four years. But if my wife will not be pleased to suffer the said nine hundred pounds to continue in trade and co-partnership as aforesaid, then I will and ordain that the said nine hundred shall be paid her within six months next after my decease.

Item, I will that my said wife shall have and hold all my messuages and tenements with the appurtenances situated and being in the parish of St Lawrence Pountney in London for and during her natural life; she maintaining the same in sufficient reparations and discharging the same of such charges as are incident and belonging unto them.

Item, I give and bequeath unto my said wife all such goods, chattels, household stuff and implements of household as she brought to me, and all such chains and jewels which she had either before her marriage with me or sithence of my gift, and one furniture of taffeta for a bed and velvet pillows, chairs and stools with velvet, and chairs and stools of needlework wrought by herself and her servants, and a bason and ewer of silver parcel gilt and a pot with a cover of silver to make a posset in with three feet.

Item, I will and ordain that Nicholas Lawrence, my said wife's son, shall have his portion, being two hundred three-score six pounds, thirteen shillings, four pence, and the sum of thirty-three pounds, six shillings and eight pence more to make it up three hundred pounds, paid unto him at the end of eight months next after my decease.

Item, I will and ordain that Thomas Lawrence, one other son of my said wife, shall have his portion made up also the like sum of three hundred pounds and paid unto him at the end of ten months next after my decease.

Item, I will and ordain that William Lawrence, one other son of my said wife shall have his portion made up also the like sum of three hundred pounds and paid unto him at the end of twelve months next after my decease.

Item, I give and bequeath unto my sister Anne Rainton two hundred pounds to be paid unto her as followeth: (that is to say) one hundred pounds thereof at the day of her marriage, and the other hundred pounds thereof at the end of twelve months next after her marriage (if she shall be then living). But if she shall not be then living, then I give and bequeath the said last mentioned hundred pounds to and amongst so many of my own five children as shall be living at the end of one year next after her marriage equally; and if the said Anne Rainton shall be married before my decease, then I will that this gift and legacy to her shall be void.

And also I will that all such legacies as I have given to my kindred and others in money (except for mourning as aforesaid) shall be paid at the end of fifteen months next after my decease or sooner if conveniently they or any of them may be.

Also I do will and ordain that my adventure in the East India Company shall be, with such convenient speed as may be, sold for the better payment of my legacies, and if need be to do it within the time limited for the payment of them; and what shall remain so unpaid of the money coming of the sale of my said adventure, I will and ordain that it shall be made up fifteen hundred pounds and put into stock with my said brother Arthur Juxon and my wife (if she will be a co-partner as aforesaid) – if not then with my said brother Arthur Juxon – and that it with the profits and proceed [sic] thereof shall be so employed for the joint use and benefit of my own five children and the survivors of them for and during the space of four years, and at the end of the same four years I will that the said fifteen hundred pounds and the profits and proceed thereof shall be paid equally to and amongst my own five children and the survivors of them.

Also I will and ordain that all my goods, chattels, household stuff, plate, jewels and implements of household whatsoever (other than those formerly given and bequeathed to my wife, and such as are now or shall be needful to be used about the refining of sugar and that trade) shall be sold within a convenient time after my decease, and the money thereof coming or made to be paid to and amongst my own five children or the survivors of them at the discretion of my overseers hereunder named.

Item, I give to the common poor five pounds to be paid to each of them three pence apiece.

Item, I do give and bequeath to the collectors of the poor of the parish of Mortlake which shall be at the end of six months next after my decease the sum of ten pounds to buy fourteen chaldrons of sea coals at the time of the year when they are best cheap, and to sell them again to the poor when they are dearest in the same year or in the hard time of winter at that rate which will make up the whole stock of ten pounds aforesaid and no dearer; that so it may remain for ever to do them good in time of need.

Item, I do give and bequeath unto my son John Juxon the great house now in the tenure or occupation of George Langham, citizen and merchant taylor of London, and also the manors or lordships of East Sheen and Westhall in the said county of Surrey, and all and singular messuages, lands, tenements and hereditaments with all and singular the appurtenances to the same manors or lordships appertaining, which I heretofore purchased off John Whitfield, gentleman, lying and being in Mortlake aforesaid or elsewhere in the county of Surrey (except and always reserved one close wherein I have lately built a brick house, and one orchard adjoining or being near to the same brick house, and one close called Brick Close and one other close called Stilegate Close, containing together by estimation five acres, be they more or less). And also I do give and bequeath unto my said son John Juxon all and singular my messuages, lands, tenements and hereditaments which I heretofore purchased off the said Anthony Calcott alias Calcocke, with the appurtenances and the reversion and reversions of the same; and also one wood or parcel of wood ground lying and being in the said parish of Mortlake next or near to a lane there called Hartleton Lane, containing by estimation twelve acres, one rood and twenty perches be it more or less. To have and to hold all and singular the premises with the appurtenances to my said son John

Juxon as aforesaid mentioned to be given and bequeathed (except before excepted) to him my said son John Juxon and the heirs of his body lawfully to be begotten; and for default of such heirs, then to my said son Thomas Juxon and the heirs of his body lawfully to be begotten; and for default of such heirs, then to my said son Joseph Juxon and to the heirs of his body lawfully to be begotten; and for default of such heirs, then to my right heirs for ever.

Item, I do give and bequeath unto my said son Thomas Juxon the new brick house now in my own occupation with all the housing on the north side thereof situated, lying and being in East Sheen in the said parish of Mortlake, together with the orchards, gardens and yard about the same house; and one little close on the north side of the said brick house late in the occupation of one Robert Chalkhill and now in my own occupation and was heretofore purchased by me off William Childe, citizen and scrivener of London; and also the said close called Brick Close and the said close called Stilegate Close and also one other close containing by estimation seven acres, be it more or less, by me heretofore purchased off Thomas Frith and lying on the east part of the said brick house; and also a little pightell lying near to the said brick house heretofore by me purchased off the said William Childe and lying on the west part of the said Brick Close; and also all the lands which was lately in the tenure or occupation of the said Robert Chalkhill, and now in the tenure or occupation of Edward Man and Edward Burges, together with the barn that standeth in the upper part of East Sheen near unto a cottage in the occupation of one Edward Pate, which lands containeth by estimation four-score and two acres, be it more or less; and also one coppice called Shorthorne Coppice containing by estimation sixteen acres, two roods and five perches, be it more or less. All which premises are situated, lying and being in the said parish of Mortlake in the county of Surrey aforesaid, to have and to hold to my said son Thomas Juxon and the heirs of his body lawfully begotten or to be begotten; and for the default of such heirs, then to my said son John Juxon and the heirs of his body lawfully begotten or to be begotten (if my said son John Juxon shall be living at the time of the decease of my said son Thomas Juxon). But if my said son John Juxon shall be then dead, then I give and bequeath all and singular the premises (given and bequeathed as aforesaid to my said son Thomas Juxon) to my daughter Sara Juxon and to the heirs of her body lawfully begotten or to be begotten; and for default of such heirs, then to my son Joseph Juxon and to the heirs of his body lawfully begotten or to be begotten; and for default of such heirs, then to my right heirs for ever.

Item, I do give and bequeath unto my said son Joseph Juxon all those my lands, tenements and appurtenances which I lately bought and purchased off Miles Frith and Thomas Frith, or either or any of them, lying or being in Mortlake, East Sheen or elsewhere in the county of Surrey, both freehold and copyhold, to have and to hold to my said son Joseph Juxon and to the heirs of his body lawfully begotten or to be begotten; and for default of such heirs, then to my daughter Sara Juxon and to the heirs of her body lawfully begotten or to be begotten; and for default of such heirs, then to the child which my said wife Judith doth now bear in her body, whether it be son or daughter, and to the heirs of his or her body lawfully begotten or to be begotten; and for default of such heirs, then to my right heirs for ever. Item, I give and bequeath unto my daughter Elizabeth Juxon all my messuages, houses, lands, tenements and hereditaments with the appurtenances situated, lying and being in Islington in the county of Middlesex, which I purchased off one Stephen Boone, to have and to hold to the said Elizabeth Juxon and to the heirs of her body lawfully begotten and to be begotten; and for default of such heirs, then to my daughter Sara Juxon and to the heirs of her body lawfully begotten or to be begotten; and for default of such heirs, then to my said son John Juxon and to the heirs of his body lawfully begotten or to be begotten; and for default of such heirs, then to my right heirs for ever. Also I do give and bequeath unto my said daughter Elizabeth one messuage or tenement with the orchard, garden and appurtenances thereunto belonging now in the occupation of John Kirrell situated, lying and being in the parish of Mortlake in the said county of Surrey to have and to hold to her and her assigns for and during the natural life of the said Elizabeth.

Item, I do give and bequeath unto my daughter Sara Juxon (if she be living after the decease of my said daughter Elizabeth) the said messuage or tenement with the orchard, garden and appurtenances in the occupation of the said John Kirrell for and during the natural life of the said Sara; and after her decease, then to my right heirs for ever.

Item, I give unto my said daughter Sara Juxon one messuage or tenement and two closes with the appurtenances late in the occupation of Sir William Foster, knight, and now in the occupation of John Wilde; and one other messuage or tenement now in the occupation of John Hill, smith, together with the barn and land with the appurtenances thereunto belonging, now being in the occupation of one Miles Frith; and also one little wood or coppice in a place called Shorthorne containing by estimation four acres, one rood and thirty-two perches, be it more or less, and is lying or being in Mortlake aforesaid, being in the occupation of Manasses Watford and George Frith, and were all lately purchased off William Childe of London, scrivener, being in the parish of Mortlake aforesaid, to have and to hold to the said Sara Juxon and to the heirs of her body lawfully begotten or to be begotten; and for default of such heirs, then to the child which my said wife now beareth in her body and to the heirs of that child lawfully begotten or to be begotten; and for default of such heirs, then to my right heirs for ever.

Item, I give and bequeath unto such child as my now wife shall have by me, and if she shall have none, then to my son Joseph, a little house situate and being in Mortlake at or near a gate called Dog Gate wherein one Arthur James now dwelleth, and the land lying to or used with it; and one cottage situate and being in Mortlake aforesaid near unto the same little house wherein one [blank] Huggott now dwelleth; and also one other cottage situate and being in Mortlake aforesaid wherein one Daniel Wingrove now dwelleth; and also one messuage or tenement and the lands with the appurtenances which Mr Henry Wethesfield holdeth of me by lease situate, lying and being in Mortlake aforesaid; and also a parcel of land containing by estimation eight acres with the appurtenances heretofore by me bought off William Childe and now in the occupation of Henry Bourne, lying and being in Mortlake aforesaid; and also one other parcel of land containing by estimation three acres two roods, be it more or less, heretofore also by me bought off the said William Childe and is now in the occupation of Hugh Woolmer, lying and being in Mortlake aforesaid; and another close in the occupation of Thomas Addams lying between the great yard of Miles Frith of the one part, and the land now or late in the occupation of Saywell, widow, of the other part; and also that coppice or wood lying or being near a place called Hartleton and containing by estimation twenty-two acres, two roods and five perches, be it more or less; and also one cottage with a close with the appurtenances now in the occupation of Edward Pate, to have and to hold to such child if she shall have any whether it be son or daughter; and if I shall have none such by her, then to my son Joseph and to his or her heirs lawfully begotten or to be begotten; and for default of such heirs, then to my said daughter Sara Juxon and to the heirs of her body lawfully begotten or to be begotten; and for default of such heirs, then to my said son John Juxon and to the heirs of his body lawfully begotten or to be begotten; and for default of such heirs, then to my right heirs for ever.

Item, I do give more unto my said daughter Sara Juxon all the land which I heretofore bought off William Jeffray which are lying and being in Mortlake aforesaid, to have and to hold to the said Sara Juxon and to the heirs of her body lawfully begotten and to be begotten; and for default of such heirs, then to my son Thomas Juxon, and to the heirs of his body lawfully begotten or to be begotten; and for default of such heirs, then to my son John Juxon and to the heirs of his body lawfully begotten or to be begotten; and for default of such heirs, then to my right heirs for ever.

Item, I do give and bequeath unto my said daughter Elizabeth Juxon one messuage or tenement together with the land and appurtenances thereunto belonging now in the occupation of one George Stapleton, and one close now in the occupation of Thomas Garway, gentleman, heretofore by me bought off the said William Childe; and also one coppice or wood called Newgate Coppice containing by estimation two acres, one rood and thirty perches, be it more or less, which premises are situate, lying and being in the parish of Mortlake aforesaid, to have and to hold unto the said Elizabeth Juxon and to the heirs of her body lawfully begotten or to be begotten; and for default of such heirs, then to my said daughter Sara Juxon and to the heirs of her body lawfully begotten or to be begotten; and for default of such heirs, then to my son John Juxon and the heirs of his body lawfully begotten or to be begotten; and for default of such heirs, then to my son Thomas Juxon and to the heirs of his body lawfully begotten or to be begotten; and for default of such heirs, then to my son Joseph Juxon and to the heirs of his body lawfully begotten or to be begotten; and for default of such heirs, then to my right heirs for ever.

Item, I do give and bequeath unto my son Joseph Juxon all my said messuages and tenements with the appurtenances situate and being in the said parish of St Lawrence Pountney alias Poultney, to have and to hold from and immediately after the death of the said Judith my wife unto the said Joseph Juxon and to the heirs of his body lawfully to be begotten; and for default of such heirs, then to such child as my now wife shall have by me; and if she shall have no such child, then to my son Joseph and to the heirs of his or her body lawfully begotten or to be begotten; and for default of such heirs, then to my son John Juxon and to the heirs of his body lawfully begotten or to be begotten; and for default of such heirs, then to my son Thomas Juxon and to the heirs of his body lawfully begotten or to be begotten; and for default of such heirs, then to my daughter Elizabeth Juxon and to the heirs of her body lawfully begotten or to be begotten; and for default of such heirs, then to my daughter Sara Juxon and the heirs of her body lawfully begotten or to be begotten; and for default of such heirs, then to my right heirs for ever. Provided always and notwithstanding any gift, legacy or bequest by me hereby given or bequeathed of any my messuages, lands, tenements or hereditaments, or any the appurtenances herein before mentioned, to any person or persons whatsoever or otherwise given howsoever, my will and mind is that all and every sum and sums of money which I have heretofore given, bequeathed, limited or appointed to be paid or employed to or for any person or persons, or any use or uses whatsoever out of the manors, lordships, messuages, lands, tenements, rents or hereditaments whatsoever above specified, or any of them, shall be paid and had in manner and form as before by me is intended, mentioned and declared by this my last will and testament, and according to my true intent and meaning concerning the same, although for brevity's sake I have not disposed so fully, plainly and largely thereof as the case might require.

Item, I do give and bequeath unto my said son John Juxon his executors and assigns, all the rest and residue of my personal estate whatsoever not hereby by me given, bequeathed, disposed or appointed. And lastly I do make and ordain my said son John Juxon my sole and only executor of this my last will and testament, and William Haynes, goldsmith of London, and the said Arthur Juxon his tutors, and to be administrators of all my goods and chattels, rights and credits which shall belong unto me at the time of my death, until he, my said son John Juxon, may in respect of his now minority prove and take upon him the execution of this my last will and testament according to the laws of this realm. And I do request my loving friends the said John Kirrell and Arthur Juxon, and also the above-named Stephen Denison and William Haynes, to be my overseers of the same. And I do give to every of my said overseers for their pains to be taken therein the sum of five pounds. In witness whereof to every sheet of this my last will and testament, containing with this last sheet ten sheets, I have subscribed my name and set my seal dated the day and year first above written, John Juxon, subscribed, sealed, published and declared to be the last will and testament of the said John Juxon the testator in the presence of us, F. Langhorne, Arthur Juxon, Raphe Edgerton, Mary Stevens, Margaret Marsh.

A note of what my brother John Juxon did the 22th of August 1626 will to be given to several persons not named in his will. And first to Mr Landford ten pounds; to Mr Thomas Stephens and his wife five pounds apiece; to Mrs Margaret Marsh ten pounds; to his servant James Stint four pounds; to his maidservant Isbell [sic] forty shillings; to his maidservant Ellen forty shillings. Moreover, that Mr Landford shall have his dwelling in the rooms he now occupieth rent free during so long time as he shall continue minister at Mortlake and preach twice every sabbath day.

Decimo octavo die mensis Septembris anno domini millesimo sexcentesimo vicesimo sexto emanavit commissio Arthuro Juxon patruo ac unum tutorium testamentariorum Johannis Juxon filii dicti defuncti et executoris in huius testamento nominat Ad administrandum bona iura et credita dicti defuncti iuxta tenorem et effectum testamenti et codicilli eiusdem defuncti durante minori etate dicti Johannis Juxon filii dicti defuncti et executoris antedicti de bene et fidelitate administrandum eadem Ad sancta Dei evangelia jurat.[656]

---

[656] The 18th day of September, A.D. 1626, commission issued to Arthur Juxon, uncle

<[margin] Probatum fuit huiusmodi testamentum coram venerabili viro domino Henrico Marten milite legum doctore commissario etc. vicesimo septimo die mensis Novembris anno domini 1635 juramento Johannis Juxon filii naturalis et legitimi dicti defuncti et executoris etc. cui etc. de bene etc. jurati litteris administrationis bonorum eiusdem defuncti cum eius testamento annexo alias Arthuro Juxon mensis Septembris anno domini 1626 auctoritate huius curiae durante minori etate dicti Johannis Juxon executoris predicti commissis racone plene etatis dicti executoris expiratis et cessatis.[657]

and guardian of the executor John Juxon son of the said deceased and the executor named in this will, for administration of the goods, rights and credits of the said deceased according to the tenor and effect of the will and codicil of the same deceased during the minority of the said John Juxon, son of the said deceased and executor aforesaid, having sworn an oath on God's holy gospels to well and faithfully administer the same.

[657] This will was proved before that worshipful man, Sir Henry Marten, knight, doctor of civil law, commissary [of the prerogative court of Canterbury], on the 27th day of November A.D. 1635, upon the oath of John Juxon, the natural and legitimate son of the said deceased person, and his executor [named in this will]. To whom [was granted the administration of all and every the goods, rights and credits of the same deceased person] after he swore an oath well [and faithfully to administer the same]. The letters of administration of the goods of the same deceased, with his will attached, granted on another occasion by the authority of this court to Arthur Juxon in September, A.D. 1626 because of the then minority of the said John Juxon, the aforesaid executor, have now expired and ceased to apply, owing to the majority of the said executor.

2 THE WILL OF THOMAS JUXON[658]

In the name of God amen, I Thomas Juxon, second son of Mr John Juxon late of East Sheen in the parish of Mortlake in the county of Surrey, being through the goodness of God in good health and memory, do make this may last will and testament as followeth. And first I do humbly lay hold upon the tender of salvation by Jesus Christ, who is the only saviour of mankind, that through His infinite goodness He will be pleased to pardon, cleanse and sanctify me throughout and present me unto God the Father at the great day of judgement clothed with His righteousness and discharged from all my debts by the satisfaction which He made in my nature unto the divine justice in His voluntary death upon the cross. And I do commit my immortal soul into the protection of the holy, blessed and undivided Trinity, Father, Son and Holy Ghost, three persons and one God, to be admitted into that state of glory which is the purchase of the holy Jesus, even the glorious liberty of the sons of God; a state totally freed from sin and from temptations and from all desires or inclinations to sin – a state of purity, of eternal and uninterrupted love, delight and praises of, in and to the undivided Trinity.

Secondly, I do dispose of my temporal estate in manner following. I do given and bequeath my mansion house in East Sheen aforesaid, with all the land thereunto belonging inclosed with a pale, unto my nephew Thomas Juxon during the life of my dear son William Juxon with the issues and profits, that he may be therewith enabled to maintain my said son with necessaries. And after the death of my dear son I give the said mansion house and lands unto his heirs for ever; I say unto the heirs of my son William Juxon for ever and not otherwise.

Item, whereas by a deed of feoffment dated the sixth of October 1670 made at Dublin between me Thomas Juxon, Standish Hartstrong and John Petty deceased, and my son William Juxon of the other part, I, the said Thomas Juxon, for the natural affection I bear unto my son did settle all my castles, houses and lands, with all and every of their appurtenances, situated, lying and being in the county of Limerick, unto him and to his heirs, paying thereout yearly the sum of one hundred pounds clear of all charges unto my dear daughter Elizabeth Juxon so long as she shall live unmarried, and also with liberty to me, the said Thomas Juxon, to alter the uses therein limited or to add other

[658] PRO, PROB 11/340/147

uses as in and by the said deed by me signed and left with the said John Petty doth and may more fully appear; in pursuance whereof I, the said Thomas Juxon, do hereby further after limit, direct, appoint. And I give unto my dear daughter Elizabeth Juxon for the natural affection I bear unto her all my said castles, houses and lands, with all and every their appurtenances, situated in the said county of Limerick and kingdom of Ireland and to her heirs for ever; to the intent that the said lands may be sold and that two thirds thereof may be to my dear son William Juxon when he shall be cured of his melancholy distemper (according to an agreement made by me with Mr Newton, where now he lodges) and not before, and to the heirs of my said son; and that he may be, in the meantime, maintained by my said daughter as she shall think good and not otherwise; and for want of heirs by my said son lawfully begotten then the moiety of the proceed of the said lands to my nephews Thomas Juxon and George Juxon of London, sons of my brother John Juxon deceased.

Item, whereas by a lease bearing date the seventh of October 1670 between me Thomas Juxon of the one part, and Sir Charles Meredith, knight, and Samuel Mollineux of the City of Dublin, esquire, of the other part, I did let and set unto the said Sir Charles Meredith and Samuel Mollineux for two years certain lands in the county of Meath and Queen's county in Ireland, and by a release bearing date the eighth of the said month and year I did release unto the said Sir Charles Meredith and Samuel Mollineux all my right etc. in and to the said lands in trust; nevertheless, and for the uses therein named, and for such other uses as I, the said Thomas Juxon, should by my last will and testament etc. declare as by the said release in the hands of Sir Charles Meredith may appear, in pursuance whereof I, the said Thomas Juxon, do hereby further limit, direct and appoint that in case I have no son by my dear wife then I give unto my dear daughter Elizabeth Juxon the lands of Dirpatrick set unto Robert Lutterrell, and the lands of the Grange set unto Thomas Hessam, for and during her natural life, and after her death to my said nephew Thomas Juxon and to his heirs; and in case I have no child by my dear wife then I do give unto my said dear daughter Elizabeth Juxon and to her heirs all the rest of the lands mentioned in the said lease and release. And I do further give unto my said daughter all the overplus of the rents and profits arising out of the lands before mentioned after the payment of three hundred pounds a year payable to my dear wife during her natural life, and after the payment of six pounds, six shilling, eight pence unto my dear sister Byfield for the term of twenty years, if she shall so long live; and after her death, during the remainder of the twenty years, the same to be paid to my nephew Tristram Davis and to his assigns; and also paying unto him, the said Tristram Davis, and to his assigns during the term of twenty years to come, yearly thirteen pounds, six shilling, four pence; which two sums make up £20 per annum – the rent of the land that my said nephew, in right of his wife, is to receive, that was sold to Colonel Thomas Coote and of which my said nephew released to him all his right, title and interest; which release is with Mr John Ramsay of Dublin in the exchequer. Out of the said £20 per annum my sister Sara Byfield hath a third part paid to her as before is said.

Item, my meaning, my mind and will is that the forementioned lands of Dirpatrick and of the Grange, after the death of my daughter Elizabeth Juxon, shall be to the heirs of my son William Juxon lawfully to be gotten before they come to my nephew Thomas Juxon; and for want of such heirs then to my said nephew Thomas Juxon and not otherwise; and that during the life of my said son they, my daughter and my nephew, shall maintain out of the said lands my said son as they shall think good and not otherwise; and for the rest of the lands shall be sold and the one moiety thereof be to the heirs of my son William Juxon lawfully begotten; and for default thereof the one half of the said moiety I give to the children of my dear sister Sara Byfield and the other moiety to the children of my cousins Matthew Sheppard, Nicholas Juxon and John Juxon.

Item, I give unto my dear daughter Elizabeth Juxon my leases and interest in the house and nursery in Mortlake with all the goods therein and thereunto belonging.

Item, I do give unto my dear wife one third part of what shall be recovered upon the statute staple of one thousand pounds from Colonel Thomas Coote unto me, and one third of what shall be recovered from his heirs etc. upon the non-performance of covenants made from him to me; and I do give unto my dear wife all my plate and goods in Dublin and going thither.

Item, I do give unto my nephew Timothy Byfield and to his heirs my farm of Barberies, with the appurtenances, lying in Danesbury in the county of Essex, and the sum of sixty pounds to repair the same and twelve pounds to pay the fine to the lord and other charges.

Item, I give unto my dear sister the rent of the lands which I bought of the Briggeses lying in the barony of Deece and county of Meath, being per annum cleared of all charges £21 16s. for and during her life; and I give unto the sons of my said sister, Timothy and Nathaniel, and to their heirs the said lands with like appurtenances.

Item, I give unto my niece Elizabeth Davis the sum of fifty pounds, to my niece Rebecca Jackson fifty pounds, to my niece Sara Byfield one hundred pounds out of the two thirds of the forementioned statute.

Item, I give the sum of twenty pounds to be laid out in erecting a monument in the remembrance of Maurice Carent, esquire, and the

Lady Elizabeth his wife, the father and mother of my dear wife deceased, in the church of Henstridge by Woodyates in the county of Dorset; provided that the lands of Toomer etc. do descend to my children and their heirs, my brother James Carent dying without children, according to the settlement made of the said estate with other land by the said Maurice Carent, esquire, and not otherwise.

Item, I will that there be erected in the church of Islington a marble in the wall near where my dear wife lies buried with this inscription: 'Here lies buried the body of Elizabeth Juxon late the wife of Thomas Juxon, esquire, daughter of Maurice Carent of Toomer Park in the county of Somerset, esquire, and the Lady Elizabeth his wife, the eldest daughter of James, earl of Marlborough, lord treasurer of England etc.[659] which said Elizabeth Juxon died the [blank] of September 1669 leaving two children, William and Elizabeth', over the said marble supported with flat columns my coat impaled with Carent and Toomer quarterly, the first argent, 3 hurtes charged with 3 chevernelles gules, the second argent, 3 bars wavy, gules and my crest upon a helmet etc. above the escutcheon.

Item, I give the sum of twelve pounds to be laid out in repairing the almshouses at East Sheen and for setting up a stone with father's coat and crest cut and coloured.

Item, I give to Christopher Cane, to Goodman Lee, to George Dally and to Goody Beavie fifty shillings to each of them; to Mr Brinsley's brother-in-law that lives in Old Brentford, to Dr Rolls[660] and to Mr Thomas, parsons of Dublin, and to my cousin William Juxon late of Virginia to each of them ten pounds.

Item, I give to my dear cousin Sir William Juxon, knight and baronet, to my cousin James Carent, esquire, to my good friend Standish Hartstrong, esquire, to my cousin Matthew Sheppard, to my cousin John Juxon, to the eldest son of my cousin John Kirrell deceased, to my sister Byfield, to my nephews Thomas and George Juxon, to all the children of my sister Byfield, to my brother Sir Charles Meredith, to my brother Robert Meredith,[661] to my sister Lister, and to my sister the countess of Mountrath,[662] to each of them twenty ounces of plate. To my dear Lady Anne Coote the spleen-stone after the death of my

---

[659] Sir James Ley, first Lord Ley 1624, first earl of Marlborough 1626, lord treasurer 1624–28; died 14 March 1629.

[660] Dr Daniel Rolls, chaplain to Colonel Sadler's regiment in 1654, minister at Swords in 1654 and at St Bride's Dublin in 1657: St John Seymour, *The puritans in Ireland* (Oxford, 1912), pp. 115, 220.

[661] Sir Charles and Robert Meredith were Juxon's brother-in-laws through his second wife, Elizabeth, daughter of Sir Robert Meredith of Greenhills, county Kildare.

[662] Charles Coote, the second earl of Mountrath, was married to Alice, the daughter of Sir Robert Meredith (above), Thomas Juxon's sister-in-law through his second marriage.

dear sister the countess of Mountrath; to my niece Farrington and my niece Kenricke, to my nephew John Key, to each of them twenty ounces of plate, and to Mr John Ramsay of the exchequer in Dublin twenty ounces of plate.

Item, I give to Patrick Corr's wife forty shillings to buy her three silver spoons, and to John Osborne forty shilling, and to my apprentice with him five pounds when he comes out of his time.

Item, I give unto the three youngest daughters of my sister Byfield that are unmarried one hundred pounds, viz. to the eldest forty, and the two youngest, thirty pounds apiece.

Item, I do give unto my nephews Thomas Juxon and George Juxon my interest in Pincocke Lane in London, with the benefit of a decree lately given by the judges in that case.

And lastly I do publish and declare this to be my last will and testament written all with my own hand containing six whole sides besides this, and I do hereby revoke and declare null and void all other and former wills, in particular my will left with Mr John Ramsay in Dublin, and I do declare my dear daughter Elizabeth Juxon the executrix of this my last will and testament, unto whom I give all the rest of my estate both personal and real not herebefore given, and my nephew Thomas Juxon the overseer, and I do give him twenty pounds a year for his care and pains which he shall take in assisting my said executrix in the management of her trust. Given under my hand and seal and dated this 6th day of June 1672, Thomas Juxon sealed and delivered in the presence of us William Doley, William Threlfall, William Witter Examinatus.

Probatum fuit testamentum suprascriptum apud London coram venerabili et egregio viro domino Leolino Jenkins milite legum doctore curiae prerogativae Cantuarensis magistro custode sive commissario legitime constituto vicesimo primo die mensis Decembris anno domini millesimo sexcentesimo septuagesimo secundo juramento Elizabethae Juxon filiae dicti defuncti et executricis unicae in huiusmodi testamento nominatae cui accommissa fuit administraco omnium et singulorum bonorum jurium et creditorum eiusdem defuncti de bene et fideliter administrando eadem ad sancta Dei evangelia [juratae].[663]

<[margin] Concordat cum originale testamento facta collacione per nos Thomas Juxon, Richard Edes. 30 December 1672.[664]

[663] The above-written will was proved in London before that worshipful and honourable man, Sir Leoline Jenkins, knight, doctor of civil law, master, warden or legally appointed commissary of the prerogtive court of Canterbury, on the 21st day of December A.D. 1672, upon the oath of Elizabeth Juxon, daughter of the said deceased person, after she swore an oath on God's holy gospels well and faithfully to administer the same.

[664] Agrees with the original will a comparison having been made by us Thomas Juxon, Richard Edes. 30 December 1672.

Received the original will of the said deceased to return according to the tenor of a bond entered into by me Elizabeth Juxon, teste Richard Edes>

SENTENCE FOR CONFIRMING THE WILL OF THOMAS JUXON[665]

Sententia pro confirmacone testamenti Thomae Juxon

In Dei nomine amen. Auditis visis et intellectis ac plenarie et mature discussis per nos Robertum Wyseman militem legum doctorem surrogatum venerabilis viri domini Leolini Jenkins militis legum etiam doctoris curiae prerogativae Cantuariensis magistri custodis sive commissarii legitime constituti meritis et circumstantiis cuiusdam negotii testamentarii sive probaconis per testes testamenti sive ultimae voluntatis Thomae Juxon nuper de East Sheen in comitatu Surriae defuncti (habentis dum vixit et mortis suae tempore bona jura sive credita in diversis diocesibus sive peculiaribus jurisdictionibus sufficientia ad fundanda jurisdictionem curiae prerogativae Cantuariensis). Quod coram nobis in judicio inter Elizabetham Juxon filiam et executricem nominatam in testamento dicti defuncti partem huiusmodi negotium promoventem ex una et Thomam Juxon et Georgium Juxon nepotes ex fratre dicti defuncti partes contra quas idem negotium promovetur partibus ex altera vertitur et pendet indecisum rite et legitime procedens partibus praedictis per earum procuratores legitime constitutos coram nobis in judicio legitime comparentibus parteque prefatae Elizabethae Juxon sententiam ferri et justitiam fieri pro parte sua parte vero memoratorum Thomae Juxon et Georgii Juxon justitiam etiam pro parte sua instanter respective postulantibus et petentibus rimatoque primitus per nos toto et integro processu alias coram nobis in hoc negotio habito et facto ac diligenter recensito servatisque per nos de jure in hac parte servandis ad nostrae sententiae diffinitivae sive nostri finalis decreti in hoc negotio ferendi prolaconem sic diximus procedendum fore et procedimus in hunc qui sequitur <u>modum</u> [crossed out] <[in margin] originale sic> Quia per acta inactitata deducta allegata exhibita proposita pariter ac probata in hoc negotio comperimus luculenter et invenimus partem praefatae Elizabethae Juxon intentionem suam in quadam allegatione articulata et testamento dicti Thomae Juxon defuncti aliisque propositis et exhibitis alias ex parte dictae Elizabethae Juxon in hoc negotio datis exhibitis et admissis penesque registrum huius curiae remanentibus deductam (quae quidem allegationem testamentum aliaque proposita predicta pro hic lectis et insertis habemus et haberi volumus) sufficienter et ad plenum (quoad infra pronuntiandum) fundasse pariter et probasse Nihilque effectuale ex

[665] PRO, PROB 11/346/136

parte dictorum Thomae Juxon et Georgii Juxon in hoc negotio exceptum deductum allegatum exhibitum probatum aut confessatum fuisse aut esse quod intentionem partis dictae Elizabethae Juxon in hac parte elideret seu quomodolibet enervaret Idcirco nos Robertus Wyseman miles legum doctor surrogatus antedictus (Christi nomine primitus invocato ac ipsum solum Deum occulis nostris praeponens et habens deque et cum consilio jurisperitorum cum quibus in hac parte communicavimus matureque deliberavimus) praefatum Thomam Juxon defunctum dum vixit mentis compotem et in sua sana memoria existentem testamentum suum in scriptis in hoc negotio exhibitis suam in se continens ultimam voluntatem rite et legitime fecisse et condidisse ac in eodem sive eadem praefatam Elizabetham Juxon eius filiam executricem nominasse et constituisse et dedisse voluisse legasse et disposuisse caeteraque fecisse prout in eodem testamento continetur proque viribus valore et validitate dicti testamenti ad omnem juris effectum pronunciamus decernimus et declaramus illud-que probamus approbamus et insinuamus per presentes necnon pro-baconem approbaconem et insinuaconem eiusdem alias in communi forma nomine dictae Elizabethae Juxon executricis antedictae habitam et factam ratificamus et confirmamus per hanc nostram sententiam diffi-nitivam sive hoc nostrum finale decretum quam sive quod ferimus et promulgamus in hiis scriptis

Lecta lata et promulgata fuit haec sententia difinitiva secundo die juridico post festum sive diem Sancti Valentini episcopi die Martis decimo septimo die mensis Februarii anno domini (stylo Angliae) millesimo sex-centesimo septuagesimo tertio per venerabilem virum dominum Rob-ertum Wyseman militem legum doctorem surrogatum venerabilis et egregii viri domini Leolini Jenkins militis legum etiam doctoris curiae prerogativae Cantuariensis magistri custodis sive commissarii legitime constituti in aula communi hospitii duorum advocatorum London infra parochiam Sancti Benedicti prope Ripam Paulinam London notorie sci-tuatam ad peticionem Magistri Samuelis Francklyn notarii publici proc-uratoris originalis supranominatae Elizabethae Juxon ac in praesentia Magistri Radulphi Suckley notarii publici procuratoris originalis sup-ranominati Thomae Juxon et Georgii Juxon super cuius sententia pro-lacione dictus Francklyn requisivit me Marcum Cottle armigerum notarium publicum dictae curiae registriam tunc presentem unum vel plura instrumenta publica exinde conficere ac testes inferius nominatos coram testimonium desuper perhibere presentibus tunc et ibidem vener-abilibus viris Thoma Exton Richardo Lloyd et Thoma Pinfold legum respective doctoribus dictae curiae advocatis necnon Alexandro Dyer Thoma Swallow et Everardo Exton notariis publicis dictae curiae proc-uratoribus testibus etc.[666]

[666] *Sentence for proving the will of Thomas Juxon*
In the name of God, amen. The merits and circumstances of a testamentary suit or a

probate by witnesses of the will or last wishes of Thomas Juxon, late of East Sheen in the county of Surrey, deceased, have been heard, seen and understood, and fully and speedily investigated by me, Sir Robert Wyseman, knight, doctor of civil law, surrogate for Sir Leoline Jenkins, also doctor of civil law, master, warden or commissary lawfully appointed of the prerogative court of Canterbury. [Juxon] had during his life, and at the time of his death, property rights and credits in several dioceses or peculiar jurisdictions sufficient in value to come within the jurisdiction of the prerogative court of Canterbury. The case for my judgment was a court case between Elizabeth Juxon, the daughter of the aforesaid deceased person, and the executrix named in his will, the party who brings the case, on the one side, and, on the other, Thomas and George Juxon, his nephews (sons of the deceased man's brother), the parties against whom this same case is brought. Since the issue between them was pending and undecided, and the case was duly and lawfully proceeding, the aforesaid parties appeared before me in court by their lawfully appointed representatives (proctors). Elizabeth Juxon's side asked and required that my sentence should be pronounced and justice should be done in its favour, and the side of the aforesaid Thomas Juxon and George Juxon asked for justice to be done in its favour, both sides wanting and pressing for a decision. I first examined and carefully reviewed the whole of the proceedings that were held and conducted before me on another occasion. Then, observing all the procedures which I am bound to observe, I thought it right to proceed to the declaration of my definitive sentence, or final decree, that I have to make in this case, and I declare my judgment in manner following [marginal note: the original has this (a reference to the crossing out of the word modum, meaning manner)].

From what has been done, enacted, presented, alleged, shown to me, put before me, as well as proved in this case, I have discovered and clearly found that Elizabeth Juxon's side has based its argument on an allegation (with several articles), on the will of the late Thomas Juxon, and on other things put before me or shown to me on another occasion on behalf of the said Elizabeth Juxon, things which have been handed over, produced and admitted in this case, and remain with the Registrar of this court (I wish these things – the allegation, the will, and the other material presented – to be taken as read and included in this case); that they have established and proved their argument sufficiently and fully (to the extent that will be declared below), but that nothing to any purpose has been excepted, deduced, alleged, shown, proved or confessed in this case on behalf of the said Thomas Juxon and George Juxon, and nothing has been said to counter or in any way weaken the argument of Elizabeth Juxon's side.

Therefore I, Sir Robert Wyseman, D.C.L., surrogate (see above), having first called upon the name of Christ and having God himself solely before my eyes, and having taken the advice of counsel with whom I have discussed this case and speedily considered it, declare that the late Thomas Juxon was in full possession of his faculties while he lived, and of sound memory; that he duly and lawfully made and drew up his will in the writings which have been exhibited in this case, a will which contained his last wishes; that in that will or those last wishes he named and appointed his daughter Elizabeth Juxon as his executrix and made those gifts, expressed those wishes, made those bequests and dispositions, and did everything else exactly as appears in that same will, with full legal effect, in accordance with the force, value and validity of the said will. This I pronounce, decree and declare, and I prove, approve and enter that will by these present writings; and I ratify and confirm the proving, approving and entering of the same, performed and made at another time in common form in the name of Elizabeth Juxon, the aforementioned executrix, by this definitive sentence or final decree, which I publish and make known in these writings.

This definitive sentence was read, published and make known on the second law day after the feast or day of St Valentine, bishop, on Tuesday the 17th day of the month of February A.D. 1674 (by English dating), by the worshipful Sir Robert Wyseman, D.C.L., surrogate of the worshipful and honourable Sir Leoline Jenkins, also D.C.L., master, warden or lawfully appointed commissary of the prerogative court of Canterbury, in the common hall of the two barristers' inn in London, which, as is well known, is in the parish of St Benet near Paul's Wharf in London, on the petition of Master Samuel Francklyn, notary public, the original representative of the abovenamed Elizabeth Juxon, and in the presence of Master Ralph Suckley, notary public, the original representative of the abovenamed Thomas and George Juxon. In addition to the declaration of this sentence, the said Mr Francklyn asked me, Mark Cottle esquire, notary public and registrar of the said court, being then present, thereof to make one or more public instruments, and asked the witnesses named below to bear witness thereupon in the presence, then and there, of the worshipful Thomas Exton, Richard Lloyd and Thomas Pinfold, all doctors of law, barristers of the said court, and Alexander Dyer, Thomas Swallow and Everard Exton, notaries public, proctors of the said court; these bearing witness etc.

INDEX

Shrewsbury (Shropshire) 74, 77
Shropshire 51
Shropshire horse, the 79
Sibbes, Richard 6, 175 & n. 652
Sicily 140
Sidney, Algernon, recruiter MP for Cardiff
  Boroughs 22 n. 128, 29 n. 188, 147 &
  nn. 553, 554
Simpson, Sidrach 65 n. 153
Sinclair, John, ninth lord 14, 126 n. 447
Skinner, Thomas 151, 164
Skippon, Major-General Philip, recruiter
  MP for Barnstaple 56, 59 & n. 126,
  63, 73, 85, 142, 152, 154 & n. 586, 163,
  164
Skipton Castle (Yorkshire) 88
Smallwood (John Juxon senior's aunt) 172,
  175
Smart, Peter 40 & n. 9
Soames, Sir Thomas, MP for London
  130 & n. 478
Socinianism 150 n. 567
solemn league and covenant 17 & n. 95,
  19, 20, 34, 44 & n. 38, 48, 70, 81 n.
  230, 85, 95, 98, 101, 102, 103, 104, 105,
  108, 113, 115, 127, 128, 130, 139 & n.
  525, 143, 145, 147, 148, 150, 151, 152,
  156, 164, 170
  retaking of 98, 102, 130, 156
Solicitor, Mr, see St John, Oliver
Somerset 3, 4, 16, 84, 86
Somers Islands, see Bermuda
Southampton (Hampshire) 58
Southampton, Thomas Wriothesley, fourth
  earl of 69 & n. 172, 70 & n. 179, 118 &
  nn. 400, 406, 120
Southwark (Surrey) 167
Spain 88, 136
Spanish 46, 48, 52, 88, 90, 97, 112, 129,
  131, 132, 134, 140, 144, 145, 149 & n.
  560, 153
Spendlove, John 175, 177
Spottiswood, Sir Robert 85
Stafford 71
Stanhope, Madam 93
Stapilton, Sir Philip, MP for Bor-
  oughbridge 10, 20, 34 & n. 224, 43 &
  n. 30, 47, 52 & n. 78, 56, 59, 60, 70
  n. 178, 71 n. 186, 75, 84 & n. 247,
  100 & n. 317, 114, 124 n. 440, 125 n.
  442, 131 & n. 481, 169
  Stapilton's, Stapiltonian party 17, 33, 34,
  35 n. 230, 84, 104 & n. 337, 154
Stapleton, George 183

States, the, see Holland
States General (Holland) 92
Stephens, Thomas 185
Stevens, Mary 185
Stint, James 185
Stow-on-the-Wold (Gloucester) 110 n. 369
Strode, William, MP for Bere Alston 54,
  85
Suckley, Ralph 194, 196 n. 666
sugar bakers/refiners 1 & n. 6, 2, 3, 8
sugarhouse 178, 180
Sunderland (Northumberland) 48
Surrey 1, 2, 150 n. 567, 174, 175 n. 655, 176,
  178, 180, 181, 182, 187, 195 n. 666
Sussex 72
Swallow, Thomas 194, 196 n. 666
Swanley, Captain Richard 56
Sweden 45, 71, 89, 131, 153
Sweden, queen of, see Christina
Swedes 44–5, 47–8, 62, 77, 91, 131, 132
synod, the, see assembly of divines

Taunton (Somerset) 78. 79. 80–1
Taylor, Daniel 8 n. 40
Taylor, Silvanus 51 & n. 73, 52 & n. 77
Thames, River 167
Thomas, Mr (minister) 190
Thomason, George 85 n. 256, 123 n. 430,
  139 n. 524
Thomson, Colonel George, recruiter MP
  for Southwark 49 & n. 64, 50, 124 &
  n. 439
Thomson, Maurice 49 n. 65
Threlfall, William 191
Tichborne, Alderman Robert 19, 90, 123,
  169 & n. 647
Tillier, Colonel Henry 132
tithes 151
toleration, religious 7–8, 11, 29 & nn. 185,
  187, 30 n. 190, 32, 41, 43, 70, 90, 95–
  6, 117, 128, 139, 148, 151
Toomer Park (Somerset) 3, 190
Torrington (Devon) 105, 107
Torstensson, Lennart 45 & n. 43
Towcester (Northamptonshire) 41
Tower of London 39, 66, 93 & n. 283, 124,
  169
  constable of 169 & n. 647
  lieutenant of 33, 71, 169 & n. 647
trained bands, see militia
Transylvania 48 n. 59
treasurers at war 32, 76 n. 211
Trent, River 50
Trier, elector of 90